BUT YOU DON'T
LOOK SICK

The Real Life Adventures of Fibro Bitches, Lupus Warriors,
and other Superheroes Battling Invisible Illness

An Indie Blu(e) Publishing Anthology

Praise for But You Don't Look Sick

". . . *But You Don't Look Sick* (BYDLS) is poised to be a major intervention in contemporary understandings of what it means to live with invisible, and often chronic, illnesses, many of which are misunderstood or marginalized by society and sometimes by the medical profession itself. BYDLS is arranged into eleven sections— autoimmune, bone, cellular, digestion, genes, heart, lungs, metabolic, nerve, unclassified and womb—with each giving a voice to the voiceless millions who do their best to cope, sometimes in silence, only to be told "but you don't look sick," a common reaction that trivializes the profound challenges, and dismisses the inspirational daily breakthroughs, that come with battling an invisible illness.

The cover, a collage of dismembered body parts superimposed by a warning—CAUTION—in crime scene tape, conveys how disembodying, destabilizing and isolating living with a chronic, invisible illness can be. As articulated in the anthology, the chronically ill body betrays often, and can also be the source of betrayal—by lovers, doctors, family members and friends who cannot, or choose not to, be an ally for the long haul. Yet, the realities of invisible illness have also fueled the immeasurable creativity that exists in the community, which has channeled its energies into producing this remarkable collection of works. . . BYDLS provides a roadmap of solidarity that shouts "you are seen, heard, acknowledged, loved and never alone."

This transnational, interdisciplinary and polyvocal anthology mounts a formidable counternarrative to social, cultural and medical forces that seek to stifle the lived experiences of individuals with invisible illnesses. By showcasing personal responses from all sides of the doctor-patient relationship, BYDLS also critiques current attitudes towards invisible illnesses, disrupts the power structure of traditional medical narratives and argues for change in therapeutics and public discourse. It exposes the gendered, racialized and class-based inequalities that persist within the realms of diagnosis and healthcare provision, while underscoring the urgency of activism, education and the ongoing fight for justice for individuals with invisible illnesses."

Dr. Tanfer Emin Tunc, Professor of American Studies, Hacettepe University, Ankara, Turkey

"'But You Don't Look Sick' explores the forgotten, unspoken and ugly-beautiful nooks of chronic illness. Because there are profound moments of horror and beauty when you're hovering between worlds, on days when you feel you can't do it anymore, in the silent hours when you really question if you're actually there, physically existing. . . Educate me. Educate all of us. We need it."

Beverley Butcher, Author of 'Sisterhood of Broken Dolls' included in the anthology 'Disturbing the Body', @boudiccapress, March 2021

"This book is not only valuable for people living with invisible illness but should be required reading for those living and working alongside them. Which is to say, all of us...

This collection spans 120 widely diverse artists, poets and writers, explaining how it isn't necessarily terminal or chronic illness that separates them from society, even as medical appointments, pain, nausea and fatigue impose their own limits. Instead, the mainstream belief that illness is a thing to be ignored, worked through or recovered from creates impossible dilemmas for those striving to manage these conditions. . .

The wellness industry has convinced the majority that with money, intention and the perfect execution of diet, exercise and hygiene one's health is simply an issue of personal choice. For people with untreatable conditions, the judgement from society is unrelenting. If their health isn't a perverse lifestyle decision, it must be a ploy to shirk the moral imperative to sacrifice themselves either to a career or to the physical and emotional care of others. But You Don't Look Sick is both beautifully crafted and a damning examination of the complex harm caused by these social biases."

Melissa Hill, Political Artist and Board Member of the disability arts charity DAO in the UK

"As a woman who has lived her life battling an invisible illness and chronic pain, I found myself swept up in the compelling collection, *But You Don't Look Sick: The Real Life Adventures of Fibro Bitches, Lupus Warriors, and other Superheroes Battling Invisible Illness*. The raw truth in each person's journey was heart wrenching, eye opening, and emotionally captivating. I found myself devouring this book piece after piece until I'd read the book all the way through.

I highly recommend this book to any person, but especially women suffering from an invisible illness. Our illnesses may differ, but our experiences are very much the same – the struggle of attempting to live a healthy life, the rejection from doctors who do not listen, the mental anguish from wishing you could be well, the isolation from friends and family who do not understand. The struggle of chronic and invisible illnesses is real, but so is the remarkable strength of the women behind the stories. Upon reading this book, I felt a sense of kinship and belonging as well as hope that I'm not the only one and I can be a superhero too."

Ravven White, Author of 'I am Ravven'"

"The diverse range of personal stories evoke despair, desperation and especially frustration at the lack of answers the medical community can give these Fibro Bitches, Lupus Warriors, and other Superheroes battling invisible illness. Above all, however, But You Don't Look Sick is a powerful human showing of how opening to one's pain generates courage and helps spread awareness. By opening the heart and manifesting compassion, this book helps drive change."

Jaya Avendel, Author & the poetic voice behind Nin Chronicles.

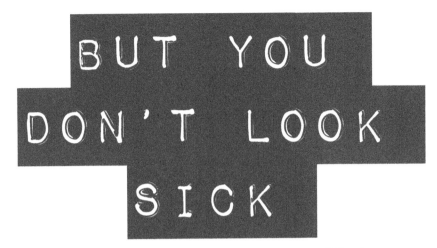

BUT YOU DON'T LOOK SICK

The Real Life Adventures of Fibro Bitches,
Lupus Warriors, and other Superheroes
Battling Invisible Illness

An Indie Blu(e) Publishing Anthology

Havertown, Pennsylvania
United States of America

ISBN: 978-1-951724-13-9 Paperback
        978-1-951724-14-6 Hardcover
        978-1-951724-15-3 Digital
Library of Congress Control Number: 2021949287

Edited by: Kindra M. Austin / Candice L. Daquin / Matthew D. Earye / Christine E. Ray / Mel Sherrer
Cover Illustration: Henna Johansdotter Sjöblom
Cover Design: Christine E. Ray

Dedication

This anthology is dedicated to those who have been misdiagnosed
and dismissed, maligned and misunderstood—
the chronic invisible illness warriors of the world.

We see you.

Introduction

In the most literal sense, Indie Blu(e) Publishing exists because of chronic invisible illness. Christine E. Ray left her high-pressured job in 2018, when her chronic invisible illness became so debilitating, she couldn't manage to shower most days, let alone commute daily on public transportation to meet the deadlines and demands of a busy neurological research center. Fibromyalgia, coupled with Chronic Migraine, left Ray physically, cognitively, and emotionally depleted. The loss of the ability to perform her job left her floundering. For those of us socialized to equate our worth through 'busyness' and productivity, chronic invisible illness can feel especially cruel. It robs us not only of physical and cognitive abilities previously taken for granted; but also of careers, hobbies, and relationships that are central to our core identity.

The shared quest to find new purpose after chronic illness led Ray and Kindra M. Austin to co-found Indie Blu(e) Publishing. Refusing to let their diagnoses define them, Austin and Ray believed fiercely in Indie Blu(e)'s potential as a vehicle to share dynamic, often marginalized voices. Long-time collaborator Candice Louisa Daquin joined the senior editorial team after stepping down from 60+ hour work weeks due to her own invisible illness. Pooling their energy, skills, and creativity, while embracing a culture of support, compassion and humor, the three have kept Indie Blu(e) vital through inevitable flare-ups of chronic illness.

Since Indie Blu(e)'s inception, the editorial team considered the enduring value of the survivor and the power of personal narrative. Survival is often our greatest achievement. The passion to create an anthology of lived experience of chronic illness was present from the very beginning; however, the journey was circuitous. After delays ironically due to illness, the team produced *But You Don't Look Sick*. It stands as testimony to the foundation of Indie Blu(e) and to all of those with whom we have worked, with reverence and respect—the invisible, much maligned and misunderstood chronic illness warriors.

Acknowledgements

Thank you to all contributors. Writing and creating art about your experience(s) is one of the hardest, bravest acts. We don't take your trust lightly. It is our hope this anthology will further awareness about the lived experience of invisible illness, but it is your courage that stands testament.

Thanks to all those who read advance reader copies of *But You Don't Look Sick* and supported this project and Indie Blu(e) Publishing's mission to spread awareness and engender change.

Special thanks to Henna Johansdotter Sjöblom for her striking cover art that so brilliantly captures the feeling of disconnection so many of us experience when invisible illness strikes.

Thank you to our guest editors, Mel Sherrer and Matt Eayre, who graciously provided their time, wisdom, and talent to nurturing this long-awaited anthology to publication.

Contents

Autoimmune

Bone

Cellular

Digestion

Genes

Heart

Lungs

Metabolic

Nerve

Unclassified

Womb

Biographies

AUTOIMMUNE

Annessa Ann Babic

Hope Underneath

As I sit here, another arctic blast freezes the city. Questionable music of my youth plays, student essays hang in digital space waiting for responses from their professor, my head pounds, and my heart shudders. I sigh the long and sorrowful breaths of a woman losing her ability to care, as once again, a physician treated me like an overweight, middle-aged woman with a history of lupus, not ill enough to matter. As my emotional pain seeps from every pore, my joints ache, my headache rages, and my stomach refuses to allow me to eat lest it regurgitates (unbecoming for social graces of any sort).

I was sixteen when this life was diagnosed, but I was younger when it began. Living with lupus and rheumatoid arthritis this long damages you in ways medical books can't (and don't) discuss. For me, I never know what day I'll hurt so damn bad, I can barely walk. Then there are the days my face is on fire with an emblazed red rash. My favorite life surprise is waking up to my pillow looking like a crime scene. Gawd, I'd say the nose bleeds are the biggest reason I stay single. Well, and that no one wants to take care of a sick girl . . . okay, well, since I'm long past a girl, a sick woman. I've never asked anyone to take care of me, yet I've had it thrown at me more than once. The sting never eases; instead, you find a sense of numbness to squirrel away the harsh reality of your reality. The last one to run from the lupus girl was the man I connected with in profound and unreal ways. As fairytales go, we had far more in common than not, but he didn't want more with me. For months we carried on, with me thinking we were moving upward and that our NYC abodes would join, and we were getting that dog.

Instead, in the middle of a cold spell, as snow fell outside, he ghosted me. I hear he's married now; while conversing with me, he met the wife, it seems. She's tiny, skinny, seems vacuous (maybe that's just me being snarky), and I know she's never been told by a physician that "Annessa, you just need to lose twenty pounds. That's what's best for you." Yeah, that was my rheumatologist, the same man who prescribes me pregabalin, steroids, and other fat packing pills. Yes, he is still my doctor. Sometimes it is easier to stay with the devil, you know. But that's a story for another day.

The cast-offs, the guilt, the shame come from all venues. Employers side-eye you; one made me apologize for having lupus, as I became ill on a trip. Friends stop asking you out, as leaving early or canceling is viewed as a more horrifying social disgrace than farting in church. Yet, when you live alone, work long and hard, stand as an activist, and continually seek to find the joy around corners of pure hell, those same people disregard you as fake or exaggerating. The deepest jabs to my soul are the regular comments of; "you are an inspiration" and "I think you handle lupus and RA with such grace." Telling me you admire my perseverance is perverse, as—honestly—there is no other way to live. Who else is going to pay my rent, cook my dinner, or pay the light bill? Well, I wouldn't expect anyone to anyway. Even my brief marriage, in my 30s, was stunted by my body's refusal to love me. I don't understand the awe, as I guess I have a bunker mentality about it all. I carry on, even when lovers run and husbands flake before the wedding signatures are dry.

The husband denied the power of my disease(s); he refused to concede I needed more medical care than the dude I divorced wanted to provide. As an MD friend of mine has stated, he's certain my health would have taken me out if the ex-husband hadn't. Though he also asserts I would have taken the husband out in self-defense. Again, another layer for another day and perhaps a women's studies case study from hell.

2

Recently, I was blindsided by a physician who sent me for a surgical consult. Side effects of the gremlins had brought on overproduction of acid and GERD and IBS attacks from hell. I am the new picture of sexy, my friends. Surgery was mentioned a year ago by a specialized physician. So, I go to the consult to be told I need gastric bypass surgery and not GERD repair. I was about twenty-five pounds overweight from my usual size, waking up from the 2020 pandemic, when nine people in my life died, including my sister. Yeah, I ate some (or a lot) of my damned feelings! I was so shocked, I couldn't even respond appropriately. I just nodded. Instead, my anger rolled over when the notes released to my chart, and in them, the surgeon claimed I denied a slew of symptoms. Since then, I've been sent back to the specialized gastroenterologist, and my physician has washed her hands of me: the problem patient who dares speak up. I feel like I was lied to and that all parties involved knew I would be told that I'm too obese for treatment and just need a barbaric surgery. Yeah, I take a slew of drugs, including an antidepressant. That isn't because life and my body hate me. That's because last year damaged me in ways I could have never predicted, even after all these years of living in a secondhand light, never being skinny enough, never being healthy enough, and never being wanted enough. The weight climbed when I started steroids, pregabalin, then I spent the entire subsequent year in a boot, cast, or brace on my foot, and then 2020 ripped me and the world over.

As these life stories go; there is no end. Instead, maybe tomorrow I won't ache to the core when I wake. Or, if my big pharma bones want to crumble up in a heap, then I know I have good coffee and creamer waiting in the wings. Hidden inside are these moments of again being regulated to a stereotype and non-starter, I choose to believe in happiness. If there isn't any, then, I would say, my life would have taken a stark turn in need of repair. A repair far greater than my failing body could question. Hence, my soul might ache from another humiliation at trusted hands, but when the sun sets, the new day's horizon has to have a promise of something more than what the previous day provided. Drugs working, good coffee, fluffy flannel sheets, warm summer skin, puppy kisses, and flourishing plants on my windowsill serve to balance out the downtrodden days. That's all I can give you. Hope underneath the darkened day. It's always there.

"At sixteen, I was diagnosed, and at nearly forty-five, I don't think the shock has worn off. Yes, I'm not as brazen about testing life and boundaries as I was then. Yet, living with lupus and rheumatoid arthritis makes you look at sunrises and sunsets with a sense of linger and love, even when they are grey and dull. Each day can change, quicker than you think."

—Annessa Ann Babic

Self-Portrait on Fabric

Christina Baltais

What is Known about M.E.

Symptoms

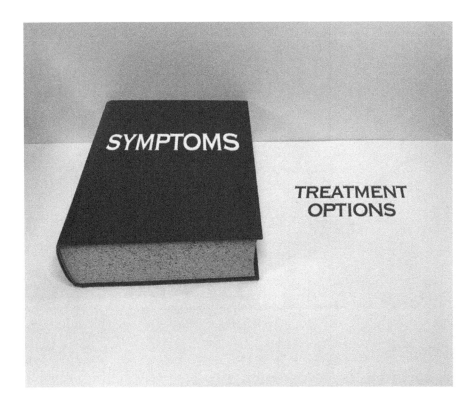

People Who Believe You

Dreams and Plans

Obituaries

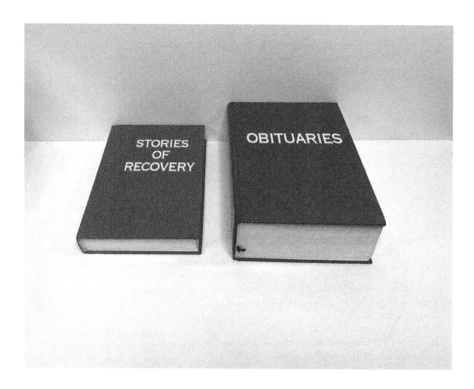

Christina came down with ME/CFS when she was 20 years old. For the next ten years, she struggled but managed to complete her undergraduate degree (Nutritional and Nutraceutical Sciences) and then nearly finished her ND (Naturopathic Doctor) degree. Unfortunately, her ME/CFS progressed and she was no longer able to attend school. At this time, she began using art as advocacy, to help raise awareness and compassion for what the ME/CFS community goes through.

Dr. Supriya Bansal

Lost in Labyrinth

Have you ever seen?
The coal-black clouds clamoring 'n clanking against the sky,
And the gnarled old oak, braiding its boughs 'n breathing a sigh,
When a seething, silver spear of lightning slashes across its core,
The sap simmers; the steam explodes, splintering its every pore,

The root retches 'n writhes, but the oak stands, sans superficial
        scars,
And the horror hisses 'n hums, clawing 'n cleaving, never too far.

I am that oaken wood,
Shaken 'n shattered, withered 'n wounded, gashed 'n gulped to the
        bones,
With no proof to parade, nothing to explain the guttural groans,
        muted moans.

Have you ever seen?
How an agitated animal gnaws 'n nibbles at its limb, caught in a
        snare?
Scrunches 'n shuns the skin, muscles, tendon 'n bone, with callous
        care,
Fatigued 'n frail, embittered 'n enraged— it swallows smithereens
        of its frame,
Helpless, hopeless, stifled, sullen, the dank darkness of its soul
        strikes aim.

Attacked 'n alienated, betrayed 'n broken, hurt 'n humiliated, the
        body turns hostile,
It stings 'n stomps, bites 'n blisters, blasts off reserves of
        ammunition by stockpile.

But You Don't Look Sick

I am that battleground,
Where my cells stir up a storm— wage an incessant inward war
      against its own,
Maim 'n mar, romp 'n rumble, my antibodies scrape 'n sunder,
      script my gravestone.

Have you ever been?
Entrapped in an inferno, a blazing bushfire pushing 'n plowing
      toward you,
Fevered, furious, the wind wobbles, smothered with soot, streaming
      through,
Your track the deer 'n snakes fleeing past, birds 'n insects on the
      lam,
Alas! You can't. You're just grass. The flames char 'n chew, not
      giving a damn.

At the dawn of another day,
Spirited, springy, the coppice flourishes 'n flowerers, after being
      razed to the ground,
Unharmed, untamed, robust, rhapsodic, resurges 'n resurrects to
      always be around.

My pain is that wildfire,
Unfurling wrath, like a bat out of hell, red-hot with ashen footprints
Sore soul, scorched skin, clogged breath; I lose everything in the
      orange tint.

My pain is also the brushwood,
Sharp to survive, even after being wiped out; never ready to retire
Its underground stems alive 'n kicking. Even in the wake of the fire.

Have you ever jumped
On solid ground but found the marsh yielding under your feet,
      yanking you down?

You tug 'n twist, lug 'n lunge, heave 'n halt, but the murk clambers
      up your crown,
Dredging 'n digging, depressed 'n distraught, you come apart at the
      seams,
Daggers dip into your dermis, holed in hell; you hang by
      strangled screams.

The rescuers grab, but fall forward, sink in the swamp along with
      you,
Gripped in the grime, you wrestle 'n wriggle till the moon turns blue.

My ailment is that quagmire,
Easy to get in, arduous to get out, I am tangled 'n trapped, but
never dead or drowned,
I lean back, my head above the mire, haunted 'n hunted by the
      howls of an internal hound.

Have you ever seen?
A candle caught in the vile, violent wind, wavering, vulnerable 'n
      weak,
While the feral gale, batters 'n bangs, whoops 'n whisks, crash 'n
      creeks,
The wind pounds 'n pestles but then suddenly relents 'n recedes,
      reticent 'n quiet,
And the flame peers at the looming malevolence scared stiff, yet
      stock-still 'n silent.

I manifest like that terrible typhoon,
Churning heavens 'n seas, earth 'n the ether, calamitous chaos
      consuming,

Vexed, waxing, waning, relapsing, remitting, ebbing 'n emerging,
      embracing.
I am also the quivering candle,

The amber hue blinks 'n beams, isolated, at loggerheads, not
conceding defeat,
Molten wax surrounds my wick— a wreath of courage 'n resolve
around my heartbeat,

Dismayed, disoriented— I dash in every direction in an inane house
of mirrors,
In this inextricable expedition, minus maps or guides, the end
doesn't seem nearer,
A labyrinth opens within me- a passage cobbled together by doubts
'n terrors.

Amidst the twines of regrets, remorse, resentment 'n rejection
I braid threads of laughter 'n joy, hope 'n dreams in my reflection.
My life a potpourri - each moment either a trial or a celebration!

"It is daunting and debilitating to live with autoimmune conditions
that have varied presentations. The painful, relapsing-remitting,
chronic progressive conditions get entrenched in various organ
systems— organ systems that are treated by different specialists
and primary care physicians. The diseases like Sarcoidosis, Lupus,
and dermatomyositis many times overlap with other medical
illnesses, and most of the time, neither the cause nor the cure is
known. It is like meandering through a tangled network of passages
and paths where you are continuously moving but not sure whether
you will find your way out."

—Dr. Supriya Bansal

Shannon Barnsley

Shadows in the Blood

Janet stumbled. The corridor seemed to stretch forever. The shadows swirled around her. Her heart beat heavy in her chest. Third blood-letting this week, and still the demons plagued her. She felt them all around her. Saw them out of the corner of her eye. Creeping. Stalking. Waiting.

She would never be rid of them, she thought, as the darkness closed in around her. She felt the world fall out beneath her, just before she hit the floor.

She wandered between worlds. Lost in some blurry half-space between living and dying, corporeality and untethered weightlessness. At one point, she was looking out of her eyes again as they fluttered closed. A man had found her in the corridor. The next moment, she was looking down at her own body as her mother attended her. Then the physician. Then the priest.

When she awoke finally, it was to prayer. A bitter tonic. More prayer. The physician returned only to tut and shake his head. In the coming months, it seemed the entire contents of the physick garden were pushed on her, one by one. But nothing helped. She grew paler, gaunter, her heart fluttering in her neck and the shadows swarming her every time she sat up. The cold hands of the grave pulling her under when she tried to stand.

"It's in the blood," said the physician. "A flaw in the blood."

"Demons," said the priest. "She's too weak to fight them."

"Atone," her family told her. *Fast. Pray. Repent. Atone. Drink these herbs. Take this tincture. Try this remedy. Accept God's will. Quicksilver should help. Maybe Mountain Ash. Atone for your sins. You must have done something for God to punish you so.*

Still the demons crept around her. Coming for her, always. In waking, in sleeping. They were always there. Chilling her. Burning her. Haunting her. Her prayers, her contrition, the medicines, they were never enough. *It's in the blood*, the words rang around her. Demons in the blood.

~

Jana shook. Her skin was cold and clammy, but she felt feverish. She took her blood pressure on her phone. It was low but not too low: 102/69. Her heart rate was 56. Not great, but it had been worse. She was hypovolemic as shit, like a used-up Capri Sun. Like she had skim milk blood.

Just sitting up made her feel awful, but she knew she had to get water. Electrolytes. Sodium. Something to eat. She burritoed herself up in her poofy, red comforter and tried to stand. Shadows swirled around her as her vision tunneled. Her heart felt like it had been seized by some ghostly hand, hell-bent on crushing it. Jana continued to stand, willing it to pass. She rocked on her feet, urging the blood pooling in her ankles back up.

She took her vitals again. 83/56. 159 bpm. Well, fuck. She swam against the dark current trying to overtake her. In the kitchen, her shaking hand missed the water filter by a full six inches. Her depth perception always went when she got like this. She managed to pour herself two glasses of water and down them with salt tablets. She filled a one liter water bottle and poured in two electrolyte packets before closing the lid and shaking the hell out of it.

She wanted some food. To use the bathroom. But the fridge and the hall to the bathroom beyond it loomed long before her. The darkness crept into her vision again.

Shadows and motion in her periphery. When they had started, she had thought it was a mouse or a bug darting across the floor. But now she knew there was nothing there, even if a thousand horror movies made her wonder otherwise. No, it was just her. Just hypotension.

Maybe she'd just have a pop-tart. She reached for the silver foil, her blood not happy with the raised arm fumbling about the kitchen cabinet. It was the last thing she remembered before she hit the floor. Her boyfriend found her and helped her back to bed. She seized, her eyes fluttering. She felt like she was going to fall through the bed or float away entirely.

He helped her drink, as her hands were too shaky, and she'd no doubt just spill it all over herself. When she'd recovered enough, she tore open the foil with her teeth and nibbled the corner of a pop-tart. She took her phone in hand and went online for support.

Go gluten-free, the screen told her. *No, paleo. Just go vegan, it'll cure you (Not being vegan is probably why you're sick in the first place). Think positively! Manifest health and happiness. What did you do to get this sick? Why can't you get better? Through Jesus all things are possible. Focus on what you can do, stop dwelling on what you can't, it's making you sicker. Raise your vibrations! Stop looking for attention. You can't still be sick. Just get outside more, nature is the only real medicine. Try this cleanse! Take this supplement! What about multivitamins? Colloidal silver! See a naturopath, I hear prickly ash helps seizures. If you were really sick,*

17

you wouldn't have been able to go to the museum last month. You aren't doing enough. Well, if I were you, I'd see a doctor.

Jana scoffed. She'd had her fill of doctors. PCPs, cardiologists, neurologists, allergists, immunologists, autonomic specialists, she'd seen them all. *Lose weight,* they'd told her. *Gain weight. POTS isn't a big deal and it's largely self-limiting. Stop looking for problems, it's like you want to be sick. Your tests came back normal again. There's nothing wrong with you. It's all in your head. You aren't trying hard enough. Do this exercise regimen. Take these pills. Drink Gatorade and eat a bag of chips, you'll be fine. Just bulk up your blood volume and quit worrying.*

Just her blood volume. Her vision swam. The shadows closed in. *You'll be fine.*

Seal Wives and Fae Women: A Parable of Lost Girls

Millions are missing
And the cooper's wife is too
So we hold our silent vigil
For a girl in a gown too blue
Lost in halls and hospitals
A silver talisman bears true
The diagnosis they doubted
With "Maybe it's just you?"

"Maybe it's your fault
Did you ever think it might?

It sure looks like anxiety
Caught in fight or flight
This isn't an emergency
I've no time to spare tonight
For another hypochondriac
Who thinks her Google search is right"

The words echo again
We've heard them all before
Generations of us girls
Lost to fable and to lore
Seal wives and fae women
Changelings left by the door
You wouldn't hear our screaming
So now you'll hear our roar

The nails in our coffin
Wrought of iron, silver, laws
Pilliwinckes and forceps
Their ever-sharpened claws
They threw us in asylums
When our ailments gave them cause
And said "domestic illness"
When our symptoms gave them pause

From hangmen down to hospitals
Aid, insurance, and the rest
They poke for holes and Devil's Marks
Scan our feeds for #Blessed
They'll find their proof in lies
Try to force us to confess
And hang their guilt and albatross
Like a noose about our breast

Heinrich brought the hammer
James of Scotland, his book good
The Exorcist echoed louder
Than *Brain on Fire* ever could
The changelings left to freeze
Fae wives used as firewood
Fallen women fall through cracks
Our entreaties thought falsehood

So when they say we're faking
Say it's just our nerves or girth
Or tests we need will cost too much
It's a burden we aren't worth
Remember all they've cost us
Down the ages on this earth
The lettings and the leeches
And gaslit twilight births

The sanatoriums and camps
The institutions where we died
The scripture and the paperwork
Where in blood red ink they lied
We paid with copay and with coin
When our symptoms we'd confide
Then they'd brand us with hysteria
And all that that implied

Even in our homes
With our husbands and our kin
They kill us to be free sometimes
Or bind us with our skin
Seal wives and fae women

And the changelings never win
Bridget Cleary's fate still looms
As their narratives they spin

Our weapon is our memory
And the silence they can't buy
Though they take our lives and livelihoods
We won't stop asking why
For our foremothers and daughters
Women lost to us and time
We will name that Rumpelstiltskin
And refuse to spin his line

In mass graves and in platitudes
Beneath a blood red moon
We will no more be buried
'Neath binding, nail, or rune
So smash your witches' bottle
Stolen memories aren't a boon
And speak the names with power
Autonomic, autoimmune

You'll not scratch out our stories
Not in hospitals or mass
Red cloaks or crooked crosses
Push us through the looking glass
Try to turn us on each other
As the "good ones" try to pass
Don't be their Gillis Duncan
And sacrifice another lass

Maybe it's your fault
My good doctor with his note
In penning your excuses

It was murder that you wrote
You left the seal wives hanging
They'd no proof without their coat
You thought that we were faking
Like they thought that witches float

Millions are missing
And the cooper's wife is too
So no more silent vigils
Don't be polite, be true
Seal wives and fae women
Owe no cooper's guilt their due
I will shout for all my sisters
Not keep silent for you

Seal Wives and Fae Women: A Parable of Lost Girls originally appeared online on the blog Salt & Iron, 10/24/20

Looking Glass Girl

Sara Kilcher sat alone, her rolling suitcase tucked under her legs, backpack beside her. She looked up from her grilled cheese. The train station was abuzz with the hum of humanity. The smell of fried food, the chatter of children, the scanning eye of the armed men with the German Shepherd, the lilt and cadence of more languages than she could name, and the ever-changing proclamations of the big board of departures and arrivals. Above it all, the great clock loomed, ticking down their time, whether they heeded it or not.

Familiar faces greeted her from the nearby bookstand. *The Magicians. The Polar Express.* An *Animorphs* reprint. Boxed sets of *Outlander* and

His Dark Materials and Narnia and *A Series of Unfortunate Events.* More Harry Potter editions than anyone would know what to do with.

A man was glaring at her for having the gall not to offer up her seat, as the precious few chairs spread willy-nilly about the small food court-style tables, were all taken. He looked in his 50s, perhaps 60s. She was nearing thirty but had never yet taken the train without someone asking what school she was headed off to. She felt his eyes on her but knew she couldn't stand yet. Her pulse had been 153, her bp 90/50, not five minutes ago. He'd probably seen her taking it and thought her a vapid twenty-something glued to her phone.

It was mid-evening, but her day was far from over. Yet it seemed a thousand years had passed since she'd signed in at the folding table in the hospital hall that morning. Her name tag had awaited her beneath the sign for the POTS patient/physician seminar. But she hadn't needed the sign.

She knew the telltale signs of her people. The plethora of sticker-clad Nalgenes and Hydroflasks amidst the Gatorades and Powerades from the vending machines or the trunks of their cars. The free samples of electrolyte supplements. The chips and apple juices on hand, lest someone's blood pressure or sugar drop too low. The zebra print and turquoise on everything from t-shirts to particulate masks to medbags to compression stockings. A spoon tattoo. The sea of redheads.

Some had canes or wheelchairs, some no mobility devices to be seen. Some bore the marks of mast cell or autoimmune disorders on their faces and skin, some no visible signs. Nothing to betray the battles they'd fought, trials endured, unending quests, secrets written into their DNA. The ones they whispered as they handed over doctor's notes, shouted like anthems at healthcare rallies, or hashtagged at 3 am— a keening call for fellow lost souls wandering the internet during the witching hour. Sara knew them, invisible as they were to those they walked amongst. The signs were there, for those who knew to see them.

23

She'd slid in beside a strawberry blonde who looked in her mid-teens. A scoopneck t-shirt that bore the words "Alice im Wunderland" over a folk art cottage had left her port visible to even the most oblivious. She'd introduced herself as Sophie, mentioning that her cousin, Gemma, also had POTS. Sara had all but done a spit take, realizing that Cousin Gemma was the GemmasWorld she'd been following on Instagram for years. They'd then exchanged handles and other kindred spirits they followed like wartime survivors trading ration cards.

For six blessed hours, Sara hadn't had to explain why she kept salt packets in her purse or zoned out midway through a conversation or hadn't "just been relaxing" or "finding herself" during the semester she'd taken off in college, despite having nothing to show for the time that had elapsed, putting her even further behind. People had told stories that might as well have been hers, no matter how different their lives looked on paper. She and Sophie had been finishing each other's sentences as eagerly as Sophie's mom was with the fiancé of one of the speakers, sitting in the row behind them.

Ancient mysteries—how she'd held her pen "wrong" since preschool, her random red-hot ear, how her skin sometimes mottled over in whitish green and bluish purple, why she'd broken her boots idly rocking back and forth on her heels when standing in line—suddenly clicked into place. As if a Rosetta stone or a full moon had illuminated some long-forgotten language or coded message.

And then it was gone. She was alone again. Invisible to the world. Her war wounds and battle scars mistaken for weaknesses, her wisdom for selfishness, her resilience for exaggeration, her victories for idleness, her explanations for excuses and complaints, her grievances for ingratitude, her chosen brandings a desperation for attention, rather than kin-seeking.

Where requests for help shouldering her suitcase into the bin overhead or asking where the elevator was when she was too dizzy to trust

24

herself on the escalator were met with suspicion or snide dismissal. Where she was Sara Kilcher, the girl whose once-promising future had withered into disappointment. Where her relatives and former classmates' parents tutted over how she hadn't amounted to anything while SophiesRealLife messaged SpoonPaladin to say what a lifesaver her survival tips were, the two already bound together in a way even lifelong friends could never understand. Like veterans from different walks of life who had never before met but who, with words like "Somme" and "Dunkirk", could finally speak a thousand silences they'd carried. Where now those words of power drew nothing but blank stares, eyerolls, or vague recognition followed by pale platitudes.

Where she tried to vanish into her grease-stained grilled cheese box as an able-bodied man shot daggers at her for not respecting her elders. She wolfed down the last bite, tied her Spider-Man hoodie about her, and pulled her hiking backpack on. Her muscles screamed in protest, despite the waist strap and cushioned back. She grabbed her suitcase, steadying herself for the long journey home. Then Sara Kilcher vanished into the crowd.

"I've been diagnosed with Postural Orthostatic Tachycardia Syndrome, Mast Cell Activation Syndrome, Ehlers-Danlos Syndrome, and Hypothyroidism. While POTS is omnipresent in these stories, it's MCAS that most ravages my life. I have severe airborne allergies to uncommon allergens, so just walking down the street or even sitting in my apartment can turn life or death at the drop of a hat. It's like constantly dodging mustard gas that no one else can see or feel."

—Shannon Barnsley

Suzette Bishop

Grinding to a Halt

"That's probably what you have," my doctor said. But I would need a specialist to concur to have my insurance take the diagnosis seriously, he guessed.

He didn't lift a finger to find one for me. I researched, called, and contacted ME/CFS support groups until I found a specialist six hours' drive away. She wasn't taking new patients. I wrote her a letter begging her to see me, and within weeks, I had an appointment in six months.

For more than ten years before this moment, my doctors had prescribed anti-depressants for the fatigue. I went through dozens: they stopped working, they made me throw-up, they made me dizzy, my pupils grew wide and dark. Other than the fatigue, I didn't feel unhappy. I liked my life.

The anti-depressants ruined two Thanksgivings where the nausea kept me in the bathroom one year and kept me in bed the next year when we were supposed to hike in the mountains with our hosts. Everyone left, and I stayed alone in the empty house that wasn't my home. The next day, we couldn't get out of town before my husband had to pull over as I heaved out the opened passenger door onto the pavement. A cop pulled up behind us, and my husband had to explain I was having a bad reaction to a medication. He was nice, concerned, but probably chalked it up to too much holiday partying. I wish.

A few years later, I was invited to apply for a full-time teaching position where my husband now taught. The one-hundred-plus student enrollment for the mostly writing-intensive college course load looked like a river, the water knocking me hard into sharp rocks. I had to decline. At this point, I couldn't do housework. I couldn't cook. Parties, dinners were stressful, to say the least. I had to leave one suddenly because of a migraine. I'd been enjoying the setting at a historic, renovated house, eating in the courtyard, looking over the bluffs at the river. It attacked suddenly and intensely. By the time my husband drove me home, I was seeing flashing lights and ended up hugging the toilet, again.

When my husband accompanied me to the doctor's office to say, "Hey, something serious is going on with my wife," *then* the doctor began the process of looking for heart disease. Just a slight prolapse was all the cardiologist found. When I mentioned I wasn't able to walk around my block without my lower legs going numb, he ordered an MS test. Normal. My lymph nodes kept swelling. I'd had mono and knew that wasn't normal. A book at a bookstore listed all of these symptoms, and I Xeroxed the page and brought it to the doctor, *Chronic Fatigue Syndrome*.

Once I got in for my appointment with a ME/CFS specialist, I recognized that woman sitting next to me in the waiting room, visibly trying to keep steady as she waited. That was me, that had been me, these past years.

I came away with a diagnosis and tests showing my immune system was in serious distress and my old mono virus kept being reactivated, exhausting my immune system further. I got worse under this doctor's experimental treatment. I switched to another doctor only a four hours' drive away. His tests showed further distress. But his homeopathic remedies were expensive, relieving my symptoms only slightly. The infusions he angrily urged me to try weren't discussed anywhere that I could find, and his wife, who had fibromyalgia and worked in the office, looked like death warmed over. I don't think those infusions were helping her much. By now, painful tender points appeared, added to the list of symptoms, and a fibromyalgia diagnosis.

I'd watched my boss have a fibro relapse and heard her say she couldn't withstand hugs from her daughters. Medication for it scrambled her brain. And there was the doctor's wife. I had been relieved I didn't have that. Now I did.

I'd have dizzy spells with driving and full-on panic attacks, forcing me to pull over. If we went on long car trips, I couldn't relieve my husband. Some of those long car trips were to see ME/CFS and fibromyalgia specialists. At this point, I *was* depressed, the pull to drive off overpasses a momentary temptation adding to the panic. I could be done with this, but my husband was often in the car. So, I'd force myself to slow down and steer straight until the next exit ramp where he would take the wheel.

There are medications for orthostatic intolerance, the likely ME/CFS symptom causing this dizziness when driving, but the cardiologist I went to refused to order a tilt-table test. I cried so hard, he changed his mind and ordered it. "See, I was right. There's nothing wrong," the cardiologist told me. My readings were normal, and my insurance company wouldn't cover it as a result. It's subtler in ME/CFS and doesn't always show up in the standard tests, the more likely explanation. Another doctor diagnosed it two years later. The medication helped for a while and then stopped helping, making my blood pressure soar.

Today, I have to spend a significant part of the day in a reclining position. Otherwise, the floor I'm standing on moves like a ship at sea. Pacing and avoiding exercise help with the grinding fatigue. I'm able to continue teaching part-time. And I'm still that woman trying to keep things steady, but my life keeps slipping into the ocean, like gardening, baking, taking a walk in the park five minutes away.

A Cardio Workout Dream

A fifty-mile-an-hour nightmare
Trying to explain fibromyalgia
To a team of women cyclists
I belong to, only in the dream.

The male coaches at their desks
Act like they've heard of it,
Saying it must be hard
Not knowing how much you can do
Before you crash,
Worried more about liability, really,
Than my crashes of bone marrow pain.

One woman, a teacher I work with,
Yells at me to take more care
With cleaning and mending my team socks.
They're just socks, I say,
They're gonna get dirty and unraveled anyway.
She looks away, rolling her eyes, rides off.

Some of the cyclists stay with me,
Circling,
As I try to put my bike back together,
But they tire of waiting for me
And take off, sleek, light-framed.

My old boss tries to find the right kind
Of screws I need,
We end up improvising a repair.
I ride back to the apartment,
A soggy, white-frosted gingerbread cake I made,
Wind and rain splinting the window.

29

Little Thunder
Based on a therapeutic horseback riding lesson for fibromyalgia

No problem climbing into the saddle for my old, short legs,
Round stirrups, leather-pressed with flowers, an anniversary
          present.

It took me a while to understand you didn't need firm kicks
Just slight, soft pulls of the reins—

Black, coarse mane, a woman's head of hair,
You are close to the ground, my fear of falling into soft dirt, gone.

Another woman says she wants to ride like me as I trot by,
I was her not long ago—leaning over the horn, body closed in—

A new look on my husband's face as he watches me ride you,
We're small, strong, thunderous.

"I'm running late, again. I look able, no cane (yet), no wheelchair,
and I park in a regular parking spot. Still, I'm grateful I paid extra for
parking, which puts me closer to where I teach my classes. Once I
return home, I'm doing an accounting of what at home and with
loved ones I can do and what I have to slash off the list—for this
hour, this evening, this month, maybe forever."

—Suzette Bishop

Wanda Morrow Clevenger

things could be worse

complications of
widely worse
such-and-what
that's how it gets you
gets you down
for the count
worms tentacles
in and out
plays Pinochle
on your snout

this is how, then
what's worse gets you
isn't the complaint
it's the tentacles

Previously published in The Piker Press – February 22, 2016

necrosis is a bony bald bitch

five months into
the pancreatitis
my hair started
falling out

my primary doctor said
rapid weight loss
wasn't to blame, just
stress he said, how
some women will
lose some hair after
giving birth

stress, he said
unconcerned,
while updating
the computer file
while
my pancreas ate
itself

Previously published in Clockwise Cat – October 23, 2014

referrals

they sail in
one after another
crisp white sheets
launched from the same
Xerox with
outstretched hand
how are you
hellos

how wasteful
the massed
expertise
made
patient pusher
bean counter

how am I?—
surely they see
the paper doll
crumpled
on their
paper sheets

Previously published in Clementine Poetry Journal – July 1, 2015

Dorinda Duclos

You Look Fine

For my Transverse Myelitis comrades, whose strength and dignity are the reasons I fight so hard to win this battle. God bless all of you.

You will never see
the silent pain, or the broken soul
who questions why
Or how or what
they did to deserve this
enormous disruption of their life.

Independence taken
away in the blink of an eye
and never an understanding
It becomes a constant battle
to make those around them perceive
the reality.

The glares of the accusing
unaware, of the horror within
the courageous body before them
They poke and tease
with disbelief and "you look fines"
without an inkling or thought
as to what they suggest.

But the strong do not give up, do not stop
the fight against a villain
who showed up unwelcomed one day
They struggle and confront the world
that looks upon them, unsure, suspicious
Uncertain

34

They are brave and fierce people
who will not let this malady define them
who will not let the constant depression
sadden the brightest days
Who choose, instead, to be an inspiration
to others who fight a similar battle
with compassion, caring…hope

"In October 2006, I awoke completely numb from my neck to my toes. I was later diagnosed with Transverse Myelitis, which is an inflammation of the spinal cord, the part of the central nervous system that sends impulses from the brain to nerves in the body. I was left partially disabled on the left side of my body, with an intense pain & numbness. However, I do not let this define who I am. Therefore, I am often told, *You Look Fine*."

—Dorinda Duclos

Jordan Garcia

More than Fine

When you look at me, what do you see?
A young, healthy able-bodied woman
What do you claim to know?
I am fine

You look "normal"
You should and can do everything
Everyday tasks are truly simple
Do not slow down
Rest is not that imperative right now
Remember what is at stake in all the work you do
I am fine

"It's all in your head"
You do not look "sick"
Your day is just not going great
Try this and you will be fine
You must be well
I am fine

Disabled?
You are not in a wheelchair
You certainly do not deserve that parking spot
You do not need to use a ramp
I am fine

You can go to the event tonight
You can plan to be there and do this and that
You do not need a nap
If I can do it, you can do it
There are no limits to what you can and cannot do

But You Don't Look Sick

I am fine

What you do not see is a sick body
Impacted by a chronic illness that chooses to unpredictably attack
Striking women of color two to three times more likely
One who yearns to be fine, day by day
I am resilient

Normal I may look on the outside, but within am struggling to be
"normal"
You do not see that I am always on guard
Wondering if I will not be able to do any task at hand
That I never know how I will feel
There is not one task that is simple
Rest is my well-being, as close to what I will ever know, of being
well
I am resilient

If only you could see that lupus purposely hides from all segments
of outside life
Covertly remaining undetected
Controlling my entire being
No matter what I do, it seeks to put me in battle
Nothing can eradicate its existence
Being able to do this and that is not my norm, and never will be
I did not choose to everyday live with a chronic illness
Just because you cannot see it, does not mean it is not worth
defending
I am resilient

Absent from your norm, is that disabilities can be invisible
I can no longer always walk the distances I used to be able to
You do not know how difficult it was for me to even get ready

You give me looks because I know, I do not look quote on quote
sick
I have had to live a novel "normal"
You do not get to define who I am
Or any part of my life. I would rather be only a sojourn
I am resilient

Please know, that I cannot do what I want
Involuntary, I survive through rest
The illness sets my limitations
I cannot plan this and that
Moment to moment, day by day
Amazing opportunities I miss
Or else I go back to even more fatigue, IVs and medication
Do you know the sun is not my friend?
Did you know my happy place is the beach, where I cannot even
entirely stay?
Imagine my annoyance
I am resilient

Do you see anything now?
You may not see it today; you may not see it tomorrow
I do not need your sympathy to change or fix things
Or tell me that I am fine
I do not question "why"
It is your understanding that matters
I am empowered.

My Reality

Chaos trembles and shakes
Light listens
But cannot move it out of its place

Fear speaks
Unapologetically overturning hope
Darkness at its peak

Hope keenly searches for truth
There must be a reason
Shadows pass of one's youth

The soul awakes
Wings of a butterfly
Bliss that remembers what is at stake
All while in ache.

An In(Visible) Truth

I am surrounded by
the unknown—
through each
and every
good or
bad
day

back and
forth, hope as strength
struggles to break
the (in)visible

fearless
I am
through each
and every
milligram

it's always
the small things.

These pieces were previously published in the undergraduate senior honors thesis entitled "An Invisible Politics: A Feminist/Interpretive Approach" on May, 2019 by Barrett, The Honors College at Arizona State University.

"Every day my true reflection is misunderstood by others. A constant battle to make visible my invisible pain. Every day, I never know how I am going to feel. It is an unpredictable war with no surrender. Enduring chronic illness, I am my own advocate mediating between the seen and unseen, sometimes against my own body to be recognized."

—Jordan Garcia

Mary A. Rogers Glowczwskie

If My Body Grew in the Forest

If my body grew in a forest
A knotted pine, you might see
But my illness is invisible
And those knots grow inside of me

If I were a maple
You might see sap run down my spine
My trunk is definitely injured
But the wounds weep inside

If I were a sycamore
There'd be spots upon my leaves
Because you can't see my illness
Often alone, I am left to grieve

If my body grew in a forest
I might grow as a canopy of trees
A place you might take refuge
Never knowing I am diseased

My Body as a Temple

They say my body is a temple
A place where a god does dwell
I wonder what deity would live here
Decaying ruins; this home, a living hell

But You Don't Look Sick

The ceiling is missing rafters
The consequence of time
Corridors lead to nowhere
But the fogged labyrinth of my mind

They say my body is a temple
Home to the Holy Ghost
I believe entities do dwell here
Hungry demons, feeding on this host

Decaying bones are the pillars
Collapsing at the seams
Arthritis and inflammation
Destroyers of hopes and dreams

In my body lies many mansions
Where hungry ghosts do roam
They declared war on my body
Now a war-torn home

They float on a blood red river
In a fortress they have claimed
They placed their flag declaring victory
Leaving my body marked and maimed

My body once a temple
The holy sacrament that's me
A place a god once dwelled
Worshipped no more under this decree

Broken in half sits the altar
Once a sacred place to rest
My body is not a temple
But a broken edifice

Deborah Dubas Groom

Strength in the Shadows

"I spent decades seeing myself through the eyes of people who did not understand invisible illness - lupus, depression, anxiety, migraines. I absorbed the negativity, condemnation, and disdain. I tried to defend myself, but I have learned. There are people who understand that I'm not unreliable, even if my body sometimes is. I'm not lazy, or a disappointment. I'm Deborah and I dream and hope and laugh and love. I'm enough and so are you."

— Deborah Dubas Groom

Sister Lou Ella Hickman, I.W.B.S.

chronic fatigue: the most forlorn of orphan illnesses
a found poem

at 43
a former science reporter:
life may well be over
pushed himself
four days
1600 words instead of minutes
vanessa li 15 years 30 doctors
I don't want to be like this forever
finally she dropped like those
who chose falling rather than flame
that engulfed twin towers
and did so with a bottle that helped her forever sleep
the reporter: *temp 102*
(mine 104 mono reactivated
the word my doctor used)
sleep isn't refreshing
oh, would it be that simple . . .
patients don't look sick
then   when we do a little   something
we crash
the litany
crippling muscle pain,   paralysis,   migraines
piercing the everything of exhaustion
no tests
to prove to scoffers   insurance   almost no NIH budgeting
no cure
for the 836,000 to 2.5 million
who live in the twilight of pea-soup fog
while lying in the prison of their bed

Inspired by 'The Tragic Neglect of Chronic Fatigue Syndrome', Olga Khazan, The Atlantic, October 8, 2015.

enough: giving a voice to chronic fatigue

i

¡basta!
my body shouted:
enough! enough already!
enough hurt
for my heart over a lifetime
and with this unvoiced word
something in me collapsed
like a scaffolding of bones

ii

i am still unlearning
my lessons of not enough
(of never enough)
and blame
like
a battered wife or girlfriend
who finally sat on the couch
too tired to cry

But You Don't Look Sick

iii

do just enough today
the unspoken warning . . .
unless you want
to feel like death warmed over
for two days
when you've done just a little too much
how often i forget

iv

now *suficiente*
for tomorrow will care for itself
sufficient is the wounded strength
hidden among the bones

First published in Snapdragon Journal, Fall, 2020.

"Thanks to my chronic fatigue, I sometimes have difficulty communicating and I have less time to write, read, and research as I must take two, two-hour naps almost every day."

— Sister Lou Ella Hickman, I.W.B.S.

Ashley Jane
this ache is my own white elephant

i tried
to sever ties,
to shake loose the anguish
bound beneath my skin,
the pinprick pain
that keeps calling my name,
stealing the oxygen
from my lungs
i tried
to burn it all away,
the torment that raged
despite the antiseptic sting
but it has settled
too deep,
making it hard to breathe
i tried
to give it away,
but no one wants it
and no words remain

i know what psychosomatic means

it's back again
scratching and clawing,
screaming for my brain
to acknowledge the pain
as if i could ever forget

47

and that's where i'm told it exists,
in my head,
a silly delusion of my own making,
a plea for attention
brewing beneath my skin

~

what i wouldn't give
to be out of the spotlight
what i wouldn't give
for one night of peace

~

but, this demon speaks
in fire and flame,
a burn that races through my veins
and i am wide awake
waiting
for every nerve to react
and every muscle to ache
and i am
so
damn
tired
of having to explain
that this is real,
that yoga and vitamins aren't the cure
that the monsters that keep me up
live in my bones
...not in my head

(but, please,
tell me again how it's all make believe)

"I was diagnosed with lupus at age 14. Since then, there have been numerous additions to the list of ailments, but I think life will always be defined by the lupus. It changed me, and I suppose that's to be expected. I was super social and suddenly couldn't be anymore. So many times, I was told it wasn't as bad as I made it, and I learned to just pretend to feel okay, so as not to bother anyone. It shouldn't be like that. I hope this book helps those who feel that way. You are not alone."

—Ashley Jane

Eva Joan

Haiku Collection

night thoughts
like liquid mercury...
not to grasp

her body shakes—
deep inner coldness
of exhaustion

these tired eyes
in my morning mirror...
i do not know them

i'm lost for words
a thousand thoughts in the head -
locked-in

sleepless—
between the hours
too much time

November years
fade into twilight—
little sparks of hope

V J Knutson

Expectant

Upright
sliding
forward

Have lived
experience
to deliver

Been knocked down
stripped bare
and bent

Landed on healing

Sure…
illness lingers
pain persists…

Have trafficked
in exes, dependency -
forget all that

None merit mention.

Expectancy is ripe.

Plea for Awareness

There is anger in dis-ease
an impotent railing against
injustice of biological systems
bent on breaking souls

This relentless drag
this mournful existence
It is not pity that we seek
nor charity that appeases

But answers, pragmatic
protocols, to dissuade
onslaught of symptoms,
unburden suffering

None of us weak
all disheartened -
abandoned medically
many confined in isolation

Our embers seething
beneath bedclothes
burning behind eyes
that have lost focus

Forgive us if we rant
if our conduct reeks of
self-righteousness, but we
are missing, millions missing

Plagued by a condition
long ignored, misconstrued,

dismissed, we are angry
unapologetically

Overlooked by
disability claims, as if
we construed an alibi
for opting out of society

If we lash out, speak out
express our discomfort
In uncomely ways, well
then listen… reasoning

Guides our voices
our disappointment
frustrated, unheeded
and very much alive –

Individually,
collectively
we wield our ire
as a cry for help

"Myalgic Encephalomyelitis is the diagnosis that changed my life. Bed bound for 3 years, a poet was born. I have regained some mobility and learned to pace myself. New diagnoses have emerged, as has new wisdom. I regret nothing."

—V J Knutson

Brandy Lane

Grounded

My aching body is failing me, my joints, my metabolism...
my thoughts race back to when I could fly.
Well, not literally, but leaping across the wooden dance floor,
watching in the wall of mirrors… not one part of my body
was touching the ground for those few, ethereal moments.

I would leap over and over again, just to feel like I was soaring.
The wind would breeze across my face as I would defy gravity
itself.
It was the closest thing to flying I could imagine.
I remember stretching, being one with my mind, soul and body.

I felt real. I felt strong. I felt in control.

I would run my hands down my smooth, muscular legs,
stretching toward my toes.
I would glide my fingers across my stomach, lean and long.

I felt beautiful. I felt healthy. I felt sexy.

Fast forward to my third knee surgery, before the age of thirty.
I was told not only could I no longer dance,
but I couldn't wait tables anymore either.
No more jobs that required me to be on my feet
for more than four hours at a time.

I was grounded, my wings clipped, I would never fly again.

Meander through a few more years,
my body no longer taut and lean, now soft and round and carrying
life.

But You Don't Look Sick

Four beautiful babies in a row.
Little toes that kicked me from within...
I felt blessed to be a woman as no man could feel this intensity
inside.

I felt empowered. I felt exhausted. I felt magical.

That's all history now.
This life giving body decided it wanted to keep growing things
once the babies had vacated: a tumor, a polyp, a cyst and severe
anemia
forced me to have my uterus removed.
No more life would grow in my depths.
That was three years ago.

I felt defeated. I felt depleted, I felt depressed.

Each day I awake, unsure of which part of me won't work;
my hip, my knees, my neck, my elbow...
what part doesn't hurt?
I try to find purpose, a reason to go on.
I think of my children, and realize that I have to...
for them.

I will admit, that there are days that I have pondered
not waking up.

There are days where I have to…
because the bed actually hurts to lie on.
There are days that I stay up
until I am so exhausted that I just cannot remain upright,
so that I don't have to feel anything when I lie down,
because I dread the way I will feel when I wake in the morning.

My dancing days are over,
they are now a hazy remnant of my past.
I take the stairs one step at a time, slowly, like I am fragile.
I am only forty-eight.
I am exhausted. I am sore. I am disabled.

I run my hands down my now empty, soft, round belly…
and I cry.

"Hidden behind the smile upon my face, my teeth grit in pain. I cry easily, because any emotion, whether it be happy or sad, is just enough to allow me to express what is always overflowing in my mind and body. I try to keep my illness hidden, because even though it is invisible, it manifests itself in my personality or the way I walk or move on any given day."

—Brandy Lane

Sudipta Maity

Keyhole

Some young seconds of life
Rolled from the eyes .
Look at the scissors
Breaking the pride
Who will stop him?
The Mirror of Abrams
In front of my mother.
The hidden screen
Moves away in tears.
There are many magic wands
In your hands
Cutting the boundaries,
All over the body.
That tip of the needle,
In an instant,
Enters the abyss
That wise head of yours
Knows whether it is important
To place of IV arm
I'm just waiting,
Mom will be by my side
In the Next Second of life.

My Enemy

Forgot about the disease
Because of the smell of naphthalene

Declined the doctor's call many times
I've come to tell the story
Of the attackers
To the doctor
In my mother's oath
After the Mystery of Egypt
Recovering the mystery of blood
We search for new liquids
In old bottles
The amount of favourite food of ants
Has increased in the blood.

Silent Burglar Alarm

I've become accustomed
To wearing striped clothes now
My body trapped in bed
Eyes on guard,
Insomnia
I tried to escape from Fibro Fog
Again and Again
But I felt like
My hands were obstructed
By handcuff made of tablets
One day the White Coat Jailer
Will be surprised
There will be no prescriptions
The day I'll get bail
From all of this
And it must be.

The call of the Thorns

In my temptation
I heard the call of Thorns
The wires of the old sitar of the body
Was tearing up
As soon as sleep is disturbed
Entering the city of pain .
Family arranged
The table of forgetfulness
The bouquet of flowers
Is slowly drying up
And so am I.
Fibro horse entered
The city for a long time
Crushing,
Storyteller's Maple spreading path
It is running across the body
Pain.

Neelam Saxena

The Light Within Me

"You are suffering from Rheumatoid Arthritis and looking at your condition, I feel that going for a knee transplant is the only option left," the Doctor said quite emphatically.

I shivered. A knee transplant at the age of 32? Ridiculous!

But then, there was no option at all. This was what was destined for me, and I had to accept it. The disease was spreading its wings. It had begun in the left ankle. It had now spread to the right knee, the wrists, the neck, the shoulders, the fingers. The list was quite long. Only a few of my body parts remained unaffected. It was almost like a slow poison spreading all through my body, making some part or the other its poor victim. I could do nothing except watch it. What control did I have over it? Nothing!

I was completely shattered. I would lie down silently and look into oblivion. Dejection and pessimism had taken complete control of my body. Thoughts of suicide often crossed my mind. But I couldn't. After all, I had a small daughter aged seven. Would my actions be justified? Wouldn't it be a gross injustice to her? God had chosen me to be her guardian on his behalf. How could I leave behind my duty and set my soul free?

What I had not noticed was that the gloom and negativity which had enveloped me, was taking a toll on my patience too. I had become extremely intolerant and edgy. While I was always considered an epitome of endurance and serenity erstwhile, here I was getting annoyed at small, miniscule things. One day my wrath showed its ugly face in front of my daughter. I slapped her for some trivial reason. She mumbled innocently, "Mummy, you have become so bad. How can you hit me? You had never hit me like this, for no fault of mine!"

I looked at her in disbelief. What was I doing? I had really become bad. How could I hit her? I was ashamed to have committed such an act. I apologized to her immediately. Taking her in my lap, I cried a lot. I had committed a major blunder.

That night I could not sleep. I was dejected and crestfallen. I was suffering. I wanted someone to come and understand my crisis. I desired someone to get me out of this mess. I expected everyone to help me in my troubles because I had helped everyone else throughout my life.

I suddenly realized that I was expecting too much, and this was the root cause of all problems. Why these expectations? I helped people because I thought that was the wisest thing to do. I did not do it as an investment over which I should keep getting dividends. Moreover, even investments can fail in life.

I suddenly realized that I did not need anyone to bail me out of my trouble. I remembered the good old times when I had succeeded despite all odds. Never once had I really lost my hope. It was almost as if a big rock had come in front of me on the path I was treading. The rock was surely too huge for me to remove. But I could change my path and come out of my difficulties, couldn't I?

I talked to my soul long into the night. It said, "Yes, there is a God within everyone. That God is my light. It is based upon the foundations of truth, honesty, and self-belief. You had forgotten me. Now that you have summoned me, I shall provide you strength to face the obstacles. Go right ahead."

I could feel a miracle happening within me. The problems remained the same. The difficulties remained. But my approach towards seeing them had changed tremendously. I was no longer worried about the mammoth rock. I changed my path. And that path was now lit by an unknown spirit, an unknown energy that continued to walk with me wherever I went.

Surprisingly, my ailment also immediately started showing signs of diminishing. My bodily pains started reducing. I did not have to go through the trauma of a knee replacement (at least not yet). It took a few years, but the pain was not even a tenth of what it was, once upon a time.

When I went to my Doctor for my next check-up, he smiled and said, "I always knew you could do it. You only needed shock therapy to rejuvenate you and your lost spirits. Cheers!!!"

"When I was diagnosed with Rheumatoid Arthritis at the age of 33, I thought that I was dying a slow death and was very depressed. The thought that I should remain dependent on someone else, made me feel horrible. However, I remembered the light within me that has always been glowing, although I've had so many difficulties in life. I let that light take me over, and today, I can play table tennis matches, walk 4-5 kms a day and do so many other things that I had thought were impossible at 33. Optimism can help slow down the progress of any disease and I wish to radiate with positivity."

—Neelam Saxena

Daniel Malito

Help, I've Fallen and I Don't Want To Get Up

The fall. No, I'm not talking about the season, or even "Legends of," but the actual thing. Falling down. Hitting the ground. Losing your balance. Whatever euphemism you choose, it means one thing when you have RA – trouble.

It happened a week ago. A fall. My stupid ankle brace got hooked on something and I went ass-over-teakettle. I hit the ground with a resounding thud and I knew, instantly, it was going to be bad. In that moment, I just wanted to stay on the floor – just pop a tent over myself, move in a laptop, maybe a soda stream or coffee maker as well and just live right there on the floor, forever. I knew as soon as I tried to get up it would become readily apparent what got shoved where and whether or not I was going to have to go to the ED.

God, nothing makes you feel ancient like falling down. Even if you are healthy, falling down makes you feel like a 90-year old. Add on the anxiety of falling with RA and it's humiliating, terrifying, and painful, let's not forget that one. Of course, I had to go down on concrete – it couldn't have been carpet or marshmallow fluff, no, it had to be the basement concrete. If I was going to pick a place not to fall, it would be there. I went down on the side, and I knew, absolutely knew, my hips got slammed, and my hips ain't exactly spring chickens.

I've had one since 1996, and the other since 1998 – when they were new the Internet was still called the "worldwide web," and Hotmail was a service that matched you with a porn star for a pen pal. And they still had pen pals. And pens. And people still said "pal." Sheesh, my hips are old. So you can see why I was concerned – one jolt the wrong way and bam! There goes the pelvic neighborhood. I'd have to get one of those new digital wi-fi hips that play Candy Crush and works your thermostat. Ugh, technology runs amok. (No, not a real thing.)

There I was, down on the floor, just contemplating the "what ifs," wondering how much time this was going to sap from my life. Because really, that's what we are talking about, isn't it? Most of the time when something suddenly impacts our RA or other chronic illness, it's an interruption. A disruption in the life we've carefully built with two things – hard work and Doritos. I mean sheer will. Also Doritos too, ok three things.

It could be weeks in the hospital if something has to be fixed or replaced, possible permanent injury that makes getting around ten times more difficult – or it could lead to any number of issues that, ultimately, interrupt life and take away more of our precious time. Pain for people like us is a mere inconvenience compared to affecting our quality of life, our daily routine, it's the real killer, and that was all weighing on my mind as I lay there on the concrete. The dirty concrete. I gotta clean the basement.

I don't know why it affected me more this time – I have fallen before. One time I took a digger in front of my physical therapy office in front of no less than seven people. It wasn't like a tiny "oops, I fell!" either. It was a full-on, ten steps trying to catch myself, wind knocked out of me, bleating like a goat, slip-and-slide level wipe out. I remember lying there, watching two of the people sitting on the bench saying, "I am not getting involved in this boy's fall," and going inside and the only thing I could think was, "what a bunch of witches." (Edited for content, this is a family site.) I wasn't worried about what I hurt or what the consequences were going to be, at least not in that moment.

Why did this latest fall make me think so much more, then? Age? More to lose? Hit my head and I was hallucinating? All of the above, I think. Well, not the last one. Thank God that pink elephant was there to help me up. I knew that the moment I moved I was going to have to deal with a whole new set of issues and things were going well, for once. Unfortunately, that seems to be the cycle with RA.

Anyone who suffers from chronic illness can agree on one thing – our illness has impeccable timing. More punctual than a British clockmaker, our diseases always rear their ugly head when we least expect it, can afford it, finally start to get things going. Basically, whenever things are looking up, it chimes in to say "can't say Par-tayy without RA!" (My RA is a bad speller.) RA always arrives already drunk and makes a scene by urinating in your potted plant and groping the neighbor's dog and then, on the way out, he burns your house down by throwing a lit cigarette in the trash can. That's on one of his less destructive trysts, too. I think we all know, RA never shows up with a nice bottle of Chablis and says "let's spend a quiet night in and just relax." It's always a fiasco, so who can blame me for not wanting to get up and light that fuse?

When I did eventually pull myself off the floor, my hips were angry, really angry. I ended up laid up for ten days or so but, on the bright side, I think I avoided any permanent damage. Now that I've said it out loud, though, as soon as I get up from this chair my leg will probably fall clean off. "RA's here! Surprise, jerk!"

How Not To Cope With Rheumatoid Arthritis

Lately, people have been asking a lot how I cope with RA and the host of adorable secondary conditions that come with it. Well, here's my answer: I just do! Awesome! Talk soon.

. . .

Hmmm, you're still here? Don't you have some jigsaws to puzzle or physical to therapy? You want more? FINE-UH! I suppose, "I just do," doesn't really do much for anyone who legitimately wants to know, and frankly, it doesn't do much for me either. I guess we'll spend some time unpacking just what goes into coping with that wonderful constellation of symptoms and conditions that make up rheumatoid arthritis, and what "just doing it" really means.

If I'm being honest, though, I wasn't kidding when I said, "I just do." I think anyone who has suffered with chronic illness for long enough knows exactly what I mean when I say that. We just do because that's what we've been doing forever (or at least it feels like it). Having to actually dissect what goes into those coping skills is a bit more difficult. I think the first thing to address rather than how, is why.

Over the years, I've been called many things – hero, inspiration, a rock, and, of course, modest (duh). All of those are inevitably followed by that phrase we've all heard, "I don't think I could do it if I was in your shoes," or something close. I usually just smile and say thanks as if someone just called me "Dennis" by mistake, but in my head I'm always thinking, "Yes, you could do it because you'd have to."

Seriously, what's the other option for me or anyone who has chronic illness? Roll over and stick my arms and legs in the air like a dead looney tunes character? Say, "Screw this!" and squeeze my buns together so hard that the RA just squirts right out of my ears? Dip myself in a tub of essential oils and walk around all glistening and slippery? Well, maybe that last one, but only for fun! The fact is that any human who gets RA must deal with it, there's no way around it, and you would too. It's what humans do: we adapt, and it's nothing special.

Now that we've gotten the why out of the way, we can get down to some of the how. Each of us has our own ways of coping and the specifics vary as much as people's preference for Coke and Pepsi. (Obviously, Coke is superior in every single way and only people who like flat brown juice that tastes like poison filtered through an old sock drink Pepsi, but no judgment.) Whether it's heat or cold, meds or acupuncture, Coke or poison, I mean Pepsi, the overall approach is always the same – we do whatever works.

"Yeah, but what works for you?" I hear you asking. Well, what works for me is a combination of a few things. First, there's pain meds, then sometimes I also use pain meds, and even on occasion I mix in some pain meds when it gets really bad.

Sorry, but there is only one thing that works well enough for me to be a remedy – pain meds. How do I know this? Well, because in the thirty-some-odd years I've dealt with RA, I've tried everything. No, really, I mean everything. Don't believe me? Well let's go through the list, shall we?

I've tried acupuncture. It didn't work for me. Don't get me wrong: if you like sitar music, plastic ferns and babbling brook sounds played from an Amazon Alexa speaker, then great, you do you. Unfortunately, lying down in that darkened room I couldn't relax. All I kept thinking about was the $125 bucks I just spent to have a full MD doctor tell me I was "so young" to have RA. Whaaaaaaaaaaat?

Besides, I had already had so many needles poked into me that I am legitimately classified as an archery target for insurance purposes.

Next, I tried diets upon diets. No tomato diet, no artificial diet, no sugar diet, no gluten diet, and the no wheat diet. None of them did anything for me, and I know I'm going to get some angry comments saying, "But the turnip diet worked for me!" and that's wonderful for you and the turnips but all that dieting never did anything but make me hungry and frustrated. Hungerated. Frusturungry?... Frungry! That's the one.

I was definitely frungry, and that word I didn't just makeup is the only thing that resulted from all that dieting. Besides, do you know how difficult it is to find something with no artificial ingredients, no tomatoes, no sugar, and no wheat at a restaurant? Keep in mind this was years ago before everyone went free-trade organically crazy. I'd order a water and...a lettuce leaf. Hold the flavor. Ugh.

Copper bracelets, yoga, hot yoga, goat yoga, hot goat yoga – look, here's the bottom line: coping with RA is as personal as your underwear – you wear what makes you comfortable and the only ones you show to people are the ones you want them to see (hopefully not on laundry day). Meditation, medication, elevation, delectation or vacation – it doesn't matter.

I know you are probably thinking, "Well this post didn't help me at all," but that's kind of the point. Try anything you think will help, and whatever helps YOU, do THAT. I can't choose for you, but I can tell you that the only person who can figure it out is the one who knows the most about your body. I'm talking about you. Yes you, the me reading this right now. That being said, I may not know how you'll do it, but I can absolutely assure you that you will do it. Cope, that is, because unless you want to simply give up and lock yourself away like some RApunzel (see what I did there), you'll have to find a way to live life.

The Handicapped Spot & "Blue Fever" (or How Invisible Illness Makes the Disabled Parking Spot a Nightmare!)

With the holiday season coming up, and shopping-a-plenty on everyone's list, I think it's a perfect time to revisit one of the most controversial 135 square feet in all of Rheumatoid Arthritisdom. Some call it the blue lagoon of disability (no one calls it that), some call it the rectangle of despair (not really). Of course, I'm talking about the handicapped parking spot, and it is a constant source of issues for those of us who suffer from this sometimes invisible illness.

Ah, the handicapped spot. That small blue polygon seems to make people lose their minds more often than any other blue-colored shape on the planet. So many regular Joes and Josies feel the need to defend the sacred honor of that little space, it truly amazes me sometimes.

What makes those with RA especially prone to looks, snorts, and notes left on windshields? Well, rheumatoid arthritis is such an unpredictable disease. One day we can be limping and almost unable to walk, and the next day we may look almost normal to an outside observer. Which brings us back to where invisible illness and ridiculous, nosy, shoppers intersect and people do things they'd never normally do to a disabled person – the handicapped parking spot.

You have probably heard tales of that storied spot and its capacity to elicit violent reactions, but I think I should give you one of my own, you know, for proper context.

The first time I really experienced what I'm now calling the "Blue Fever," was years ago when I was at the drug store. It was a heady time, when most of America was still offline, and pagers were how people got in touch on the go. If you got a page that said 911, you better answer. Or get a beer. Either or. Anyway, at that time I was still driving what my friends affectionately called the "Meat Wagon," (for reasons that will not be covered in this lesson) which was an old Ford Aerostar, one of the first minivans made. It was suggested to me that I obtain a handicapped parking placard to make life easier after my hip replacements, so I did, and it was good. For a while. This brings us back to the drug store.

It was a sunny day in the summer, and I was actually feeling fantastic. Nothing was hurting, spirits were up, and it was about to be the weekend. So, I pulled into the handicapped spot and hopped out of the car like a normal person would. I wasn't showing any outward signs of RA, as many of us don't sometimes, and I went into the store to get my DVD of Braveheart and a magazine to catch up on the OJ trial.

When I got back to my car, there was a note on the windshield. First I thought it was a parking ticket. As I got closer I saw it was actually loose-leaf (that's paper with lines for you younger readers), and I realized that unless the meter maid got really desperate, it probably meant someone hit me. I just assumed someone dinged the Meat Wagon, but as I angrily grabbed the note from my wiper, I remembered the ol' wagon had more dings than a doorbell store. Confused, I opened the note, and it read:

"Handicapped spots are for disabled people! You should only park here if you are really disabled you jerk!"

Hmmmm. My first thought was "Do they mean really disabled like no arms or legs, or really disabled as in actually disabled? That's just poor grammar." Once I parsed out that mystery, I realized whoever wrote this note took the time to watch me get out of the car, went to their car, took out a pen and some paper, and then thought up and wrote down two sentences which they then folded over and put under my windshield wiper. All because they felt the need to defend the virginity of the handicapped spot. Also, I get why they might have assumed I wasn't disabled, but a jerk, really? Talk about insult to injury. Literally.

Ever since then I've noticed the static I get for parking in that most holy of spots. Stares, sometimes even from people who are obviously using the handicapped spot to run in for a quick item, are the least of it. I get huffs and puffs all the time, pointing, and of course, the ubiquitous sidelong glance/rolling eyes. It's so bad sometimes that I throw on a pronounced limp when I get out, you know? Gotta give the people what they want. It's shameful and I shouldn't do it, but sometimes I just don't want to deal with the looks, and in a perverse way, it kind of makes me feel like "ha! You thought I wasn't handicapped, but I am, you ass!" It's the little things in life, you know?

Why do people do this? It's a question I've considered a lot. What I've settled on is that it makes people feel like a hero, when they really are doing nothing at all. There's really no downside for them, and no upside for the person they are sniping at. Think about it, at best, even if they did stop some unscrupulous handicap placard user with a pencil-thin mustache and an eye patch, they wouldn't even be there to see the fruits of their labor. So they drive off feeling like they just saved the world from overarching evil, and yet couldn't care less what happens after.

Of course, we all know, most people who use a handicapped spot actually need it. My mother had access to my placard for years, and made a point of not using it because "it wasn't right." I think most people would agree but still, that goodness doesn't seem to apply to people minding their own business and certainly doesn't apply to not making assumptions which make an ass of, well, you know the rest.

"'Invisible Illness,' has always struck me funny. Why? Well, for most of us our illnesses are anything but 'invisible.' They are visible. Eyesore-creating, landscape-altering, plaid-with-striped pants level visible. But there are good days when others may not realize by looking that we have chronic illness. Unfortunately, it's yet another example of how disability and chronic illness is defined, many times, by those who do not experience it. Hopefully this book helps to change that!"

—Daniel Malito

Marion Michell

Advocacy poem

Imagine the most hushed, unrushed procession possible,
flocks of people with severe M.E. filling the streets
on berths, bunks, beds, futons, beanbags, sofas, wheelchairs –
crash pads all, running on dreams and discipline.
Tens, hundreds, thousands, and those who cannot leave
the rooms they lie in, there with their walls around them,
curtains drawn. Housebound, occasionally out;
bathed, unwashed, half-dressed, PJ's or Sunday best;
some with bedpans or commodes, some with feeding tubes;
speaking, humming, silent, eyes closed, eyes wide – all of us.

No drums beaten, nor banners waved.
Instead see our bidding magnified
on bedclothes, headboards, eiderdowns, and,
if the sun is out, scrawled all over the big blue:
urging serious commitment to medical research,
increased support, and being heard.

We're too tired for a riot,
and only up to rallying sighs.
But a simmering rage is in the air –
no more waiting!

bond

when breath sprawls next to you
in long sinewy strings
you know your body is straining.

what you take for decorum,
are bored by, chest rising, falling,
rising, falling; what you neglect,

drunk on technicolour dreams
of skipping out the door,
encounters, speech in dazzling tongues;

what you don't see, forever pining:
how body labours,
steady as an old love.

Forks

Early one afternoon, when light has long outlasted you, a person comes to claim a parcel. They'd caught a glimpse of you the year before and do not blink when you appear in Sunday flannel PJ best: carmine roses on midnight blue, on a weekday too.

Struggling to stand, hunting stick in hand, you hug the door, and, when asked how you are, reach for words and find - none. Your legs mask fading shafts of prickly particles. Stumbling along the fallow field unscheduled conversations have become, you can feel their hum.

Turning to leave the person says: you look well, you must be better!
The pull of gravity is pitiless. You're keen to push another fork into
the bedroom wall, but, alas, your arms lack oomph.

Knot

I won't write an ode to my old hiking boots, no, I won't.
Nor to the paths trodden, forest, coastal, city-wide;
the scents encountered, the views, the people;
the shared or solitary pleasures; soundscapes, silences.
The intense but never deadening tiredness after walking
in all weathers, mile by snaking mile;
the blisters, scratches, bruises, nature's exuberant citations;
lungs filled with yonder; real hunger; deep and satisfying sleep.
What use retracing steps if grief trumps grace?

"Myalgic encephalomyelitis (M.E.) is like a burglar who steals from
you every minute of every day. Its booty is your energy, half a
sackful of cognitive functions and whatever else it can find. Out
goes your profession, your social life; your mobility, vision, memory;
your ability to look after yourself without help; your idiosyncratic
vitality – in short: the way you were in the world. Hardest: when
your intelligence curls up in a ball and rolls out of reach."

—Marion Michell

Ji

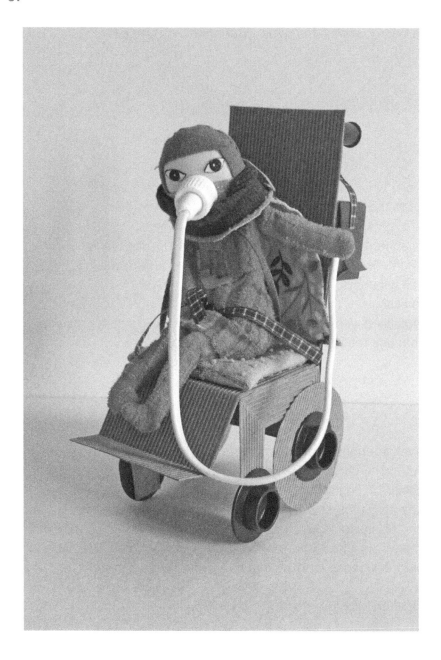

PT Muldoon

Second Act

"It's incurable" is just a phrase
Until that phrase is said to you
Then all that once felt possible
Quickly melts into "all through"

But slowly you find meaning
As you meet em one by one
Warriors from your new tribe
On the quest you have begun

The stakes you face are higher
Each loss will break your heart
But here inside this battlefield
Every warrior plays their part

You search for little moments
You loved back in your prime
The one thing that evades you
Is the chance to turn back time

On days the monster beats you
Driving pain deep thru your skin
You take a rest until you're able
To rejoin, then fight again

Incurable defines my foe
I've accepted that as fact
But if you think I'm beaten
Just watch my second act

"One of the hardest parts of living with Myasthenia Gravis (MG) is that you never know when it will flare up and when that happens all plans can evaporate in a moment. The meds I take to counter the effects of the disease quite often make me very sick. Learning to accept what is out of my control and work with what remains has been my greatest challenge."

—PT Muldoon

Christine Obst

Tattoos and Scars

I was diagnosed with Lupus when I was 31. I was living in Los Angeles at the time and showed up at my doctor's office with a rash, the size of a dime, on my face. After swimming in a pool at friend's house, I swore I had ringworm, but after the doc ran some blood tests, he left this voicemail at my apartment:

VM message from the doc: "Hi Christine, its Doctor blah blah. Yeah, your test came back positive for Lupus, but no big deal. I'm headed to Greece for vacation and we'll talk when I get back."

My first reaction was complete confusion. Little did Doctor blah blah know that a friend I was working with at the time, her mother had died from Lupus at 72. Imagine my heart in my throat as I could hear it pounding in my temples and ears.

When I moved back to Philadelphia from LA, I went to see a new doctor and told him of the discovery in California. He ran some blood work, a few times, and proceeded to say, "nope, don't see it, I think you have more of a "Chronic Fatigue Syndrome." Just for frame of reference, for those of you who watched The Golden Girls, on one episode, Dorothy goes through a ring of doctors then she finally gets diagnosed with Chronic Fatigue Syndrome, I guess it was the safest disease they could come up with that wouldn't shock their 1980's audience. They later did a bit where Rose thinks she has HIV, so kudos to them.

At one point, I had pneumonia for the third time in a year and could not get in to see my regular doctor, but the nurse was able to set me up with his partner. He looked through my file and asked me if I ever had rheumatologic blood work done. Of course, I didn't know what that was and replied, "I don't think so".

According to my file it was evident that I did not have these tests done. Long story short, he ran the tests along with an MRI of my brain, which showed high ANA and RNA numbers.

The MRI showed a lesion in my right brain matter. The report stated, 'Least likely MS, most likely Lupus'. He sent my results and reports over to a local rheumatologist. I met with him and found him to be snide and aloof.

He proceeded to tell me that I ONLY had 6 points of the 11 for Lupus and he needed all 11. He then told me that I probably had Fibromyalgia, but "we all know that's a bullshit diagnosis." I went immediately back to my doctor and told him to give me the best, which he did. My current rheumatologist is wonderful and told me he only needed one point of Lupus to diagnosis. The bad news was yet to come, though. After his tests he told me I had Lupus, Rheumatoid Arthritis, Fibromyalgia and Osteoporosis.

When I look back on receiving those diagnoses, I remember how calm I was, because I didn't have Cancer, because our society is conditioned in such a way that if you don't have Cancer you don't have any problems. What is not understood is that Cancer is also autoimmune. If we cure one autoimmune illness, say Diabetes, we cure Cancer. Maybe it's not that simple, but it would be a start, but does our society really want to do that? When I started to research and look into my illnesses, I got angry. Which wasn't helpful for my conditions.

When you realize you have a life-threatening illness, and its not Cancer, there are things you need to let go of. For me, I had to let go of my expectations of others. You tell people you have Autoimmune Disease with this look on your face of dread. Their reactions range from: What's Lupus? To "But you can't die from that, right?" I had to reel myself in and just "do me" as they say.

I had to learn to say 'no' and relinquish my FOMO (Fear of missing out), but most importantly, I had to redefine my idea of a "good time." People thought I looked good so how could I possibly be so sick?

Lupus is one of those "invisible" illnesses. You can't see our scars because they are embedded in our muscles, our tissue, and our bones. People think there are magic pills that heal, so why complain? I had to let go of anger and resentment.

The first thing I did was decrease my friend group. Those who had stopped inviting me to the party were the first to go. Don't get me wrong, I still maintain contact, but from a distance and yes, I forgave them for their lack of understanding.

I looked into exercise and stretches that would help with pain, I took yoga classes, and even painting classes to see what new hobby I could get into. What was so wonderful was this disease actually helped me find my way back to writing. Writing is the one thing I can do that helps me with anxiety, depression and even pain. I look forward, now, to going to bed and reading a good book and waking up in the morning and writing a few paragraphs for the memoir I am working on. In a way, I have Lupus to thank for that, it allowed me to see the joy in my surroundings. I still have to work on it, because I still have those angry moments, those expectation moments, but I'm closer to being mindful of my surroundings, telling people I love them and creating work I can be proud of. We are not here forever, and with my illness, I've lost years, so I want to go out having known I created, loved and discovered joy on my terms.

"It takes everything I have to get out of bed in the morning. Most days I don't know if Lupus has come to visit, or Rheumatoid Arthritis is in control. Fibromyalgia is just an added bonus. My pain speaks to me on a deep level. I've given up careers, friends, and hobbies to be with my illnesses. It is an abusive relationship that knows no bounds. I live for today; in this moment."

—Christine Obst

Jess L. Parker

Miss You Already

I'm foreign in my own skin. Alien invasion—
the limited edition. Headlights in fog. I drip
drowsily into the next day. Into the,
into the next day. Blinking over hills I'm
bobbing for my resting place.

You were bleak but I was bleaker. Drowning
in that empty glass of water. When my engine sputters
don't revive me—I'm not meant for this world.
If you would, survive me. I may have spent it all or nothing;
check the mattress, walls, and ceiling.

If you would, lead me into some repetitive song;
I'll follow you there. Hold hands with the snare drum.

If you would, cure me like bacon.
My head is such an apple in orbit.

It's spinning and I
miss you already…

"On days when I feel well, I might struggle to articulate the illnesses that I suffer from (migraine, chronic fatigue). On days when I am suffering, I look much the same. This is part of what makes invisible illness so slippery…

as the title of the anthology suggests, when we are not ill in ways that others readily accept as valid, empathy comes slowly if at all, even from ourselves."

—Jess L. Parker

Lilan Patri

Boredom

When I'm at my sickest, all I want is the absence of anything: sunlight, e-mail, the neighbor's footfall, the lifting of an arm.

Chewing.

I don't know bored then. The void is my salvation.

Boredom won't come till the virus ebbs. She's a whisper. A dim star. The promise of "better." And the virus does ebb—before it flows. That's how it works, this tidal existence. The sick never stops. The four walls stay my sandwich. But me, my body, forever we're fluxing. "Better" comes slow: My frontal lobe blinks. The mitochondria rustle. My heart stops popping. And everything outside of me is less sharp a blade.

That's when boredom gets eager. Boredom gets antsy. She tugs at the sleeve of my soft cotton chemise. I have to shake her off.

Not so fast. No DOING. Not till the chills leave my spine, the lead-weights my limbs, and brushing my teeth is an act I can take for granted again.

Boredom's not pleased. Her glare is an itch. But if I don't scratch it? If I keep the black-out curtains sealed, mold the Ohropax to fit the ear, if I lie here mummified…

One day soon, I am donning a bra. I am chatting with my caregiver Marzena. I file a bill. I dance the cat-angler. I am DOING! Boredom belly-bounces on the bed. She lobs glitter at the ceiling. God, I want this party. Let's DO. I order nail lacquer, I water the ficus, I write six e-mails, I watch every Friends clip I can find. Boredom sings

Hallelujah, and I do and I do and I do, until my eyes are sinkholes, my breath's a heave, my adrenals flip backwards, and the words go missing every time I speak.

Why, hello, says the virus. *Whoosh!*—all the force of the Atlantic behind it. I fight the tide. I deny it. But there is a weeping beneath my sternum that means I've already gone under, and now boredom—my spark, my Lorelei—doesn't look me in the eye. By tomorrow she'll be gone. She won't bother to say goodbye.

Closer and Closer to the Core

I never thought I'd lose my words. Now they hang like half-chewed cherries from my lips. Stones and flesh.

"Whereitwhereit went," I say.

I claw for sentences that will not come. Half-formed thoughts that used to slip out smooth and fully formed twist and snap before they reach the air.

My caregiver Barnaby learns to read the blips.

"Check the white whisker basket," I tell him. "Whick—?"

"Got it," he says.

Pinned in the dark, I chase down synonyms, adages, clichés. I just can't remember anymore how we say what we say.

"You sure did tackle the belly of the whale!"

I dream of a bird, caught in the left lobe of a friend's brain. Its wings gleam turquoise, silver tipped. "But can they get it out?" I ask. She shrugs, unfazed.

I wake and I *know* that bird. It once chirruped and rustled in its cage. "Peacock... peacock... no. Canary? Peacock... pppp... PARAKEET!"

The next day I forget all over again. "Peacock... pea... *Dammit*."
I scramble as I write this. I am feverish. My neck sweats.

A social worker visits, keen as nails. For an hour, she hammers. I stumble, defending myself. Words refuse reach. Syllables drop, flip-flop. I am in tears. "I was 38 years old," I say. "I thought I would get better. I thought I had a future."

When she leaves, she takes with her my voice.

Every day, Sylwia comes. Or Marzena. Or Barnaby. I check-mark their list of tasks in advance so I need say nearly nothing. Still, sometimes I have to ask: What did you feed Leopold? Please bring me a bottle of water. Throw this away... or that.

Every day I measure the cost. If I ask for the bottle of water, my larynx burns all hours. If I rise and get it myself, shivers rush my limbs. I buckle. There is no best direction.

Seasons fall away. My voice rises, slowly. Not the same. Never the same.

I keep thinking of my Grand-mère, at 90, 95, 100, her bookbinder's fingers which had once creased each page to perfection, fumbling now, failing her, reduced over time to no more than tearing thin strips of radiant Japanese paper that her caregivers then glued on cards.

They were so beautiful, those cards. How she hated them.

Leopold mewls. "Shall I open the door?" I ask as I unlatch the window. He bounds across the sill.

I did not know, so many years ago, what it must mean to watch the pieces of yourself get shaved away, the so-you-you-always-took-them-for-granted pieces, the closer-and-closer-to-the-core pieces. The loss is immeasurable.

And I am afraid.

He Calls Himself M.E.

I live inside a house, a house that has no door. My captor is an illness, with the build and the might of a minotaur.

His name is Myalgic Encephalomyelitis. He calls himself M.E.— because once he has found you, your own myself goes missing. He takes away your me.

He keeps me locked in shadow. He lays himself on top of me. I cry out. He crushes a filthy palm against my tongue. I try to kick. He pins my limbs. I am buried under the weight of him. Gnats roam his pelt. They pinch my skin. I want only not to feel.

At night I hear the other women, their stifled howls in other rooms, rooms I cannot reach. Down halls built labyrinthine, his footfall thuds like mallets.

M.E. has henchmen, naturally. They call on me all hours.

Postural Orthostatic Tachycardia Syndrome, he goes by the name of POTS. His stride is long, his cloak a wing. It seems to hum and whir.

He waves his arms. His sleeves flip back: fine-boned wrists, a cloud of black. Tiny red-eyed vampire bats. They flap in a fury against my ribs. Fanging for blood—before it pumps the heart, before it sates the brain.

I reach for a wall, brace myself, fall into a crouch. POTS laughs. He pokes my shoulder. I tip right over. I am wan. I gulp for breath. POTS whistles high and tight.

His bats rise. They're gone. I can't stand up.

A phantom flutter bites into my breast.

Hashimoto's Thyroiditis is fat as a slug. He blinks real slow, like a man who can't be bothered.

Outside, the sun bakes the sky—except I wouldn't know. Hashi controls the thermostat.

My room is brisk as January.

I tuck my comforter under my feet, my hips, my forearms, I pull it to my chin.

No matter.

But You Don't Look Sick

Hashi is here, greasy strands slicked across his scalp. He gives the blanket one small tug—he's got hold of my fingers, hold of my toes. Their tips take on a glacier's sheen. A chill rolls into the all of me.
On his way out, Hashi snaps off a fistful of my hair. He lets it drop.

Whatever. He doesn't care.

Adrenal Fatigue used to row crew. She sports collegiate sweats—exclusively.

Nights, she nudges me awake. Every two hours, maybe three. Mornings, a paper bag gets crammed over my head.

If she's feeling punchy, she might just cut two eye holes. Mostly, I stare at empty brown. This, she says, builds stamina.

Either way, I'm never not exhausted.

By five, she lets me take it off. She's not so bad then, really. She tells lewd jokes. She pets the cat. She teaches Texas Hold'em.

At nine, she slaps on pounds of lard. My thighs, my butt, my upper arms. She likes her gals chunked up.

I tell her I want the skinny back.

She laughs. Vanity? You think you're allowed *that*?

M.E. has three teen daughters: Leaky Gut, Gut Dysbiosis, Candidiasis. Big into arts and crafts, my intestines, their pet project.

The eldest likes to scrapbook, her scissors sting like flame. She has me buckled over, weeping for the pain.

The middle one inflates my tummy: a balloon she papier-mâchés. I am relegated to elastic loungewear waists.

And the youngest with her bedazzler! Dime-store rhinestones geyser out my bowels.

I've culled my diet to five stewed foods. I gorge on lactoferments. Regardless.

My stomach lining is macramé, my intestinal wall is paper lace. Each snowflake the sisters cut, another toxin in my bloodstream, another nutrient gone to waste.

Epstein Barr wears Tony Lamas. He's always watching. The mean is in his eyes.

He watches for when I get busy, he watches for when I show joy, he watches most of all for when I *carpe* the damn *diem*, and that is when he strikes.

He slams me against the door frame. He kicks me to the floor. I'm curled at his feet, I'm begging: *please, not this time, no, I didn't mean to, really.*

He lights an American Spirit. He flicks the match head at my face. I shut my eyes. He laughs. The heels of his cowboy boots click away.

The air is coarse with tobacco, my mind all soot and blur. I cannot move. I cry three days.

It's two weeks before being alive feels kind of okay.

My immune system was once a vision, her muscles lean and coiled. She roared into battle, her arrows thrummed. She never knew a loss.

Twelve years she has hunted M.E.'s henchmen, she has chased his band of miscreants—Borna, Parvo, Entero; Chlamydia Pneumonia and Mycoplasma; Ehrlichiosis, Humanes Herpes 6.

She has thrown herself on M.E.'s back, she has stabbed his sides, she has pierced his neck. For what?

She has been flung against walls, she has broken three ribs, she has lost the skin off her knuckles.

She is hunkered in a corner now, barely aware who's in the room or whom she's supposed to throttle—maybe she's the one who started it, maybe she's what's wrong, she's why I'm still here?

She pounds her temples. She tears her gnarled hair. She rakes her own arms.

Take that, you, she says.

She lives in a house, a house with no door.

Her captor has the build of a minotaur.

On a Late Afternoon in June

June sweeps in, and she's a beauty. I want to cup her cheekbones, I want to know her close. I want to touch her blue sky skin.

I have not been outdoors since February.

I have been pushing myself, cloistered and nocturnal, for months. I have read a book. I have read it twice. I have kept a journal. I have watched TV! *Ellen*, Graham Norton, the stuff I could find for free. Banal, I don't care. *Funny!* I have launched a blog, I have written five posts, I have drawn little drawings, I have cut out each. *Precision scissoring.* With my cousin I have collaborated, I have edited in translation, I have PR'd her article all over the Web.

I have done everything I am not supposed to do. Everything I'd relinquished the past four years.

The sun reaches long and low across our garden wall. I unfold a plaid blanket in a triangle of light. Weeds and wild grasses bend soft beneath me. An ant trails across my ankles.

I wear my Bose 15 C noise cancelling headphones. The construction site beside us works late hours. A snarl of engines, the clank of steel girders come to me muted. I wear my Bose 15 C noise cancelling headphones, and I pretend that this is enough. I forget what I had remembered every afternoon, the summer past.

My eye mask is indoors.

It should have destroyed me months ago: the everything I've done that I am not supposed to do. But it keeps *not*. And so I keep on. My brain is snap-crackle-popping, my body all edges. It's a vitamin B complex that does this. I cannot rest as I must, I cannot meditate either. The current is too fierce, the hunger, after so many years' abstinence, for a mind that gets to churn again, fiercer still.

Of course I am unwell. Brittle and chilled. Feverish. Yet, the valleys I slide into—between all the doing—are shallow, their slopes an easy climb. And I am brazen.

Now June curls up like a cat, lays her weight upon my eyelids. They haven't felt this warmth for years. I want it never to end. Hot tears roll into my ears. I think: I shall write a post about grace. I shall write a post about the grace of the sun on my eyelids on a late afternoon in June.

The next morning, my eyes catch flame. For weeks they blaze. I cannot stay the pain.

Something is terribly wrong.

Oh, but the Germans dance toward World Cup glory! I dare to watch. Götze's left foot slices the sky. My body quakes, my body falters. And then, everything breaks.

I do not write about grace.

"I was diagnosed 7 years too late, and even then doctors mocked me, refused treatment, accused me of replicating Christ's suffering like monks in the Middle Ages. This is part and parcel of having ME/CFS. As I lay isolated and brain-fogged, wrung dry by fatigue, normalcy turned to a memory, and what had made my life mine fell away. Two decades on, I cherish anemones and sunlight. Standing upright. And every soul who believes me."

—Lilan Patri

A. Shea (Angie Waters)

Courage

I can't compare this exhaustion
or define every pain,
but I know some days
it is courage, sheer courage,
that wills me to fight again.

Fate

I am resigned
to no fate
but rather to take back
every day
in some small way
that reminds this disease
who is in charge

"My health is compromised by Lupus SLE (Systemic Lupus Erythematosus), to the point I am no longer able to keep a regular job. It includes seizures, heart issues, chronic migraine, extreme brain fog, immobility and many other complications. I am currently on disability and doing my best to create a life I can be proud of, in spite of lupus, by writing and creating art."

—A. Shea (Angie Waters)

Eira Stuart

Myalgic Encephalomyelitis

I. The Cavern

I'm broken,
my body is aware,
full of sensations I cannot bear.

Stolen are words,
language is null,
from the outside there is no one,
understanding is gone.

Protest is futile,
they cannot see,
past the wholeness of my being,
to the broken me.

Neurons firing inside my brain,
voices are burning,
lights do the same.

In darkness there is shelter,
a refuge of peace,
from the bombardment of the outside
but inside there's no relief;
the sunburn in my brain,
the crawling shocks of pain,
the patients who claim,
the system is to blame.

I'm broken, I'm broken
on the inside,
but on the outside all they see

is a despondent soul,
inwardly writhing in agony.

The protestors still march
while I sleep in my bed,
some campaign for the truth,
the rest say it's all in my head.

Well, the only thing I can say is
perspective has given this game away,
I have seen reality,
from politics to pure empathy,
I will carry on my torch
in hopes of a better day.

II. The Grace of Suffering

At the depths of despair there is laughter,
when the pointlessness of suffering dawns,
yet there is no escape from these unyielding prisons
crippled by disease not yet known to man.

They say in suffering is hidden mercy,
but I don't see it;
all I know is my body is slowly unravelling,
and my soul is endlessly wailing,
as each breath unstitches a semblance of my being.

This cruel torment that can deceive
and make you look well with one surge of adrenaline,
that moments later has you crashing down
the stairs of this unending fortress;
isolating, abandoned and yet so painfully Misrepresenting
its emaciation for antiquity.

How can you see what is being consumed from within?
You think because you care about me
that makes me invincible to the fate of so many others?
It does not.
This is not some notion.
Stop telling me I'm beautiful.
My suffering is not a palette
and my pain is not a work of art.

I keep crying to you in the stillness,
but no one will hear me.
No one will hear me in this silent storm.
My suffering is muted in the cavern of my being,
the burning sun scorching me from within.

My body is for them
to mask reality;
my skin a painted veil over a raging fire;
to feed their denial,
to fund their somatoform lies.

How can so much be concealed by so little?

I fear they will not cure M.E.
before it is too late,
until I AM yet another human form,
consumed like volcanic ash.

IV. Hippocratic Oath

The darkness is my shelter,
it shields me from the harm of light,
the scorching, burning, pain
is relieved only by the night.

My spine is like an iron rod,
full of spasms and pain;
muscles like barbed wire,
so weak and quick to fail.

My Hypothalamic-pituitary axis
is utterly disrupted,
by Myalgic Encephalomyelitis,
still a mystery to doctors.

M.E. is a Neurological disease,
affecting cellular mitochondria,
brain-stem, spine and muscles,
it is not feigned hypochondria.

It is also systemic,
and occurs in pandemics,
what we need is a polemic
shift, in the view of medics.

Yet worse than all this suffering,
is the disbelief I must endure,
the constant accusations,
and the fact there is no cure.

I am told that I "play dead",
and that "it's all in my head",
and "I can if I try",
and "perhaps I'm in denial".

I wish that they could see,
through the eyes of M.E.

They only wish they could lie in bed,
though my life is of the waking dead.

IX. Carousel

The Christmas carousel has arrived at my door,
it is a time of year I truly abhor.
As the children go around merrily,
my head begins to spin incessantly;
from the hurricane of noise in my diseased brain,
from all the singing in the rain,
the carols bring me no pleasure;
the torrential noise is simply too much pressure.

I cannot read my Christmas cards,
opening the envelope is much too hard,
when I'm in pain in my very bones,
the last thing I need is to hear them gloat:

The friends who forget me all year long,
suddenly write to flaunt their victory songs;
of their mortgaged homes and new promotions,
and their new found parental devotions,
to their new born progeny,
you would think their three year old is a prodigy,
for pooing in the potty and eating a biscuit,
well my life is really no different.

I am thirty three and wear a diaper,
and eat puree food from a beaker,
no I do not have a fetish,
I suffer from M.E and it is hellish.

Eating a biscuit would be a momentous achievement,
my long lost life is my constant bereavement;
of dreams gone up in smoke,
and financial pressures like a yoke.
Buried alive before I'm dead,
forced to live in a lonely prison bed,

no one has any time for me,
I am pulled around like a piece of property,
no companionship is ever offered me,
except my own lonely soliloquy.

Just in and out at record speed,
the corporate bodies are full of greed,
to maximize profits with minimum resources,
despite it being a crime to the labouring work forces.

It could even be classed as modern slavery,
to extricate hard manual labour with little pay,
lucky for them I have no say.

For if I did, I would make them listen:
No more slaves of minimum wage!
No more forcible isolation in a prison-like cage!

We need national minimum standards in social care,
and qualified professionals
who are kind and self-aware!
No more task based checklists and mechanical airs!
What is needed is person-centred care.

Such are the joys of an M.E sufferer at Christmas,
only biomedical research will ever redeem us.

XI. Effete

They enter my sanctuary;
a cacophony of relentless noise oscillates through my spine
seeping into every nerve,
unravelling into a furnace of sensation,
ebbing at the shores of sanity;
in perpetual darkness.

But You Don't Look Sick

The slamming refuse bin breaks the silence
alleviating the night vigil;
the torturous drone of the hoover,
hissing doors on creaking hinges,
CBD oil in plastic syringes;
effete by a bloodless invisible massacre
achieved by mere vibration.

How I wish to summon Newton from his grave
and ask him to review the laws of physics.
In my own private universe they certainly abide by chaos theory –
(Castaneda eat your heart out!)
Was it not vibrations in the primordial fields,
in the false vacuum that caused the Big Bang?
Well then,
vibration must be the most powerful force in the universe.

Screeching footsteps approach;
a languorous walk, the epitome of nonchalant youth.
No hello as she shoves the tablets in my mouth
unceremoniously followed by concentrated orange juice;
the essence of oranges once fresh and whole,
pasteurised, preserved, mummified,
devoid of essence;
an allegory of my own life,
a mark of a profit driven business
masquerading as a care institution.
But who really cares?
Certainly not this young woman
feeding me breakfast in between sips of coffee
and bites of her sandwich;
using my room as an escape;
her own private refuge.

Welcome to the M.E. café!
I'm of no consequence,
as good as any other inanimate object;
a human table perhaps?
How's that for personification?
It will have to suffice.

I cannot move, speak, sit up or chew.
No visitors, no telephone, no T.V.,
just existing in suspended animation;
in perpetual darkness
to calm the inferno of inflammation
coursing through my nervous system,
drowning in nitric oxide;
that accident that ruined my life,
altering my fate; stealing my destiny.

An inanimate object was all I could hope to be,
an accessory for careless youth to delight in
and shun as worthless,
as it sates its sloth at my door.

IV. Carrot

Carrot; a postmodern parody

In my sanitorium the food is bland,
often orchestrated by an unknown hand,
on my palate, the tastes amalgamate,
a conundrum that gluttony itself cannot substantiate.

But You Don't Look Sick

And then one day a roast dinner appeared,
I ate it with gusto, though my energy fell in arrears,
from Myalgic Encephalomyelitis
which spelled an end to my career.

I did, however, wonder if a carrot would present,
would I be able to chew it?
Or would it further my descent
into the abyss of post-exertional neuro immune exhaustion
despite my best intents?

While I began to chew, a chunk titillated my tongue,
the glory of caramelized vegetation
a lost anomaly to the young
whose senses have been clouded
by MSG, artificial sweeteners and E's 1, 2 and 3.

Beta carotene, a light in the darkness,
a tonic to the isotopes, the retinal cones,
decoding a myriad of transient sensory kaleidoscopes.

Endorphins dancing the light Fandango
throughout my ravaged brain,
the essence of the carrot was probably to blame,
I thank it heartily for the sacrifice it made,
for its delicious happening,
right upon my plate.

F. Cade Swanson

Fullness

For years after I came out
my mother would ask me if I was sick.
"You're too skinny," she would say.
It was an accusation more than an observation.
But my gaunt appearance
was not due to the sickness she imagined.

And while my gay drove me to be lean,
as if my self-doubt consumed all of the nourishment
my body needed,
it would be years before the virus she feared I had
contracted
would appear
unexpected
in my no-longer gaunt body.

Self-doubt had been replaced by comfort.
Fullness of parenting
Fullness of relationship.
Comfort opened up new vulnerabilities.

Unknowingly
I let HIV in,
delivered in a package of kindness and warmth,
an extra ingredient in a meal of validation.
I had eaten too much.

First step: confession.
I bring my husband to get tested.
Negative.
I tell no one else.

But You Don't Look Sick

Unsure if I could deal with their reaction.
Shame Pity. Shock. Disgust.
Rejection.

Next step: acknowledgement.
It takes me more than a year to go on meds.
I was not ready to accept my new reality.
I was not ready to have my kids find my pills
and ask what's wrong.
Afraid of
"you look sick,"
the words my mom used to say to me.
Afraid of dying.

Final step: acceptance.
And so now I lift weights
And eat lots
And take my meds with meals as prescribed
And worry about bone density and kidney function
And cholesterol levels.
And worry about my kids.

And while the meds keep the virus in check
Undetectable
I secretly work to keep my illness
Undetectable.

Still afraid perhaps of being too comfortable
Or too full
Because that didn't work out so well last time.

*First published in Day Without Art 30. Pandemonium Press.
December 2019*

Hoping to not be too Weird

"Bring your raincoat," I said to Jade.

My daughter was finishing up her morning routine: brushing her teeth, pulling her new braids back into a ponytail and laying her edges. The familiar smell of coconut oil meant she was almost ready to go. I heard the squeaky door on the shoe closet open and looked over. She reached past her Nikes to grab her Adidas, then remembered the field trip and pulled on her boots instead.

Today started especially rainy. A dense petrichor filled the room as we opened the front door, quickly overtaking the pleasant coconut smell. It was going to be a very wet, muddy day. I was hoping those black leather boots were going to keep her feet dry.

Raincoats are not cool in Seattle- they're a sure sign that you're not from here and only just better than an umbrella, something a local would never use. Hoodies are okay, but not ones made out of nylon or rayon or polyester blends. The sound those fabrics make as your arms glide effortlessly past your sides is like a not-so-subtle reminder that you do not belong. Still, I knew we'd be outside all day, and I also knew Jade wouldn't want her braids to get messed up. Protecting the hair won out and the purple rain jacket went on.

The first time Jade had asked me to chaperone a field trip, she gave me clear instructions: *don't be weird*. Because I'm one of *those* dads, she knew it was important to lay down a few additional rules:

107

1) Be friendly, but no funny stories about when she was a baby.
2) Dad jokes are strictly off limits.
3) I may not pick her up at any point unless asked.
4) The field trip is not about me.

I felt confident based on her feedback from the last field trip, after which she simply stated: "thanks for not being too weird." Still, it felt a bit like walking a tightrope, and I was starting off a bit unbalanced, having insisted on the raincoat.

Earlier that morning, I had gotten up to make breakfast for her and the boys, as I do every day. Jade likes a toasted English Muffin with a fried egg where the yolk is just soft enough to run, but hard enough to not drip all over her hands and nails. Noah always has oatmeal and Jaylen has eggs with toast. My meds are to be taken with a meal of at least 450 calories, so I make myself two eggs and toast with a slice of turkey. I wash down my antiretrovirals with coffee and a chaser of probiotics and vitamins with a protein shake.

I worried a bit about the cold weather and the dozens of kids who awaited me, with their inevitable sniffles and coughs. Having convinced Jade to wear a raincoat, I felt okay wearing mine. *Not weird*. I practiced fist bumps instead of high fives, because it felt a bit safer, like I was less likely to get a hand full of snot or germs that way. I was feeling good, though, and my immune system was strong.

When I first got my HIV diagnosis, Jade was just two years old. It was unexpected; I had survived years of animated urban gay life before marriage and kids, and managed to avoid the plague that had killed so many of my contemporaries. I was so careful at this point in my life, so calculated about my risks.

I was overwhelmed by feelings of shame and guilt, and allowed taking care of the person whose HIV had been shared with me to distract me. Late night phone calls overflowing with his emotions and tears were an easy way for me to avoid my own feelings, and also allowed me to shift to an easy default for me: being helpful. Having buried so many friends with HIV and AIDS, I was not clear how my life should continue, but I didn't want to think about it. I acted as if my illness was invisible, allowed the rainy grey skies of Seattle to soak deep into my bones like a local, convinced that the way to still fit in was to pretend like I was unaffected.

I hoped that I would somehow be unaffected.

I worried about getting sick, but I worried more about my kids finding out I was sick. I worried about dying, but also convinced myself that confronting my sickness by going on meds was too risky. I didn't want my kids to find my pills and worry about me. I didn't want them to think I was going to die.

Hope is fickle, though, and my body called my bluff, said it couldn't fight on its own anymore. It forced me to make some hard choices and start dealing with my illness, to accept that I couldn't pretend everything was okay, even if my illness was not obvious to others.

Which doesn't mean I like the smell or taste of the meds, even years later, any more than I like the smell or feel of nylon rain jackets. And it doesn't mean that I like the sound of my hand clicking open the top of my bottle of antiretrovirals, any more than I like the sound of my arms gliding effortlessly against my waist in my raincoat. And it doesn't mean that dealing with my illness makes me feel any less like an outsider than how I feel walking around in a raincoat on a wet Seattle morning.

But it does mean that I can focus my energies, at least for now, on a different hope: to not be weird, or at least *not too weird* for my daughter to spend time with me. Because even though I'm *that* kind of sick, I'm also still *that* kind of dad. And not being weird still takes a lot of hope, and a lot of effort.

"While HIV works to destroy my immune system, the stigma of living with HIV is a much larger battle that keeps my disease hidden. Sometimes I wonder if the shame I've been told I should feel is ultimately the thing that will take me out, other times my commitment to being a cranky old grandfather one day keeps me swallowing pills and focusing on long term survival."

—F. Cade Swanson

Brent Terry

21st Century Autoimmune Blues

Even the flowers are trying to kill you.
Even the bread. Even the cells in your nails
conspire to drag your hands to your neck, enwrap
and enrapture your song-encrusted throat.
Your fingers make palpable the shadow
that seethes beyond the Earth's voracious curve,
play the blues that stipple the tender flesh.
It's a brand new year and histamines are all the rage.
Corticosteroids are the new black.
You've become allergic to yourself. It's body
vs. antibody, that same tired tango,
and it's way too late for dancing. Your twisted mister
blinks back from the bathroom mirror,
doesn't bother to floss. Your future is encrypted
in the walls of your bone-vault, you bury your feelings
but have to admit that things are getting grave.
Whispers pass over your body like hands.
The tossed postures of your everyday
play shadow puppets on the kitchen wall—Punch
and Judy headlining the Armegeddon room.
So you spend what's left of your youth laughing
until you cry. Your eyes itch. It's just your body
trying to kill you to save you from yourself.
You're caught between a rock and a hardly place.
You're going to name your new band
Systemic Inflammatory Response, your first album,
What's Been Eating You Lately?
Maybe it's tick-borne. Maybe a fungus. Maybe
you're a character in a DeLillo novel. Your affliction
is so postmodern. You're so meta it's killing you.

111

"For twenty years, I have been dealing with an elusive and nebulous autoimmune disease, an illness further complicated by allergies, mononucleosis and Lyme disease. The syndrome took away a professional athletics career and for a bit, my sanity. Writing about it has been a big part of dealing with something manageable, but never vanquished."

—Brent Terry

Nicole Townsend

Stagnant

I remain stagnant,
Tired day in and out,
I have to be quiet
When I want to shout.
I remain stagnant,
I want to cry,
But I have to stay brave,
I have to cry inside.
I remain stagnant,
Everyone moves ahead,
But here I am…almost,
Always restrained to my bed.
I remain stagnant,
Sad and alone,
The independence I once had
Is almost gone.
I remain stagnant,
My hands shake uncontrollably,
To the point where it's hard
To hold my sister's baby.
I remain stagnant,
I feel chained
And weighed down,
I want to fly, jump, soar…
But my body won't allow.
I remain stagnant,
These four walls are all I see,
The world outside is waiting,
I want to be set free.
I remain stagnant
But not my prescriptions,

They seem to be growing
Every time I look at my nightstand.
I remain stagnant,
Fatigued and depressed,
Medicated and weak,
Pained and stressed.
I remain stagnant,
I've learnt to fake a smile,
I even pretend I'm ok
When I'm tearing up inside.
I remain stagnant,
I'm so confused,
Is it Lupus? Fibromyalgia?
Or is it just something new?
I remain stagnant,
Today I'm too tired to fight,
Today I just want to rest,
Maybe tomorrow I'll try.

Previously published in the Unseen & Unspoken poetry competition on September 8th, 2017.

"Being diagnosed with Lupus at 15 was devastating, not understanding what it was or what lay ahead of me but I was prepared to fight. 15 years later what a battle it has been, I have a long way to go and I am determined to win this war that Lupus has waged on me. Along my journey I try my best to educate and support, I've suffered countless losses but I've had beautiful gains."

—Nicole Townsend

Ullie-Kaye Poetry

But You Don't Look Sick

but you don't look sick.
my eyes were clear as sunlight
and shimmering as moons,
rippling amongst ancient tides.
fields of wheat tethered
to wide, open skies. dancing.
i sounded like freedom. most days.
i sounded like morning. and songbirds.
and deep holy waters.
and it was magical almost -
in ways that speak not of clever hats
or white rabbits.
but rather secrets becoming illusion.
the silent whimper. contained.
mascara left unapplied.
for fear of running. spilling.
catching the lonesome tear
that refused to hide.
to mutate into something or possibly
anything that the world deemed strength.
i knew enough about the world to know
that i carried it daily between these
shoulder blades.
in these lungs that gasped for breath.
i carried it in the grip of my fists
that absorbed the shockwaves
just enough to stifle my gasps.
i carried it in the wounds that had
no other name but "i'm sorry".
i'm sorry that i could not punctuate
my sentences with abbreviation marks.

but in truth, it was only because
there was never an ending.
and it just hurt too much to
take the time to string words
together coherently. to explain.
a thousand times. or more.
and so i just woke up.
and said, "good morning".
and made banana pancakes.
and turned on the radio. and sang.
while thunder tore at my bones.
and hurricanes scattered the
debris of years of accumulation.
ravens perched inside my chest.
s c r e e c h i n g.
fighting over the remainder.
what is left to devour?
i bit my tongue to keep it in.
i dried my tears on my own skin.
i did not want to let you in.
it's why i don't look sick.

"At 29, after giving birth, my body and mind entered havoc. I began to lose weight rapidly. My hair fell out. I would find myself lying in the bathtub during showers. I lost muscle mass and my limbs became weak. A year and a half later, my eyes began to protrude and my vision doubled. I was diagnosed with Graves Disease, an autoimmune disorder. 14 years later I was bitten by a tick, which embedded in my spine. Although I recovered from the initial paralysis, I began to get drunk-like episodes. My sensitivities exploded. Burning. Tingling. Numbness. Hot and cold spots. Stabbing. Biting. Crawling. Migraines. I am still fighting every day."

—Ullie-Kaye

Juli Watson

Adaptive Response #1

photo credit: Nicola Hunter

Adaptive Response #2

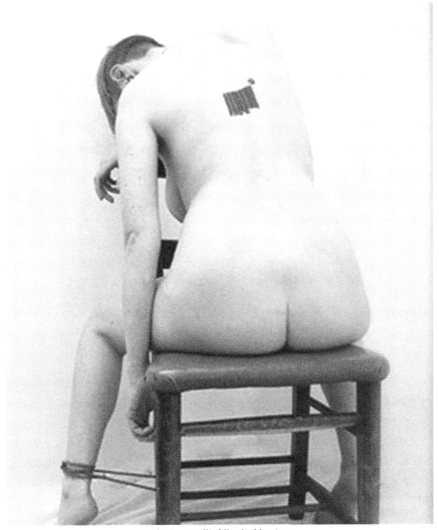

photo credit: Nicola Hunter

Adaptive Response #3

photo credit: Nicola Hunter

"I have M.E./Chronic Fatigue Syndrome and have also suffered from depression and anxiety since my teens. These illnesses can't necessarily be seen by looking at me, unless I'm using my walking stick, my portable folding seat, crying, shaking or hyperventilating. Looking "normal" or "well" belies the everyday pain, both physical and emotional. Please don't judge my book by its cover; I am more than I appear."

—Juli Watson

Julene Tripp Weaver

First Cohort Long Term Survivor: My Body as Experiment

In 1997, with my T cells around two hundred and my viral load at 161,000, I was told I'd be dead in less than ten years; given a 71% chance of death. My lump of spirit condensed to save me. The wisdom in my bones turned to salt. So important to stay alive while dying. Intentionally I watched my numbers through an anonymous program thinking of my body as an experiment.

I considered myself lucky, it's a word I've used, but I am knowledgeable and privileged. From my history as a lab tech in my first career, a Masters degree in counseling, and my work at an AIDS Service Organization, I learned how to navigate systems. Privileged because I'm white, I've had continual access to the best medical care, and used programs to track my labs before they were on official records. I learned my status early so made life style and diet changes. I've used every system to my advantage because I had the knowledge they existed and understood how to access them.

It takes a lot to advocate for one's self. Everything a hurdle to overcome. An HIV/AIDS case manager, I knew why my clients got so tired, they were tired to start with and the systems overwhelm people who are disabled, tired, poor, or living with AIDS because they are set up to limit access, even when they say the opposite.

Although I am not middle class I feel and appear middle class. A baby boomer I've had two full careers and periods of working odd survival jobs, my degree is paid off and I own a home. I identify as bisexual and queer and claim this community. Why? Because I identified as a lesbian earlier in my life, and my work has primarily been with the queer community. I've been in an interacial relationship with my current partner, a man, over three decades.

121

We have negotiated contracts through the years to be open or closed.

My survival comes from education, hard work, and a history of privilege. My father was able to buy the house I was raised in from a veteran grant. My family owned three houses in my childhood, that were eventually sold off by my sister to support my mother. She was on Medicare and Medicaid for fifteen years in a nursing home after a stroke. If we were other than white, my mother and I might have fallen through the cracks.

Less than a year after finally starting Western meds I developed resistance to a whole category of antiretrovirals, the non-nucleosides, it was hard to take two doses a day. After changing regimens my partner started to take a vitamin each morning so we could take pills together. Taking pills daily for the rest of one's life is difficult. In chronic conditions fifty percent stop taking medications. With his help, and keeping my pillbox at the table so it is obvious when I sit down to eat, my adherence improved.

I'm a long term survivor from the first cohort of people infected. This means, before the cocktail approach was discovered in 1996. Because of this, I'm on an old regimen, meaning I have a higher pill load than most people who are newer to the disease. Luckily it's a once a day dosage. Though it's rare I miss taking my meds, it still happens occasionally. My cholesterol and bilirubin are high, and my liver enzymes elevated, most likely from the meds. An ultra sound showed nothing. The liver filters medications, the doctor says I've been stable too long on this regimen for it to be the cause, but there are many unknowns, especially about the long term effects of these pills. My body is still an experiment.

Skin problems and postherpetic neuralgia from shingles are ever-constant. My nerve cells were damaged so the right side of my head is chronically itchy and painful. The itchiness has spread and my face breaks out. A biopsy confirmed a diagnosis of eczema and seborrheic dermatitis, I have a prescription for cortisone, which the dermatologist said is the only thing that works. Of course I try alternatives.

There was a time I thought if I had a chronic illness I would give up everything and go into a war zone to fight for the disenfranchised. But I am in a war zone living with HIV in my body. HIV keeps a body in perpetual inflammation, it speeds up the aging process. Everyone with HIV, even with modern meds, is essentially ten years older due to the strain on the body from fighting the virus. My thoughts have changed, I need to preserve my health through the end.

I waited a long time to start Western meds and the methods I've learned and use have helped me survive through a time many died. The Wise Woman Tradition has been my cornerstone; using daily nutritional infusions and vinegars, along with wild harvested food such as nettles in the spring, Oregon grape berries, a variety of mushrooms, elderberries, rose petals; and I integrate Chinese foods and medicines. Elderberry syrup is a year round staple to prevent the flu. Adaptogen herbs tonify my organs; whole milk yogurt with bacteria for a healthy gut; commitment to prevention is my way to maintain my health as long as possible. Now a person with HIV/AIDS can live a full life with medication; I consider myself lucky to have survived.

All these years later, after one of our wonderful meals my partner commented how lucky we are—we don't have chemical sensitivities or allergies or asthma, we can eat everything. He's right. A part of me still feels that I spoiled our life by getting HIV. But getting HIV/AIDS has been a lesson, introducing how to live beyond what a doctor predicts. No matter what comes I feel better prepared than the average consumer of our medical system.

Living a Life Invisible While Surviving AIDS

AIDS was visible in the 80s and well into the 90s. People lost weight down to skeletal bone, got dementia and yelled in the streets, turned a gray pallor like a ghost, used walkers and had tubes wired into their bodies for life support. ACT UP made a racket, carried coffins through the streets, closed down Wall Street, showed up en masse at St. Patrick's Cathedral, disrupted daily activities because people were dying and nothing was being done by our government.

Now with modern medications AIDS has turned largely invisible, the history mostly forgotten. People with AIDS die from heart disease or cancer, normal causes like the masses do. But stigma and fear are very much alive. In a recent poll of Millennials, 28% reported they didn't want to hug a person living with AIDS. They were born after the visibility, they hold the stigma, and no one has taught the history of the war so many of us fought.

Being a woman living with HIV that progressed to AIDS, I have always been invisible. Doctors didn't think to test women unless they were drug users or pregnant. Thirty years living with HIV/AIDS no one asked, "Are you HIV positive?" I don't know what I would have said if they did because I kept my status private; cautious about who I told. Health information is private and I did not want to ruin my life by having it leak beyond a certain sphere of people I trusted.

For thirty years I kept my secret close. The people I felt most comfortable sharing my status with were gay men, especially HIV positive gay men, and the positive women I sought out. In grad school, studying counseling, my class started with fifty-two, the total of our school was over one hundred each semester. I told three people. Two were gay men, one was positive the other's partner was positive; the third, a confidential counselor the school provided. In my daily life I wanted more support, so I shared my status with a straight man who was a nurse, one of the first people I met in Seattle and a neighbor. His response was, "I hope you don't expect me to take care of you?" Far from needing care, this had never entered my mind. Hurt and angry I didn't even know what to say. Given he worked in the medical field I expected empathy and understanding. Sharing was going to be complicated.

Realizing I would have to get my support through the gay community, I attended groups at Seattle AIDS Support Group (SASG). The groups were filled with men, which was not the kind of support I needed. What I really wanted was a group of positive women, but positive women were rare. Despite that, I reached out to find other women, asking the Director of SASG, she connected me with a woman who was gathering names of positive women. We started a group of five or six of us who showed up regularly to potluck dinners. We called ourselves Babes, and started a peer support organization.

Then there was the work world, I needed to learn how people died from AIDS. Lucky or destined, I got a job at Northwest AIDS Foundation, the biggest AIDS Service Organization in the Northwest. The gay man who entered me into their system was open about his status, so I shared mine and asked, "Can I be open here?" He gave me a surprised look then said, "No, I wouldn't share it if I were you." I trusted his response. He died later that year.

My first client who died shook me to my core and I did not have support at work. My boss was concerned and didn't think I could handle the work as an AIDS case manager. That was not the question, ever. I could handle the work, I needed to process the first client who refused to go into skilled nursing when he needed it. He had been in and out of the hospital for blood transfusions, he could barely walk. The day before he died I was at his house watching him hobble room to room holding the walls, gray and skeletal, shaking and cold, I tried to rationalize how being in care could help him. Feisty and defiant he refused. The following day he was dead. I was rattled. Now I've seen many people die, clients, friends, coworkers. It's not easy to watch. There were hundreds. I kept a list.

I'm one of the lucky ones from the first cohort of people infected before the cocktail, a triple regimen approach, was discovered, and before Protease Inhibitors were approved. I did not take AZT because I knew it killed people. I watched and stayed invisible opening up to gay men I trusted, who understood the disease and wouldn't stigmatize me.

I had ongoing skin problems and lymph node swelling, then when my counts were low, my first opportunistic infection, shingles over my eye. It was terrifying, but invisible because shingles are well known and common. It left postherpetic neuralgia, constant pain over my eye and on the side of my head. I've tried everything but nothing helps.

I have eczema, seborrheic psoriasis, insomnia, increased cholesterol, bilirubin and liver enzymes; all this equals anxiety of the regular things ordinary people also live with. I do my best to make them not show and carry on. When it was time I left the work world, not from disability, but at retirement age. Now I'm semi-retired. As a result I felt free to be more open about my status and published a poetry book with my personal poems about AIDS.

"My poetry book, truth be bold—Serenading Life & Death in the Age of AIDS, offers a view from inside the AIDS epidemic. Today many do not remember the history or the advocacy that stemmed from such anguish and death. The vaccine for Covid-19 was created faster due to the groundwork of ACT UP. As we face variants, and new viruses due to climate change and species jumping, understanding our history makes us better prepared."

—Julene Tripp Weaver

allison whittenberg

Death

you greedy motherfuker
seems like
you're always around

                        harvesting

with your miscarriages
lurking defects
lingering complications
accidents
and the light
the way you up and leave everything
unfinished
like the ending
of a good miniseries
surprising...
inevitable...

"I had vaguely heard of this disease that I have before my diagnosis. It's an odd sounding word - scleroderma. It gives the impression that it may be something terrible or may be just a minor irritation. As chronic illnesses go, it is rather rare -- lucky me, right?!"

—allison whittenberg

BONE

Amie Campbell

Paradise

They say that Paradise is a place with no more crying or tears
A place where your injuries and old wounds are healed
And sickness and pain leave your body
But I think that Paradise is when you walk into a room
And you're accepted exactly as you are
Scars and Pain
Illness and insecurity
Each accepted
As a tile in the mosaic
That makes the art of you

Laying in Wait

My pain creeps in like a thief for my joy
Trying to steal even the tiniest jewels of happiness

I try to lock all the doors and make sure the windows stay shut tight

But sometimes, when I long for the cool Autumn breeze
I start to think it'll be safe to crack a window or two
Surely the thief can't squeeze in some place so small

But true enough, he's wily and snake-like and he slithers his way in
while I'm napping or washing dishes

I don't see him enter or even leave

But the tiny gemstones of peace are missing when I turn around
The last diamond of a pain-free day, nowhere to be found

So I close the windows again
Check all the locks
And buy a big dog

For a while, I think he's gone.
There are no rubies or sapphires for him to steal
And I begin to think he will leave me alone

Until I wake up at night
And see that he's slithered into my bed
And made a nest of my pillows
No longer content with my joys and my days

He's lying in wait to steal my life away.

Aunt Edema

Edema- sounds like an old lady name.
Welcome to the quilting circle, Miss Edema!
Oh, Grandma Edema makes the best apple pie!
My Aunt Edema still makes her gravy from scratch with biscuits
        every morning.
Edema, an old lady name, for an old lady disease, in what feels like
        an old lady body.

I'm not ready to be an old lady yet; and certainly not one with a
name like Edema. I want to feel young and full of life. I want to have

energy past nine o'clock at night. I want to raise Hell and live a life worthy of talking about well into old age.

I don't want to be old Aunt Edema in the rocking chair, don't get up
       without your walker.
I want to be old Aunt Edema dyed her hair hot pink again.
Old Aunt Edema pulled the fire alarm this morning, so she could flirt
       with the firemen.
Old Aunt Edema's playing tricks on the nurses again.
Old Aunt Edema's got so much life left in her, don't you dare call
       her old.

When the Pain Is Gone

My pain doesn't slide down a scale of 1-10
It doesn't slip or slither or creep or crawl
It doesn't come or arrive at all

It's simply there
Like the air in my lungs
Or the hair on my head
I do not notice it until it's gone

When the pain is gone,
I find I cannot breathe
Though my lungs expand, they bring in no oxygen
They don't know how to support a non-hurting body
How do they expand and contract
Without the twinge of pain, to know the rest of the body is there?

My pain doesn't sneak in like a burglar
It lives here.
Like a hermit who never leaves
Content to stay in this broken-down shack for the rest of time

And when he leaves
Steps out into the world
The shack shudders with its emptiness
For is it truly a shack with no hermit to inhabit it?

"I live with two congenital spinal deformities, psoriasis, asthma, arthritis, muscular contractures, chronic digestive issues, and lymphedema. My body was born "wrong" and doesn't know how to work "right". My poems in this collection are part of my coming to terms with my body as it is, accepting its limitations, and determining to live my life in harmony with my body, instead of in spite of it."

—Amie Campbell

Deborah Hetrick Catanese

Car Crash

When ache became a given
and easy days as rare
as a bluebird
singing on my windowsill
in January,
I switched from expectations
to pride of survival,
though it's not quite enough
to compensate.
For my loss.

Deep Heat on Horse Dung

Each day I arise in Iceland
Surrounded
by open fields of unfenced horses
by pervasive clouds
by grasses growing where lava used to flow and may again,
by dark waves that pummel
hardened lava into black sand,
further disintegrating what's left of who I am.

And in the ever-changing sameness
of long bartered nights
of endless molten flow
I'm laden
with mystery pecking at my bones

with goosebumps shivering my skin to sweats
as if a moon-calf called my name,
a name now sounded beyond all recognition
in a language as forsaken as the land.

While each new morning, I try myself on again,
to see if I still fit.
And in which world.

Road to Tough Hoe

I will not ask for forgiveness
though my reactions have let you down,
increasing anger and frustration
without alleviating a shred of my pain.

And while no one has asked
for my forgiveness,
I will not grant anyone the amnesty
I refuse to give myself.

Short Cut

The due date for her paper fast approached.
Eventually she just had to ask -
How do you define 'short cut' for this assignment, Dr. Huber?

The imaginary Palomino moved strong under me
as I rode Western,
trusty Maryjane right behind me
on the black stallion of her dreams.
We reckoned those evil town twerps Pete and Paul
were closing ever nearer to our cache.
'Let's gallop', Janie called out,
'and head them off as they come winding down the hill.'
We needed a short cut through the woods, and fast.

Crumpling a page of crossed out lines,
she sought a current feel for the term *short cut*,
but had none.
Other than wishing she could
find a short cut
like young Maryjane and she had done.
A short cut through pain, through trying to find help.
A short cut to the other side of anger.

She would have to plow through.
Seeking true words to soothe
to express her pain
to embrace her life
even when she felt as crumpled as her rough draft.

She held onto that wild child inside her
still riding that galloping Palomino,
still taking that short cut to protect her cache of gold.

And Intellect

I do not feel obliged to believe that the same God who has endowed us with sense, reason, and intellect has intended us to forgo their use.
        —Galileo

I do not feel obliged to explain
How I was robbed
How he was driving drunk
How it changed me
And why I am stronger than you,
though my gait may say I'm weaker.

I do not feel obliged to act dumb
To let it slide
To allow you to tell me how it is
How life could be better with a better attitude
Or with prescription drugs,
when you have no idea.

I do not feel obliged to paint it pretty
Though pretty I can be
While you say I "don't look handicapped."
Perhaps you failed to look beyond my visage
At my tale of daily struggles
and how I didn't just get by, I overcame.

I do not feel obliged to care
whether you do or do not choose
to understand.

"I was hit by a drunk driver running a stop sign, when I was 32 years old. Decades later, failed by mainstream medicine, I live with it daily. Since my disabilities, pain, and fatigue are invisible to others, many can't or won't understand. I often feel weak, but ultimately, I am forged-by-fire strong -- I have overcome. Writing poetry helps me express the pain, the anger/frustrations, the loss, and the superpower of feisty wisdom I've gained."

—Deborah Hetrick Catanese

Tiffany Elliott

Myself, My Body

unconscious across the plaza grounds
across the grasses
clinging to my hem like the children
I'll never have, I drag
myself, my eyes focused
on nothing—or everything—
lamp-hot, concrete rasping, calloused
fingers, the shadow of a man
watching as I struggle with myself,
pulling my finger bones from their sockets
pulling my corpse, deadened to the New Mexico sun,
pulling my weight to the church steps under the loud shadow
of an inglorious gong

If Uncorrected

Once she told me about a magical bottle
of olive oil blessed by a priest
(though she was no longer Catholic)

and her earache and the way her mother
refused to take her to a doctor. A miracle,
she said, a miracle. Sometimes I use

olive oil that wasn't blessed by a priest, hoping
God doesn't mind, hoping he still heals earaches
and scars. My grandmother grew up

on a farm and didn't believe in calling
for doctors. At 15, my mother fell over
nothing on the basketball court

C-Curve Scoliosis
one twist
fatal
if uncorrected

She was short-listed for the junior
Olympics, the year they filleted her spine,
six vertebrae fused. To this day,

the spine is uncurved. She does not
pour olive oil on the abalone scars or pray
for healing anymore.

a vase of burl wood

unusable unstable
rocking
on festered mounds

I do not flower
red poppies, do not hold
steady stately roses

In the window of
a downtown boutique

But You Don't Look Sick

my walls warmed

the sunlight lacing through
patterns netwing on my
weightless side

Roopali Sircar Gaur

Agony and The Search for Ecstasy

The sun scorched sky was a blue
deeper than the ocean's hue.
The snow filled clouds had taken flight
From the melting heat of a summer afternoon.
A sudden clarion call
and an ecstatic Icarus, had flown into the deep sky
flapping wings, jet-propelling him into infinity.
The Fiery God glowered at this blasphemous over-reacher
the laser beams began to beep
and the wax singed with heat
the tips of those wide wings.
The wind under the flapping wings, fanned fire rings
and a seared and sizzled Icarus came headlong down.

I woke up, wax dripping from my wings
drowned in formalin, in a white room
with blue winged angels moving on soft clouds.
As sharp needles pierced my skin
screams echoed, waking the dead.

That invisible, throbbing, continuous pain
still wracks my body
and through corridors of excruciating pain
memories rest on wheelchairs
pushed past fragrant Duty Free shops
into airplanes full of strangers.
And now this limping, undulating body
this greying orthopedic stick
this synthetic ankle without
the jingling silver anklet
gifted by my beloved.

Since then, the pain never stops,
the throbbing flesh beneath which
my bones lie dead, nailed together with titanium.
The pain no eyes can see;
no hands can feel; no heart can read.
I am just another agonized Christ
nailed to a cross, seeking ecstasy.

At the Airport in a Wheel Chair

"Stand up!' The young security official looked at me in the wheel
chair. "If only I could", I thought to myself.

She gesticulated that I stand up and walk to the booth. Not many
steps away.

My grey orthopedic cane with the jingling beads, my constant
companion, had taken a ride with my passport, my purse, and my
laptop. It now stood forlorn on the other side, waiting to be claimed.

I was a nobody without them. Panic seized me.

Restless feet and disgusted eyes were queuing up behind.

An official hand gestured me to get moving.

The now anxious, kind chair pusher helped me stand up. How I
hobbled, cobbled those miles, I cannot recall. Sweat poured down
my neck. I felt the heat of the sun. My wings were dripping wax.

Behind the curtain it was terrifying. The medical certificate was set aside. Every inch of me had beeped. Those 32 pain throbbing, hidden titanium nails. Now the long humiliating inspection, the lifting, the pressing, the tapping, the gloved hand moving all over my distorted body.

The deafening silence. You see, I could be a human torpedo. I could just rip through the aircraft. Quite bruised of heart and body and mind, and in acute pain, she let me go without a goodbye. She had turned into a robot, and I was still human, my pain palpable.

The anxious looking pram-pusher looked sadly at me. She seemed to understand my pain. All day she pushed people like me, up and down and down and up, on eerie elevators past the aroma of freshly ground coffee, the fragrance of perfumes, those evening gowns and pashmina scarves.

The smell of sandwiches and freshly baked bagels, on a hungry stomach.

Unseen, her body must ache too. A comradeship of pain held us together. She was my witness.

And I, hers.

"A freak accident broke the important bones in my lower body, and changed my life. It first gifted me a wheel chair, and finally a stick. "You have changed so much," they complain. Don't you see I hurt all the time? When I get out of the car at a wedding, pull out that stick, I am sad. Then I see a guest in a wheel chair, and I know I am fortunate to have only a stick."

—Roopali Sircar Gaur

Deepali Parmar

Dangi Story – 2001/2002

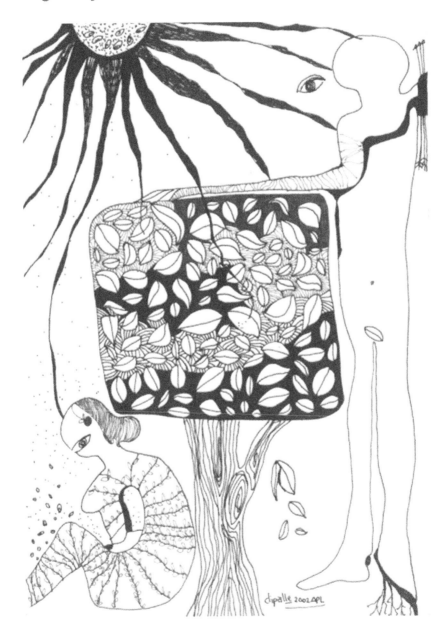

Birthing Death – 2001-02

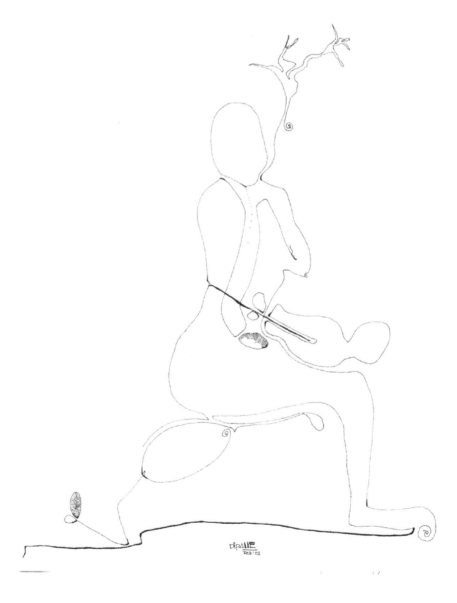

Lost at Home

CELLULAR

Laksmisree Banerjee

The Phoenix and The Cacti

Survival is a gruelling task
when severely injured through
cruel negligence of another

One more day of their hot-eyes
scorching erect as a black reminder
afflicting me into perpetuity

Their glare, a knife in my flesh
though they often hoped
against my pulpy softness

I managed to return the spike
with struggling deliberation
against destiny and the doers

Their eulogies, emptiness, flowers
exploded to envious slips of flame
ignited callously behind my back

Pushing them into some unknown
judgement day I am sure of
yet my injuries remain irrevocable

On that haunting day of hailing the Visionary
with unforgettable cramping memories
of arrogant pomp and no vision, or empathy

Their incendiary pavilion full of
meteor-eyes fuming, as if to

have me burnt to ashes

When the flames ate my flesh and silk
someone enthused:
"but isn't she scarred beyond recognition?"

That day I garnered my realization
from the ruins of reality

The fire tearing at my spirit and body
writhed upwards and inwards
like a hungry, lascivious female ---

My arms and soul outstretched
an umbrella hard to open
to save my only fledgling

Time has gone by since that inferno
but I have risen with the rainbows
in rain and sunshine from the ashes

A tigress or a phoenix? I do not know
never debilitated, nor sunk
yet unable to cremate

The charred corpses still inside me
bristling, crowding like cacti

Repairing a Burnt Body

The doctors saw my body,
scarred, naked
and shamelessly identifiable

The scorched moon dying
with the rising sun
in my blood

My splintered self
breaking under the scalpel
with my simmering corpuscles

A lump of flesh examined
closely by burn specialists
while I made my consciousness
and awakening
wait outside—

The body had to revive
and the spirit to die

Though I never allowed
the hard rocks in me
to ever wane or dissolve

Photographs of my
snake-skin grafts
helped Dr. Bhargava
to fetch his degree

Masters or Doctoral
in the skilled art
of redeeming
burnt bodies

I wailed in searing agony
with outstretched, disheveled limbs

While he pulled off my bandages
to snapshoot my bleeding wounds

Bouquet of Flints

My body feels like a grave
    With sprouting flowers
Adorning its lovely crafted facade
    My mind a lonely peak
Free and breezy at the summit
    In its dizzy stance
Of world-watching
    After the storm.

The cinders inside have
    Caused efflorescence, transformed into
Endless contentment of victory
    And forced tumescence
At having known and conquered it all.

I have learnt to walk on burning coals
    And feel yet, the icy cool,
The balmy wind playing on my face
    And the slag of black pains
Which I have waded across
    Gathering still in memory
The aromatic white sprinkles
    Of the Springtime grounds.

I have faced it, fought it,
    Learnt to accept the scars
Of hidden illness as trophies
    To make my bouquet
Of flints and sparks

  Now I see
    A scintillating, slim ray
Across an endless forest,
    Perhaps my fractured sun
Will rise yet again
    From the violent billows
And touch me with his baby-pink
    Soft incandescence
To light my thorn-ridden path
    Perhaps, perhaps---

"I am extremely glad and grateful for being given the opportunity to use my Poems for Social-Transformation and Awakening for being able to put in my efforts to unveil the ruthless maladies and disorders that people suffer due to no fault of their own yet do not receive any love or care from a totally negligent, cruel and exclusionist society. Thanks to the Editors for making just wonderfully Humanitarian Anthologies."

—Laksmisree Banerjee

Susan Bellfield

Biopsy

Name, birthdate, left or right?

My body, chalk outline on a stainless tray—
not dead but allegedly diseased
face half-turned toward remembering
   the numbness of fever
 when everything felt larger.

Before laminated boxes, there were tin trays—
frozen dinners
   my mother heated in the oven.
Turkey and stuffing,
  meatloaf with mashed potatoes.

Your safe word is, Sharp!

My breast compressed
between steel plates
   the incision, a tangle
of cells extracted
   confirming their suspicions.

Alone in a room of technicians, if only
 I could scream,
tell them it's impossible
on my mother's side, no history of cancer—
   dead nonetheless.

Ice packs for swelling; Tylenol for pain.

Still bleeding. On the highway, I miss the exit
face half-turned toward the sun
   or an oncoming semi
I no longer know how to tell you
   what I feel.

Radical Mastectomy

As a child, I taught myself to sew.
Wind the bobbin; thread
nodes through the nipple
in nuclear blue. Pin
fabric pieces, leaving room
for breath. In pre-op
softly sobbing. Lower the foot
to lock fabric. Curtain swishes—
another gurney exits. Press
the pedal to start. Swallow
your tears. Return with finished
seams puckered and uneven.

Lost in Transition

       Approach carefully
as a mislaid bomb.

       Pretend you have survived
like an infection.

       Forbidden words accumulate, use them
to name things you love best when your hands
       are empty
give birth to silence.

Slippers of human hair leave
no footprints.

You know better than anyone
    a bone-pointer's curse
precedes the ritual burning.

Parody

In the infusion room
our features morph
into resemblance, an
        unholy marriage
of flesh and toxin

sprig of rosemary
   scrap of red cotton, we
     bathe in   tumbling
locks of hair   spiced
with paprika   and chili pepper

prick   a vein with sterile pins
   sear sage
to consecrate the ache
   and embrace
its crush and splinter

      collect the pieces
     hide what matters
   then, count backward
to erase.

Dissolution

In the fluorescent blue
of the dressing room
I inspect my torso
   for recognition

baptism by tracing
   what only I have known
for decades, now scab   now scar
      now surgical glue   silicone

somewhere   inside me
      a land mine
            buried just below
the surface   trip wire set

a sudden sun   ignites
the myth   fractures
            the dream of ever
after   exposing

        amputated   bits   of   flesh
sewn hastily together.

Promise

Autumn's end witnessed
a house on fire
                    a dream from which I
            half-woke, my hair undone
        writing on the pillow
        uncertainty clenched
between my teeth.

It began with a circle cast
during the gibbous moon
                    a jar of sharp objects—
            needles, broken glass,
        razor blades—secreted
under the sickbed.

I shelved a season beneath
frozen ground.
            Now the butterfly wing
                    and the scent of lilac.

"A couple of months after my breast cancer diagnosis, I received a call from an acquaintance who wanted to catch up. After telling her about my surgery and treatment she replied, "Oh breast cancer is an easy cancer." It was the last time I spoke to her, and the last time I revealed my health struggles to anyone. Sometimes invisible suffering is less painful."

—Susan Bellfield

Natalie Cummings

Sea Glass—A Journey

I did not begin the way I am today.
The fragment before you wasn't always this way.
I was once whole, true, and fully content.
Naïve was my soul, life's rhythm was constant.

One moment serene, radiant, and intact.
Then suddenly I changed; now damaged and cracked.
Unexpectedly broken, blunt, and torn.
I wander aimlessly; weathered and worn.

Abruptly swept up by the sea's merciless tide.
This passage a daze, with only waves as a guide.
I rolled and swayed; my relentless journey ensued.
Completely unprepared for the storm's magnitude.

Phases pass when I float with little resistance.
In them come instants baring strength and persistence.
There, too, arise occasions I question my fate.
Terrible mindsets of defeat, doubt, even hate.

I fear no relief from continual churning.
Reprieve a mere wish amidst tossing and turning.
This voyage was one I'd never chosen to take.
How truly unfair, the pang of each snag and break.

Quiet comes slowly, all movement suddenly ceased.
Clear transformation appears, bringing subtle unease.
Resting in the warm sand among the shells from the sea,
I can relax, stop moving and am able to breathe.

But You Don't Look Sick

A soft, frosty, dulled haze, in a pastel hue,
has replaced the luminous gleam I once knew.
Lost is the flawless shine I had worn with such pride.
The cracked edges turned jagged, have been smoothed by the
ride.

Relief is fleeting, as I ponder what is to come.
Will I know normal again, or must I succumb?
Can the remaining portion of me that exists,
withstand the heartache and pain of all that I miss?

I crave my previous, unaltered entity,
And mourn the being I was before this journey.
Alone, I await dark to consume the setting sun.
Fixed on fear, surrendering to the damage that's done.

Day breaks, the surrounding air freshly renewed.
Skies vividly transform as light beams break through.
Absorbed by the beauty and potential it brings,
the sunrise softly whispers of new beginnings.

Unexpectedly encased in a supportive hand.
An unfamiliar embrace raises me from the sand.
Instinct reassures this grasp is not by mistake.
In the comfort it provides, I feel tenderly draped.

Unable to ignore my newly altered state.
Reality surges back with thunderous weight.
For nothing has improved, I have not been mended.
Fearfully, I await the fall, time suspended.

Yet this nurturing grip remains firm and intent.
Soft comfort awards a hint of ease and content.
Set gently alongside salvaged souls just like mine.
Each is unique, distinct; details one of a kind.

Despite the occasional strife over valid woes,
an ultimate outcome, only destiny knows.
Rest assured though, exist ones on which you can lean.
Be not dismayed, purpose remains yet to be seen.

Jane Dougherty

Have, have not

I have all my limbs, my hair,
an air of good health,
and nobody sees the clenching
against the cold,
the depression
that comes from weariness
when the blood breaks
into tiny useless pieces,
or the hidden tears
that blur the small joys
and the splendour
of wide winter skies.

Bad blood

It grips when the sun fails and the summer fades
and the chill rises from every shadow
and the blood shatters, corpses of corpuscles
floating in the wilted yellow of the eyes
and the blood fails to carry the breath
so the breath fails and with the weariness
the lassitude that darkens every glimmer
so nothing smiles, nothing rises above the mud
and the hand clenches into a frozen fist
squeezing the colours into a desert of black ice
with no respite and the dead blood retreats
to the core, curled where the first men crept

169

in fear of the dark enduring cold, hoping for
the warmth to return, life to course
with the rising sappy sun and the squirming
dread that perhaps this time it will not.

What you don't know

I hate it when I say, I suffer from the cold,
and you say, me too,
and I say it makes me ill,
and you say, I'm sick of it too,
and I say it's a disease that gets worse in the winter,
and you say, yes, I have that, we all miss the sun,
and I say no, it makes me anaemic, it drains me
so my feet drag in mud, and my mouth fills with silt,
and you say yes, it's tiring, I can't wait for the spring,
and I say it's a disease that destroys my red blood cells
and makes my body think I am dying of cold;
my blood deserts me and hides, and the shivering
extremities go red then white then black,
and you say, you have poor circulation,
you need warmer gloves,
and I walk away, and the depression
that walks with weary people whispers in my ear
with a voice brittle with frost,
It's just you and me and the dark.

"Having a disease that destroys my red blood cells means constant fatigue, chronic anaemia and frozen extremities. It doesn't have to be cold, just cool; the disease has its own thermostat. Then it gets worse. You can't see anaemia or heart flutter, like you can't see exhaustion or the depression it digs. I hear the incredulity though. We all hate the cold; I'm just the wimpy one who complains about it."

—Jane Dougherty

Carol H. Jewell

Bladder Cancer

I hate gambling.
I hate the garish machines, one-armed no more, that draw you in
with their bright lights and colors.
I hate the endless, continual loud sounding soundings sounds
continual reminders
--English is a funny language. How synchronistic that "sounding" is
the word instantly thought of,
and so appropriate—
you said the odds of recovery were 80%. You said, "I like those
odds."
I nodded—it seemed the thing to do—but I was unconvinced.

Now those odds seem laughable, laughing at you, laughing at me.
Neither one of us is laughing, now.

Tripping the Light Fantastic

Just when I thought it was
safe to come out
as a crone,
my body cried out,
"Guess again!"
And I have to grow anew
from this altered place.

New things to do: VATS Lung Biopsy,
high-frequency Chest Wall Oscillation.

New words to learn,
medical jargon: fibrosis,
noncaseating granulomas,
Sarcoidosis,
incurable.

Grief is not linear, thank God.
Grief is a bittersweet dance around the room.
I am my own partner.
Little by little, I learn
not to step on my gamboling feet.

"I have more than one invisible illness. That is, they are invisible until they make their presence known with non-stop coughing, pain, muscle weakness, pain, tremors, trouble breathing or shortness of breath, speech difficulties, and, did I mention? Pain. But you can't see pain unless you see me writhing in pain, or crying out, or eating Tylenol like M&Ms. My invisible illnesses include migraine, sarcoidosis, degenerative disk disease, irritable bowel syndrome, as well as anxiety and depression."

—Carol H. Jewell

Donna Motta

I Was an ER Nurse

I was an ER nurse.

Self proclaimed

Bad ass.

Judging was
My job.

And I was good.

Headache?!
Really?

Backpain?
Legs hurt?

Let me guess…
Depressed?

I thought so.

Well,
Tell me please

How may we help?

But did I care?
Was that what I meant?

But You Don't Look Sick

I'd like to
Congratulate myself
Yes…

But truth…

I meant-

Seriously?
A headache?

Could you
Not deal
With this
At home
Yourself?

I do...
Oh never said out loud
But thoughts screamed out proud—

You don't look sick to me.
Life is weird
And Karma's
A
Bitch.

One minute

You're

Strong

Then
SWITCH…

But You Don't Look Sick

Sides changed…

Muscular Dystrophy

Is a teacher by theft.

You lose

Til what's left

Is a faint trace

Of what was.

Strength and ability

Lost.

Wisdom comes at great cost.

Yet more precious than gold

Once the bill's paid.

In wake of disease
I miss many things.

Yet- my old bad ass self
Thankfully took wings.

And left in her place
Is an understanding sage
In the process of making.

Myotubular Pieces

The sneer
I receive
Hard to believe

I was once
A beauty
To behold.

To hold--
And bold
I was so very bold.

Former
Arms
Of strength
Pillared
Limber
Legs.

Flexible
Mind
Heart
Body
Soul.

Mosaic
Myotubular
Myopathy.

Myo
My
Middle
Myopathetic.
Mosaic
Art
Fresco
Piece.

Pieces.
I am in pieces.

My myopathetic pieces.

Empty parts
Quite literally

Empty space between.

Empty space
That robs the place
Of strength.

Nuclei
Anucleated.
Abated.
Abdicated.
Negated.

Looks so good on the outside.

Still empty insider replicates.

Yet
I live.

Fortunate
One.

I will live
And not yet die.

I live without
Apology.

For my weakened state-
Though,
From it arises question.

Please know
As I look serene
Inside I would scream
If not so numbed
From the dull thrum
Of chronic painful
Disease.

Please be gentle
With your thoughts
And words.

I measure my own. No
bitterness shown As
that would drive those I
love
Away.

I brace and breathe
And calmly believe
The empty spaces
Filled
With the strength
Of love
And peace.

Trying to breathe

Trying to breathe—

In
Out
Focus on the breath

My breath
How many breaths left?

Robbers of breath
Youthful ignorance
Chemical ignorance
Chem trail
comet tail
Long trail on horseback

Slow down
Focus in

But You Don't Look Sick

Medication
Steroids
Bitter liquids
Inhale deep
Forming crystals
on tongue and teeth

Hands shake
Knees weak
Shallow gasps
Try to speak

Every expansion of chest wall
Cause emotions
To rise and fall

Solitary
Lonely
This task is mine

Passersby ask my welfare
Oh, I'm just fine

For if fine I'm not
Then dead I'll be
If dead I am
This all for rot

I am alive
I live
I will live
well and hard

But You Don't Look Sick

Long white legs
Now bent
Feet blue

Clear white sclera
Congested map
Red lines
Of airway maintenance

Breasts once milky mounds
Old Cold Mottled wine skins

Ovarian fruit hangs low
Slow falls
Soggy glops
From dragging branch

Smooth hands
Gnarl now
Clutched grasp
Over plastic pipe

Strange matriarchal
Vaping visionary

Dark horsemen
Circle round
Glaring threat through White chemical
Mountain mist

Threaten not
My immediate corpse

Rather

Radiant maiden bodies
Who thrive within
Safe glow
Maternal warmth

Awaiting the ravage
I must stave off
The ravage of
The camp

So

Trying to breathe
In
Out
Focus on the breath.

"I have had Muscular Dystrophy for years- and thrive in spite of. However; many humans do not realize my limitations, and therefore pass judgement. I used to feel I had to excuse myself, and spent much of my time doing so. Over the years, I have realized loving myself is the best way to communicate my worth if only to myself… who matters most. Much love."

—Donna Motta

Smita Ray

Insomnia

Nights seethe underneath the Kilimanjaro
And her wide open incandescent eyes,
A gatekeeper of 10 am office
Quietly smouldering
By an ivy door.
She watches
Sanguine forest
of surreal dreams
Going up the flames.
Spreading like a wildfire
Tall flames of a blazing pyre
Drifting across the gurgling Ganges
Her indigenous demons then silently sidle over
Her squashy pillow as she longs for
Placidly falling into long-awaited impetrated slumber.

Cancer

Please, don't avoid eye contact
And tiptoe around how you feel
It makes no odds,
All bodies meet a similar fate
The beauty of disease is
It won't detract from our strength
We still stand our ground
I am still winning

But You Don't Look Sick

One day I, inadvertently, arose from the anesthesia
Weren't we always supposed to die?
To be aware of it when others slumber
To be conscious of the presence of death
Which was growing within this body
Along all those years
Is having an edge over others
I can't afford to miss the opportunity
To savour my intensified life.

Sanhita Sinha

Warrior

Malignant rose that bloomed
in her soil,
Spreads its thorns silently.
The blue aroma that slowly metastasized from soil to her soul
Could not wither her smile.
Syringes never fail to kiss her
on any occasion.
Embroideries of stitches,
Onco-words and the graphs
Narrate how brave she is!
Colorful capsules and pills are now
the nests of her chirping happiness.
The pink ribbon shines like a diamond brooch
on her barren chest
That once showered elixir
for her child
and she smiles like a warrior!

DIGESTION

Candice Louisa Daquin

When birds fly into glass

What if she's me? The woman screaming without reprieve?
And what if she's you? The body beneath the sheets lifted by
strangers?
Every time the phone rings, I see in my mind's eye, your prone form
this fear I inhabit is years in coming
your fragility creeps up on us like a wetted shroud
once so strong, you'd take me in your bronze arms and
press me to you, where the sound of your powerful
heart beat assured me nothing would erase or remove
your certainty
then the sick hiss and whisker of machines
a tube down your throat, a glazed look, no recognition
slack hand filled with needles, empty eyes void of life
I felt you moving away, even as you stayed
gone and still there
the taste of your lips changed
as if blistering over from sudden Winter storm.
As time ticks down, we look up
to salvation, prayer and hope, when maybe nobody listens
I stand over you as you sleep
your little bluebird chest rising in dream
I want to climb on the bed and laugh, as once we did
now the dust has settled and we still
scattered pictures, cannot see clearly
all around are shadows and shorn warnings
easy to lose ourselves in fears glory

like gathering a bird who has fallen from glass
stunned and dying, pressed in our hands
death on us now, like unsought reflection
glinting, glinting, glinting.

I miss you, the you I knew, better than I know myself
who would turn in her sleep and touch me without waking
such was our eternal fuse, one into the other, no boundaries
and time is a fickle fellow
taking you and keeping you sickened
welded to pills and paper casts of closed theatres
we stand apart, at times nearly severed
I would sacrifice all to make you well
but I have given everything I know
it is clear we go in different directions
one is the end and you drift like wind on frigid water
while I continue to swim upstream
I cannot, you see, let go
your bright feathers dull and still I look up
when birds fly into glass

Hell is hospital food

Chrysalis
they sapped her energy
dried once buoyant skin into folds
go on, put her away, to turn to ash
after all; "you're supposed to be dead"
said Radiation
blinking green by hospital bed
"I tried to exterminate your core
scrape marrow out
electrocute protest
so take a seat
lick a pen

see it glow
have another glass of radioactive hello
go on
it won't hurt
for long ..."

Chemotherapy smiled
beneath yellowed eyes
her pet needles quivered
ecstatic for the chance
"Me! Me! Me!
Can I puncture her heart?"

Scalpel sneered
scoffing at the play
I'll have my chance, he thought
hankering to slice, cauterize
taste a little sliver.

Sharp knife, Sharp knife
run away home
surgeries closed
patients escaped Thunderdome.

The window faces another wall
pigeons crowd, grey sponges on thin sill
too healthy to enter where sickness resigns people to ingenious
methods of;
is it Hell?
Torture?
Relief or regret?
When put together with twine
do we survive their best attempt?

Walking unsteadily, back exposed
feet on lino, red dye #5 turning pee to blood
we transform into sorcerers in our alchemy with God.

Suppose, just suppose
I chose not to yield to thee
would dying be different next time?
With rolling sky above us
where we rinse poison out
remove tube, catheter, IV, drain
be once more, free and unchained
dancing barefoot in sprinklers.

Encroachment

*The year after being in the ER every week & finally diagnosed with
a form of Gastroparesis, during a routine visit to the eye-doctor I
was told I had premature Macular Degeneration. Confirmed by 4
specialists & a genetic test. 3 out of the 4 doctors said I would be
blind within 10 years. I'm not even middle-aged. I choose to believe
the 4th doctor who said, nothing is set in stone, or as I like to
phrase it: Fuck that for a laugh.*

You saw your disintegration, in the shrouded reflection of a store
window, already losing custom

and for years prior, women adjusted their hose and children's
grubby faces wiped, in that much smeared glass. It held, decades,
like high cheekbones, will shore up time in a beautiful face

But You Don't Look Sick

I saw my eyes fail me, in the encroachment, of some uninvited
color, as if the sun, greedy for attention, had left a permanent
marker.

The doctor, with his accent-less voice and starched fingertips,
probing my retina, for answers like tarot card reader, will shuffle
and cut her deck

declared me prematurely blemished, stained by time and
inheritance, imperfect, going blind, wrapped in yesterday's
smudged newsprint.

And I laughed, the same laugh my grandma had, when terrible
news was delivered, along with cold dishes and

empty seats where once our ancestors sat, filling the roost of our
quaking bones, marking time and Advent

she would raise a thin-lipped glass, of *'this n' that,'* --- To Gods and
Monsters, To Plato, the *Ten Sefirot*, Communism, the *Bhagavad
Gita* and Woody Allen (before we knew we was a pedophile)

there should be a preface to every memory, she said; toasting
turpentine shadows, swilling away horror, like a rinsed mouth will
always be, more kissable, come New Year's Eve

where we'll forget our enemies and join shoulder-to-shoulder,
kicking long multi-gene legs into space to the chime of twelve and
ghosts. Not yet knowing, what will become of those flung into the
future, to forge ahead alone

unsupported in ancestry, just the sound of voices, a snatch of tune,
the smell of half-finished dinner, paused forks suspended in song,

stewing pears over cheap white wine, her hands red like mine, from
scrubbing too hard

that blemish, it won't come out, so, it sinks, orange streaks of
sunlight beneath green orbit and a stranger in a bar once remarked;
"you have gorgeous eyes like they came from the depth of sea, all
green and lost"

I think of loss, a stray button, a missed appointment, a fallen hem, a
blind future.

Maybe I won't return, to the doctor who found my stigmata,
bleeding like a fish cut on rocks, into the very bones of earth.

Do you see? Because I don't anymore. Not well, getting glassy like
my old ted, with scratches making mosaic overlays

increasingly, my eyes look inward, to the old days we toasted with
depression era pink glass, it was all anyone could afford, and I
remind my American friends of this, poverty after the war

a tendency to never feel safe, like city foxes

scour, empty feral streets, for scraps and squint

at the harsh glare of amber streetlamps

attracting insects, bleached yellow

by the piercing quality, of their need to

magnify.

"Invisible illness matters because we dismiss it and people suffer more. We equate 'health' with strength, and by default, 'illness' with being weak, both physically and mentally. Yet people with any illness are often forced to be stronger. Formerly rare illnesses are becoming a silent epidemic, striking younger and younger. Only awareness will make any difference. We need to support each other to prevent the emotional fallout of physical illness."

—Candice Louisa Daquin

Kelly Glover

Chronic Disease: The Child You Never Asked For

The thought of having a chronic illness that never goes away is not something the mind can easily accept. So, when they tell you that you will be sick forever, it doesn't sink in immediately. It is as if you are handed an unexpected newborn child that you must now figure out how to care for, for the rest of its life. The process of moving from diagnosis to acceptance can be a lengthy and difficult one.

When you first receive an incurable diagnosis, you just can't comprehend it. The mind cannot seem to process forever. Sadly, that's part of the reason the divorce rate is what it is. Slowly you start to realize that your symptoms are not going away. In fact, they may even be multiplying and dividing into more than one disease. You start to doubt your own pain, even though it is very real. *Is this all in my head? Do I really need to go to the emergency room?* There is always a fear that other people will not believe your agony. We often suffer needlessly because our pain is mostly invisible.

Even though you may have experienced excruciating pain in the past due to your disease, it is almost as if your body doesn't let you fully remember it. It's like childbirth. If women could readily recall the physical pain, they might not be so eager for child number two. Something in our nature blocks out the memory of that intense pain. It is the same with chronic disease. You block out the pain in order to remain safely in denial about your condition. It is easy to try and pretend it doesn't exist, that the pain you feel is not a flare up of your disease. But like a toddler, if you leave it alone, unattended, there will eventually be hell to pay.

Slowly and painfully you begin to realize that your condition is never going away. One of the first indicators that you have an incurable disease is that you begin to spend too much time in the bathroom. It is an around the clock affair taking care of a lifelong illness, just like

198

taking care of a kid. That doesn't just go for those with my affliction, Crohn's Disease, but people with any chronic illness will tell you the same.

We take extra hot showers and long baths trying to relieve our various types of pain. We spend hours clutching a wastebasket to our faces, begging for the nausea and pain to ease. We don't want to leave home because we will be too far from our favorite restroom.

Unfortunately, my bathroom has become my most frequented room in the house. My sick oasis. I try to keep it as comfortable and inviting as possible. Fresh vibrant paint and live plants can do a lot for your well-being. I try to surround myself with beauty for when I am at my ugliest.

Another sad realization that comes from a lifelong diagnosis is that your stamina and physical abilities will at some point become inhibited. You simply won't be able to do what you once could. Again, it is like taking care of a newborn. You never seem to get enough rest and the baby is always in need of attention. You spend hours figuring out how to soothe your child, or the many symptoms of a disease, whichever it may be.

Many autoimmune disorders have sister diseases that eventually manifest, either naturally or drug induced. We learn to recognize the many symptoms of our various diseases. For example, the drugs I take to manage my Crohn's Disease have led me to develop psoriasis. We learn to differentiate each symptom with its corresponding disease and treat them accordingly. It starts to take up much of your time. When you aren't physically dealing with your disease, it is always in the back of your mind.

After some time, like with every other turning point in life, you begin to find acceptance. Nothing you do will change your diagnosis, so there is no sense in worrying about it. You must learn how to best take care of yourself. A lot of times this includes getting the correct medications and nutrition into your body. You have to figure out how to create a balance between your body and your mind. Yoga and meditation are great tools, as well as talk therapy. There is no shame in speaking with a therapist to help you gain an acceptance of your disease and future. You must always advocate for yourself. Speak up when you aren't being heard. No one knows your body or condition like you do.

Acceptance will come. It may take a while, but just like learning how to be a parent, you will learn how to be a chronically ill person. It's too bad there is not a manual for any of it. You are on your own in the school of incurable disease, but it is not the end of the world. As long as we are living, we can have a worthwhile life. The other option is giving up and chronic disease warriors aren't built for that.

Diagnosis Day

There are certain days in a person's life that alter their existence. A wedding day forever binds one human to another. A funeral forever separates. The birth of a child adds and multiplies love, while the birth of a disease subtracts hope. There are days that we all know for sure are in our future, like the day our parents die, for instance, that devastate and leave you different than the day before. These are the days we don't want to think about, but we know are coming. There's another day, though, that's never expected. It's diagnosis day. That one always comes as a surprise.

I remember being wheeled back into my hospital room after a CT scan, groggy from the suffering and pain medication. A faceless, nameless doctor darkens the threshold and enters the room. "The results are indicative of what we find in patients with Crohn's Disease". There it was. Finally. He continued speaking with my mother, who was sitting just to my left, but I tuned him out. Maybe that was to quell the shock of what I was hearing. I had heard of Crohn's before, but I had no idea what it was. I had the next week to learn about it, lying in that hospital bed.

I had symptoms of this disease all throughout my life. Mysterious manifestations that were never defined. Overabundant nausea. Radiating back pain that moved from the back to the front, if that makes any sense. It didn't to the numerous doctors I went to over the years trying to find the root to that pain. This disease would rear its head every now and again, but never enough to raise any alarms to my medical providers. That is until my marriage fell apart and I sank into despair, emotionally and physically.

My body began to scream, violently. I lost 60 pounds in about three months. I had diarrhea that entire time, maybe even longer, but I didn't really think anything of it. So much that it had become my normal. I guess I was under the assumption that it was all stress related and I used over-the-counter medications for pain and bowel control.

Seemingly overnight, my hair became brittle and thin, and each day brought more exhaustion than I could ever explain in words. I started to look as sick as I felt, gaunt and pale from lack of nutrients. When the blood first arrived in the toilet, I knew something was seriously wrong and I started actively seeking medical help.

I didn't get any answers, not even a clue, until my diagnosis day. I was begging for help to anyone that would listen. I went from urgent care, to general physicians, to specialists, each to no avail. Maybe it's an ulcer. Indigestion. Hemorrhoids. Take some acid reducers and call me in the morning. Needless to say, that did not work. It was like trying to throw an ice cube on a forest fire to extinguish it.

Finally I couldn't take it anymore and went to the emergency room where they performed a CT scan and later a sigmoidoscopy, which is essentially a shortened colonoscopy. The doctor who performed it could not go deep into my colon because of all the inflammation, but was able to take a sample for analysis. The biopsy is what gave me the definitive diagnosis I had been searching for.

What followed was a strict diet of liquid and pills. Weeks of prednisone would leave me a puffy, sleep deprived, anxious mess. As I settled in my hospital bed that week, trying to process all this information I was hit with, I mourned the old Kelly. The one without a chronic disease that would leave me with a 75% chance of needing major colon surgery. I was in a dark place, and this became evident to one particular hospitalist who saw through the diagnosis and into my emotional pain.

Dr. S, as he called himself, came to my room almost every day to check on me. He took the time to explain things and made sure I understood what was going on. He sat on the side of my bed and held my hand as I wept. I cried for the loss of the woman I was, and I cried for the woman that I had become. To this day, I have never encountered a doctor that showed more compassion. One day he came into the room and jerked the curtains open, letting the sunlight in, and made me get up out of the bed. My legs were weak from lack of use, but he forced me to find the strength to climb out of the pity party I was having and start rebuilding myself.

I started to see my diagnosis as comforting. All the years I didn't know what was wrong with me. I was always so tired, but I thought I was just being lazy or unmotivated. The back pain and incessant nausea made sense. I finally had answers, and though they weren't what I wanted to hear, I was on the way to acceptance of my new life. The best things often come out of the darkest places. What I encountered before my diagnosis day made me strong enough to endure the woman I became after. Now I am even more prepared for the next life altering days that wait quietly in my future. Crohn's cannot take that from me.

One Thursday Morning With Crohn's

foul vomitus
erupts from my stomach
purges from my esophagus
burning my throat
retching in the bowl

breathe. is it over?
never even begun

heaving, heavy breathing
when does my yoga breath activate?
hyperemesis
again, again, again

minutes. hours.
gagging on the nausea

regurgitating the pain
over and over
unyielding disgorgement
blood vessels explode
my hands are tingling
legs going numb

help. I need help
call. they come

same questions repeated
get up! she says
I can't move, I can't talk
get me up! can't you see these Jello knees?
the ride is cold and bumpy
too long. only sympathy. no help

But You Don't Look Sick

I don't remember one face
I didn't look at anyone but my son
his face buried in his pillow, as they pulled me away
no dignity resides, snot flows freely
into my emesis bag, my forehead resting on it
my head bobs with the bumps in the road
the man beside me holds my back so I may sit up
to hurl nothing but noise into my little green bag

no fluid left to come up, only my peace
being violently emitted
iv's inserted in limp arms
blood pressure high, blood pressure low

begging for help, help or death
whimpering, spitting blood
no liquid left for tears
no one cares, no one stops

still no help. 3 hours so far. 2 hours more before
finally the drugs. I drop the bag I have been clenching
and spitting my insides into for so long
head lulls, still no liquid left for tears

another scan showing no answers, you are fine!
but now there is something wrong with your heart
yea I know it's been broken
working on repairing it and they tell me it's still fucked up
I'll write about it. it's the only way I know how to heal it

what the fuck have you got next for me body?
kidneys? you got stones?
pancreas, liver, you two ok?
hang on there brain, you are the best of what we've got
hold on, even when everything else rots

Six Weeks

Every six weeks
These drugs do creep
Into my veins
A supposed antidote seeps

Chronic dripping
The needle threads
A singular tube into the crook of my arm
As I stare at the wall from my hospital bed

Everything is a continuous standoff
From insurance and infections
To side effects and symptoms
My body beats itself out of spite

Every day is a fight
For things that will eventually disappear
From happiness and health
To love and life

I am defeated
On the days I remember
The life I had before
This disease rendered

Ailment one
Requires compromised immunity
Opening the bolted door to
Voracious viruses vaulting my viability

The cure breeds disease two
A simple strep infection
Pulls it from its slumber
My skin succumbs to burning plunder

I am illness personified
Every step I take
Is backwards straight out the gate
Unhealthy is my new life

While my body rots
My mind stays sharp
Enough to cut these thoughts
A guillotine for my insanity

My schedule revolves around
Six-week intervals that
Break me down
Juice from a mouse makes me a rat

Gnawing at the insurance and drug companies
Biting at their cures and placebos
Sniffing at unaffordable dreams
Of health and heroes

The Dragon

The cycle begins. Hour one. The first flutter of nausea starts to
grow, stretching its angry wings within. Something will soon be very

wrong as the body prepares to void. An application of heat to a tender set of intestines, lends hope that the wave of retching will be absolved. The trash can a holy chalice in which to spit. Hour two. Antiemetic drugs like children's Tylenol for an elephant's pain. Any attempt to stop the Dragon is thwarted. The purge begins.

Hour three. Denial still floats the boat. The stomach now an empty quivering cavern. Maybe this will be the last time vomit is induced. There are no more nutrients to lose. Trying to utilize the power of breath but ceaselessly failing. I am stronger than this hateful beast. Hour four. Never mind. Call for help. First from my own flesh, then from an ambulance. Into focus come two pairs of black boots with no faces, asking the same questions. Don't they have a file by now? What is your name, your birth date, your medications, your problem? A blood pressure cuff grips a limp arm, sounding a high alarm. Hoisted up from the chilled tile floor, it's time to go for a bumpy ride, buckled up tight, with the sickness that never subsides.

Hour five sees a backup in the emergency department. So many emergencies with so little sense of urgency. Already failed antiemetic drugs are repeated. Bile burns the back of my throat, as it bubbles up through flared nostrils. Stomach contractions clench at dangling sanity. The door stands open, but no one enters. So busy, but so quiet? Alone again with the retching. Hour six. Hour seven.

Pleading for someone to care, to hear, to help. Only met with glances of contempt. The title "Junkie" apparently branded on my chart. Narcotics the only thing to assist, the only thing kept out of reach. Just a nuisance that can't stop begging for help in between moans. No pharmaceuticals. No fluids. No compassion.

Hour eight. I give up the torture chair that is forever at an odd uncomfortable tilt, and take up residence on the cold, unkempt floor of triage room #5. Wishing for death or the attention that was needed hours ago, whichever comes first.

Hour nine. A picture hanging above my head asks which number rates my pain. A laminated poster full of the various emotions of smiley faces, mockingly asks what a nurse does not. I request a blanket to huddle under, hoping to hide from the pain and am met with an eye roll of irritation. Hour ten. How much longer? There is a six hour delay and you've already jumped line, go back to the waiting room if you can't stop the whine. And besides, it's shift change on the busiest day of the year. The Dragon drags on, dragging me down to drown in my own tears, bile, and fears.

The eleventh hour. Still choking on my own fluids, a once pretty face is haggard, mottled with broken blood vessels. The taste of digestive juices linger on the breath. Where does the mucus end and the saliva begin? Fluid just leaks. The limits of human endurance are tested over and over until there are no more tears.

A brief interlude. A moment of sweet spontaneous relief as I pass out from exhaustion. Hour twelve. The man with a mission speeds in with his sword drawn high. He will be the savior. Three minutes in the room and he's gone. How can there be a six hour wait if the doctor barely even looks at one patient before he's on to the next? It's an assembly line of absurdity. Scans are ordered before the cycle takes over again. The brief reprieve was only a tease. Hour thirteen creeps in with an admittance, acceptance that this girl needs some help.

Hour fourteen. The correct drugs are finally administered, and the cyclic vomiting abruptly stops. The scan, of course, shows nothing. Just a bug, they say. Here are some unnecessary prescriptions, they say. How would you like to pay, they say? With a fistful of middle fingers and enough curses to make Blackbeard blush.

Hour fifteen brings a dark ride home. A body beaten into submission by itself. Sips of ginger ale, the nectar of that fairytale some call heaven. Another test of endurance ends with me as the victor, but it sure doesn't feel like a win. The Dragon slain, if just for today. What happens next is a waiting game. Crohn's Disease lives and breathes on the exquisite pain.

"Living with an invisible chronic illness such as Crohn's Disease is like having a shadow that follows you around, even on the cloudiest of days. It demands attention, and if neglected, the consequences can be long term. I certainly have a greater appreciation for my health since being diagnosed with a lifelong disease. Once it's gone, you often can't get it back."

—Kelly Glover

Jennifer Juniper

The Silent Army

We wear fatigues, alright.
Stripes signal our invasions
not by us,
but into us by
People we just met
barely know
but are asked
to trust.

Intimacy with a perfect stranger
No candle, but
they do dim the light
before the CT scan

Battles and victories and losses
We march to the beat of
our shared vulnerabilities

"Crohn's Disease. That's the diagnosis. My body attacks itself, against an enemy that isn't there. Placing me permanently on a rug that can be pulled out from under me at any time. This is my decision: In between drinking dyes and shooting EpiPens into my thighs, I shall have epic moments. I have no qualms reaching for the biggest and best life has to offer; make no excuses for milking the littlest things for happiness."

—Jennifer Juniper

Marjorie Maddox

After the Diagnosis,

the doctor who dismissed her
complaints now calls every morning,

brings Cookie Dough ice cream
to the hospital; on his lunch break

arrives with cheeseburger and fries
bathed in grease and gossip

about his other "loser" patients, the not-
pretty ones who don't garner such attention.

With a boyish smile, he tosses out
quick comments to coax

her skeleton body to eat, regain
lost confidence and weight,

her blood cell count swimming
swiftly toward death and lawsuit.

Though we demand an end
to such solicitations, the phone

keeps ringing, his shaky voice,
she tells us, both arrogant

and scared, asking far away
on the other end, "And how

are we today? And how
is our favorite patient?"

". . .my daughter began experiencing debilitating stomach pain. The public response? "She looks great!" "What a beauty!" "Getting a little thin, maybe." "It's a teen thing." For years, the pediatric and GI doctors were no better: "All in her head." "Just nerves." "An eating disorder." Despite our proactive approach, it took an ER doctor and a simple test to finally arrive at a Crohn's disease diagnosis. Of course, no label captures the physical and emotional ramifications of remaining "unheard" for years."

—Marjorie Maddox

Pankhuri Sinha

Covid Curse for Digestive Ailments

The world had barely stood up
On its feet
Finding cures to measles and diphtheria
Jaundice and typhoid
Inventing, vaccinating all its kids
Against polio, hepatitis
And was so often brought to its knees
Frantically, searching for remedies in stem cell research
For forms of cancer, unexpected
In form and in the people it afflicted
Erratic, without reason and pattern
When covid struck
And locked all people
Inside their homes
Closed the offices
Deserted the streets
Crashed the world market!

A disease so deadly
It could kill like jellyfish
Stuck in nostrils
Maim our limbs and organs
Threatened badly and brutally
And so, we sat at home
Reading about it all
Hooked to gadgets and wires
Reading of vaccines, research and trial
Cutting our walks outside
Dropping the gym
Tough decision, terrible restriction, safety imposition
For those of us, used to the gym
To the weights, the lifting, the cardio

In and out, the fresh air
For those of us, with slow metabolism
The work out is a boon, fresh air a cure
Confinement slumps digestion
Well, in my case
The war of Immigration
Gave me diseases of fancy names
I had never heard of
Called the 'Irritable Bowel Syndrome'
At least, it was good to know
They knew what I was suffering from!
It was susceptible to conditions outside
Responded directly, communicated with my habitat
Could be spiked with stress
Cured with happiness
And the long visa wait
In the holy land of Canada
With provinces like Yukon
And mountain parks like Jasper
Where the air was so clean
You could smell, the pine and the fur
And longed to buy a condo
Get your papers together and settle down
Get a car, Get in and drive
Cause the roads were so empty
And the Rockies so beckoning
Instead, just waited
For a little more control over your life
And did not get it
Have you read the report
On the first nations genocide?
Aboriginal abuse?
Did not get it, the visa
The life, and the control over it
Because of the sick old academic politics
Which had already robbed

214

But You Don't Look Sick

Robbed of the nicest thing in my life
My US visa, my approaching green card actually
Being processed by the then husband's company
Which I had dropped unbelievably
To stand all over again
In the Immigrant's queue
But trust me, I needed to make
The dreaded, 'I can do it myself' statement!
Sure, a sudden about turn in love
Can have a toll taking effect
And I had decided to walk out
Out of that relationship of
High school romance
And still be friends!
But that path was taken
From right in front of me!
The country suddenly did not exist in my travel plan
Visa cancelled, the house, I had been living in
Since the last six years, was declared not mine
I an illegal alien, standing in front of it!
And among the many things difficult to digest
Injustice is the hardest!
Have said so with a smile
In the doctor's office
And will say it again!
And isn't there a trauma form
For past emotional setbacks!
That can help diagnose
This weird thing, this syndrome
Which borders on being a disease and a condition!
And there are drugs for it!
Addiction to over the counter drugs
Can be a disease in itself!
And trust me, how bad covid has made it!
Have tried to eat properly!
It's a lot of work!

Laboring the double flight of stairs
For that walk! And that piece of sky!
Air included! Having to count the basics of life
Like this! What an age! What a time!
Who would have thought
A disease so contagious
Could come our way?
And look how it got us!
Took some very dear precious lives
From all around us!
So we quietly brave the stairs
Though stair climbing is strictly forbidden for me!
Did I tell you that when I did reach the lovely
Government funded public health care system
Of socialist Canada, after being technically out of it
On a visa awaiting status
They told me I was Iron deficient
Did some infusions and did not charge
Felt good but did not solve issues
Neither border nor a failing digestion
Well, if not that then one severely weakened
Which required me to walk for two hours
For my usual, simple meal taken
The gym lost its flavor, its fragrance
And aroma, but was still a savior
I understand now, even the one here
Downgraded, down sized
Life itself, split in half
That's right, I took a break
From the 'condo in Canada' dream
The North American dream!
Except it wasn't a dream!
But my life! And how does one take
A break from it? Am still learning!
And as I dream and as I plan
The journey back, I strengthen

With food and love in motherland
As much as I can! And so
When the pain around my knees
Began to hurt more than the heartbreak
I called the doctor! Stood and lied before the x-ray machine
And was told, there was cartilage damage
Depletion! Well, first about the cartilage itself!
Coz who knows? The joint in the knees is bound by them
And wear and tear could really hurt!
I was in tears, when the doctor said
Walk no more! But thankfully
He also said cartilages are rebuilt
At least, erosion can be checked
With high protein diet! 'they had been used
As protein, by a protein deficient body
And perhaps you can rebuild!
If not, stop the erosion!'
So here I am, not just eating my fill
But eating along the prescriptions
And wellness guidelines!

While it has always taken me
Double the time to eat the
Normal course served simultaneously
To friends and colleagues
And twice as much digesting it
It takes longer now!
So what the hell, I labour hard!
To be fit and fine!

GENES

Lorelei Bacht

Hypothermic

August, April - it is always cold.
I detect every draft, breeze, flutter
In the air. Aware of how short
Or thin every item of clothing is,
I make notice of the slightest
Fluctuation of degrees. I know:
When shirts are unbuttoned,
Collars slightly ajar. Adjust
And readjust the scarf that keeps
Slipping to one side. The shower:
Unbearably tepid - pockets
Of cold air in between the drops,
Picking up the towel a leap of faith.
My hands, now: shades of blue,
Purple, black lines visible through
Their translucent envelope -
"Your hands are cold", the usual
Greeting. And yes, they are. I nod
And take my place right next
To the radiator / oven / fire - I spot
The warmest point of any house
As quickly as the cat. She stares,
Stretches, accepts companionship.
We share patches of sunlight.
Outside, I determine the vertical
Territories of butterflies, stand
At the center. As for my enemies,
I know to avoid rain, wet clothes,
Rubber boots and puddles—
Any form of weather found in England.

Medicalised

I sit high in stirrups, the doctor snaps
Her latex gloves - this is not going
To be fun. My mother smiles,
Her dreams come true: I am a medical
Complication, obscure combination
Of Latin words made flesh. I spend
The next decade in reclining chairs
Hospital beds, and medical tunnels,
Where I am told to hold my breath
For far too long by someone on
A microphone, watching me through
Tinted glass, injections of unnamed
Chemicals tracing white diagrams
Along my veins against the black,
Strictly for the trained eye to decipher.
My insides are hung out on a clothesline
For everyone to see, assess. Blood
Tests, vial after vial - afternoons at
The hospital, a plastic tap
Conveniently inserted in my arm.
I drip blood, precious only to me,
To everyone else, a matter of scientific
Curiosity. Turns out my mouth was made
To swallow pills, in varied shapes,
Colours, sizes. "We need to adjust your
Treatment." Humbly, I concur, having
Grown used to reading my life

In mmol/mols. I am a pie chart,
A bar chart, a graph. I quickly learn
That I am never right.

Molly Fuller

Family History

1.

What is father? (half the genes)	What is mother? (dying men call out for her)
Genetic encoding (moth	cocoon) of dominant traits (traitorous)
single-gene (acid washed jeans)	disease caused by pathogenic (trail)
variants (Christmas ties)	individual (I) (you)
autosomal recessive	autosomal dominant (disorder)
(Snoopy dressed as	reindeer with red wine stain)
or X/Y-linked (cuff)	pattern of inheritance (monogrammed silver)
painful disorder (out of)	tissue is similar (my hands are my
grandmother's)	familiar to what (familiar to whom?)
(define the word *disorder*,	if you are going to use it)
lines the inside of the uterus —	(a pussycat is also called a familiar)
the endometrium —	grows outside (disorder again: unruly genes)
(high-waisted 70s style bell	bottoms overthrow the patriarchy)
a mutation (what	is normal?) effects in brain,

But You Don't Look Sick

spinal

cord, retina, kidney, pancreas

and reproductive system (if you are a

woman, everyone asks when

are you having kids) (A: *joke's on you*)

ovaries, fallopian tubes (fig. 1

like the textbook) the tissue lining the pelvis

chronic: can last for years

or be lifelong (nightmare parade of priceless

family heirlooms you should

keep in your small house (I mean womb)

condition can't be cured

(they burned women alive for less)

thickens, breaks down, bleeds

tissue has no way (out)

to exit the pained body

(what does *not* pain even feel like?)

becomes trapped (an animal)

(no cure) (treatments are temporary, painful)

abnormal (the canary dies)

organs stick to one another (red velvet cake)

frameshift permutation (you

saw this movie already) unexpected affect

cellular proliferation

(it had Leonardo DiCaprio in it)

invasive survival

potential cells multiply uncontrollably

(*Inception*) structural

chromosomal abnormalities categorized

(MC Escher)

deletions, duplications

translocations, inversions, or rings   (staircases that lead nowhere)

unbalanced complements   of genes thereby

causing problems   for the progeny (loop) (looping)

2.

Malleable memories
entail the most mundane
such as second-guessing
whether I really did
turn off the stove

~

Protean
Readily assuming different forms or characters;
extremely variable

(initial capital letter) of, relating to, or suggestive
of Proteus

Protanomaly, protanopia, protasis, prote-, protea,
protease, protease inhibitor, protect

See: An amoeba is a *protean* animalcule

As in: Humans crawling into existence out of the muck from single-
celled organisms

~

Epigenetic memory / epigenetic inheritance
Environmental genetic changes / can be passed down
fourteen generations in C. *elegans nematodes*
(roundworms)

Epigenetic inheritance: the question is:
how long-lasting these inter-generational effects
last

~

Great, great, great grandfather: Solomon Cutler

Solomon: "Man of Peace"
Alternative spelling: *Salomon*

Related *names*: Suleiman, Sulayman, Salomão, Shlomo, Soghomon,
Salman, Zalman

Solomon is a common given *name*, surname derived from Aramaic

Cutler: English: occupational name for a maker of knives, from an
agent derivative of Middle English, Old French co(u)tel, co(u)teau
"knife"; Late Latin cultellus, a diminutive of culter "plowshare"

Americanized spelling of German Kottler or Kattler: of uncertain origin

~

Existence
entity, reality, individuality, animation, duration
continuation, continuance, endurance, presence, perseverance,
permanence
essence, subsistence, survival, journey
real world, rat race, the hand one is dealt, the big game, the long con
something

as in: something that exists

as in: actuality

But You Don't Look Sick

as in: being

as in: breath

~

Inheritance
uncertain origin / a set of good knives
Did I turn off the stove? Did I turn off the stove?

3.

What is daughter? (girl) (female) (me) What is sister? (girl) (addition)
(younger) (split images)   Problem with (association) (smell of
        gardenias)

central pain increases   (value of health) sensitivity (hot) (cold) (scent)
or perception (prophetic)   Brain processes pain (being torn apart)

reacts to given triggers (catch) (bracelet) (necklace) (band of painful
        muscles)
Test (trial) (symptoms) set off (adorn) eleven out of nineteen (cardinal)

identified body parts   fatigue (break) unsatisfactory sleep (inoperative)
cognitive problems (evidence) ongoing (chronic) (days spent watching

birds at the feeder out the window) (immoveable) May (prediction)
be hereditary (memory) (body) (swimming in the lake at sunset on land

my great-grandfather bought in 1934) (my grandmother's diagnosis)
Exact (solution) cause is unclear   Nucleotides (string) not divisible

(disunited) by three (me) (mother) (sister)   Gene (pool) or variant
expresses different signs (semiotics) (car crash) (accident)

(post-traumatic) (whiplash) (variable expressivity) mild (merciful)
manifestation or severe (excessive) complications Mitochondrial (thread)

inheritance strictly maternal (trauma) only egg cells (incite) developing
     embryos
Females pass on (track) mutations to offspring (epigenetic) Fathers (men)

do not give the disorders (confusion) to their daughters (xy) to their sons
     (y)
May take (cheat) years of painful (inflict) tests   What is autoimmune?

(against) What is immunity? (inviolability) (the portrait of my great-
     grandmother
in my childhood bedroom) (she holds a gardenia) the exact mouth I see in
     the mirror

"Fibromyalgia is a chronic pain disease that overwhelmingly affects women (80-90 % of people diagnosed are female). Fibromyalgia is difficult—the loss of control, the loss of focus, the loss of a "normal" functioning body. The trick for me, eleven years in, is realizing that there is no trick. I have adapted my process as a writer to work through my illness, rather than against it—creative flow—acknowledging and accepting both loss and growth."

—Molly Fuller

Monica Marie Hernandez

Scanxiety

The anxiety never leaves,
no matter how many years pass.
The fear of hearing the words,
the cancer is back... is always in mind.
Every day seems too short, knowing in an instant, everything can change.
Some days, hope is elusive but still I go on... life is too precious to waste a single moment.
My story may not be long, but it will be well-lived.

...and then she said

The days pass too quickly when you know your time is short... so many moments to remember in place of ones never to be experienced. Life speeds by when all you want is to stop time for a few minutes. Words left unspoken and unwritten, silenced forever by my constant companion, Death. Though darkness may threaten, still, I hope. Love, life is too precious to give up so easily. So to Death I daily say these words, "Hey, Darkness, my friend, you may have me tomorrow but not today... today is all I have and that you will not take." And I walk away without a backward glance, except for a single finger uplifted in defiance.

"I have a hereditary colon cancer syndrome (Familial Adenomatous Polyposis) which has been the cause of most of my over two dozen surgeries, cancer and many other complications and chronic illnesses. Even through all that I've been through, I try to live by my mantra of 'There's always hope and a bright side to every cloud if you look hard enough.'"

— Monica Marie Hernandez

Tracey Koehler

All in Your Head

Pain has been my eternal companion. It never disappoints; through highlights and challenges, it endures, always alongside. My loyal confidante, privy to my most intimate thoughts and feelings, able to witness that which remains invisible to the rest of my world.

Childhood complaints resulting in specialists who prod about and filch my blood, my urine, my skin, thrusting me into machines to scrutinize every ounce of my small body. Specialists who lose interest when tests prove negative and declare the problem is all in my head. Psychosomatic, hypochondria, psychological disturbance, depression, narcissism, nothing rooted in medical reality, nothing but a waste of their precious time.

Parents who refuse to indulge my suffering or validate my distress as my illness progresses through the years. I fight through the pain and weakness to avoid their contempt, their vile sarcasm, their condescending glances. I go on with bottled emotions and dreams of debunking theories. One day they will fathom my strength and implore my forgiveness. Until then, I will go on.

As the years pass, I witness sympathy, kindness, compassion, solidarity with the diagnosed. Grief and resentment infiltrate my thoughts and I am filled with bitterness. I am chastised for my selfish need for attention and charged with comforting those who are visibly ailing and diagnosed as such while I am forced to endure my misery in silence.

My body continues to degrade through the years into middle age. I have raised three amazing children alone. I have put myself through college. I have worked my way from an entry-level position in my career to one of the highest in the company during my 16 years of employment; giving every ounce of strength I can muster, only to collapse with my age-old friend, pain, when I return home for the evening. He hugs my body until I lose consciousness and find relief in the bliss of sleep.

In my 49th year I received a diagnosis from the Mayo Clinic, a rare genetic connective tissue disease called Ehlers Danlos Syndrome. Defects in my genes affect the strength and formation of collagen, a main component in the connective tissue in your body. It has caused several secondary diseases such as fibromyalgia, dysautonomia, inappropriate sinus tachycardia, and reactive hypoglycemia. I live with pain and weakness every moment of my life. My body cannot properly regulate my heartbeat, blood pressure, digestion, body temperature, sweating and other "automatic functions", my memory and concentration are ruined. The discs in my spine break down, causing stress fractures. My immune system is very weak, leading to the frequent contraction of viruses with extreme complications. There is no cure.

I had searched for a diagnosis my entire life, something to prove that it was not "all in my head", not just for others, but more importantly, myself. And, while none of my family or friends have recognized my strength or implored my forgiveness, I have. I look at the accomplishments I have made in my life while being under such dire circumstances and am amazed. I once waitressed for two weeks with a broken foot, thinking it was just another pain. I worked for four months with a broken back, traveling all over the country – I thought I just needed to strengthen my core muscles. It required a double fusion to repair.

I am amazed at my strength and tenacity, and I know that I am in a very small group of amazing people who must also go on with their invisible illnesses. We are perceived as whiners, as weak, as self-centered, as hysterical, delirious – yet we are the strong among the masses.

HEART

Rachael Z. Ikins

Boundary Violation/Heart Surgery

I entered the machine.
On my own soft feet.
Murders of black robots like crows rustled and hummed,
exhaled frigid breath.
They stripped me,
taped me, needled and sprayed me.

And I laid my body down
in this glass room. They kept me awake. Bitter herbs.
A white rabbit larger than a man
grinned vampire teeth,
hammer in one paw to pound my heart.

There were balloons, liquid nitrogen,
a suggestion of microwaves and my secrets exposed on a 52"
screen as snakes slithered through my skin into pathways only
my blood should whisper.

They told me to breathe.

The next few nights I did not sleep.
Fearing the rabbit.

Where they planted a monitor in my skin, glued next to my cat
tattoo,
bruising spread, my left breast a purple Picasso masterpiece.
I did not sleep.

The monitor tattles my secrets all night after midnight.

But You Don't Look Sick

The third day exhaustion took me. I slept hard, unaware when
 I woke of the day or time. I followed my mother into a field. She
 disappeared down a woodchuck hole.
When I called, she popped out, a large lynx with Mom's
 three-years'-past-dying eyes, juicy dead bird in her mouth.

"Eat, baby." She said. I was hungry.

Last night while the monitor betrayed my irregular rhythms
though I camouflaged myself well with dusk,

I arrived on Cape Cod. My husband and I argued and then
I was running, running to the ocean, water to my waist. I embraced
a mossy cliff.
Salt-tinged rivulets flowed down my sore throat.
I need. I need. I need.

When I climb to the beach, fog obscures the world.
No way back to him, our motel, or not to fall off a cliff.
I slide one bare foot at a time along pavement, sand grinds skin.
My feet must be bleeding. It stings.

A cottage looms. Woman bows her head over artwork
she crafts by lantern light. I stand unseen, back to the shingles.
I shiver, fingers spread, full of splinters and peeled paint, to wait

for the sun to burn the fog away.
To find my way.
Heart-percussion syncopates/ocean's song;
beneath a May moon.
I pray
for peace.

Some Magic and Mystery: waiting for a heart to beat

You squeeze your fist, magic erupts.
Does magic make it happen or is it your act?

Power and sparks, glowing, glowing.
Burn and glowing.

Some say two billion magical
shocks happen in this current that flows a life-time.

How long is a lifetime? Never-enough.

You clench your fist, remind yourself to breathe.
Everyone knows oxygen fans all flames. You thought

you had forever. You thought you wouldn't wonder,
except in theory, about dying, not this October.
Instead you lie in the dark, your body listens:

for clench of spell cast and when it pauses,
smack your chest open-handed to jolt;
Magic drums, the raft that carries you through this night

239

"Imagine being on the Aspergers spectrum, not knowing until you were 53. Imagine 25 years of psychotherapy and drowning in constantly changing high doses of multiple drugs for mental illnesses you didn't have. Until those drugs damaged your central nervous system permanently and the electrical circuitry of your heart. Imagine feeling every heartbeat skip and pause 24/7, and a pulsating traveling numbness tingling head to toe. Nothing is ever still. Exhausted, anxious. Nerves heal very slowly, if ever. Grit your teeth, keep going."

—Rachael Z. Ikins

Antonio Vallone

Hospital Prayers

This summer, I had five stays
in three hospitals and one rehab center.

In each, hospital clergy
stopped by my room, asking

if they could pray
for me. Even though I don't believe

in any organized religion,
I always said yes.

One time, my wife
who shares my disbelief,

was visiting in my room.
When I said yes, again,

and the clergy member closed her eyes
and started an unusually long prayer

over my hospital bed,
my wife looked at me

like she was a petite question mark
and walked out into the hall.

After the clergy member left
my wife returned and asked

"Why
did you let her go on like that?

You don't believe."
"True, I answered.

"But she does."

My Wife, the Feminist

Washes my feet,
Shins, and calves, then slathers them
With moisturizing creams

Between Women's Studies
Classes she teaches
Three days a week

Using Zoom
From her new COVID classroom--
Our dining room table--

And between more
Than her fair share
Of household drudgeries,

Some I'm slowly reassuming
As I heal
And regain strength and balance.

But You Don't Look Sick

My dry skin
Started after the amputation
Of my two toes,

And dialysis draining
Liters of fluid
Out of me

Three times a week
Every week,
All the summer's

And fall's
Illnesses
And hospitalizations,

Plus another never-
Ending Pennsylvania winter
I've not grown to love in 30+ years.

Neither of us
Finds anything the least bit
Ironic in her actions.

We know
Love is not simply
Theories for living

Equally.
For people like us,
Love is doing for one another

Whatever needs to be done,
Whenever it needs to be done,
However it can be done.

"Unless you saw: scars hidden under my shirt, you wouldn't know I've had a quintuple heart bypass and a cancerous kidney removed; my wife dropping me off at the dialysis center, you wouldn't know I need dialysis three days a week, four hours a session, for the rest of my life; you saw me standing and walking wobbly, you wouldn't know I have vertigo and two toes on my left foot needed to be amputated."

—Antonio Vallone

LUNGS

Trevor Flanagan

The beast within

Festering and seething in the dark, I wait.
A hidden debilitation bringing decay and misery.
Your physical and mental degradation nurtures me.

Crawling and itching between the filaments.
My calling cards, like leaf ants
invading your airways.

Wheezing, coughing, and choking.
These are the tunes I play.
Like a poorly tuned set of bagpipes.

I'm caged and all alone down here.
The beast within.
I rule over you.

Beware. If I catch you, I will rake your life.
I will constrict as a boa would its prey.
I will rip all hope out of your throat.

We are alone, you and I.
An unwanted symbiotic relationship.
Yet I am needed, in part, for life.

You search for an unobtainable cure.
Yet, suppression of my fortitude is futile.
Slithering from place to place, I avoid detection.

Friends and family can only watch with dismay.
Your tolerance and moods fluctuate with the
ebbs and flows of my life like a malignant tide.

Sooner or later you'll slip up, and I'll be there.
A lightning strike darkening your world,
I'll lie here, in the dark.

"I've had bronchial issues since childhood. In 2013, a severe chest infection exacerbation led to a diagnosis of bronchiectasis. Coming to terms with the condition was a huge learning curve for me and my family. For the most part, I hide the condition from public view, not because I'm embarrassed about having it but about how I have to deal with the symptoms day to day. For more information on the condition, see: https://www.nhs.uk/conditions/bronchiectasis/"

—Trevor Flanagan

Vandana Kumar

Burning out

I have seen illness
Like an asthmatic tree
In dense forest
That caught fire

I have choked
On the fumes all around
The chronic tree
In me
Kept burning
Long after the fire was doused

Friends shrunk
As the list of things
I was forbidden to eat
And the list of sports I couldn't play
Far exceeded
The lists of those I could

The remedies on offer
Increased
As cures decreased

Far better the heart that drops
With a thud
The candle put out
By pinching the wick

The asthmatic tree
Waited a lifetime
To exhale

Lahari Mahalanabish

Battling for a Whiff

The alarm screeched through the rhythmic roar of the waves, the hush-hush monologues through the conch shells and the slapping of rubber slippers on the wet sand. My blinking eyes skimmed over the undulating blanket tickling the fuzzy walls of the mosquito net. At once I became aware of the stinging sensation in my mouth and the itching in my throat. My nose was clogged. Runnels of water shot out of my nose and hung over my upper lip. I hastily put on my slippers and ran to the sink. After rinsing my face, I brushed my teeth and squeezed my nose repeatedly, hoping the invisible obstruction would uncork my nostrils. My mouth popped open and shut like a hapless goldfish's mouth as I struggled to channel in the air shunned by my nose. My ear holes itched, as well. Earlier, I would raid the bedside table drawers for the box of ear-buds. Now I knew the culprit was not earwax, but the same allergy assailing my nose, mouth and throat. And I kept my ears clean in any case.

I changed my clothes to offer my morning prayers while water continued to noiselessly drip down my reddened nose. I unrolled the jute mat, patted down its creases and stroked apart its stubbornly clinging tassels. My sneezes exploded through my silent chanting while I prayed. It was difficult to keep focus, but I soldiered on. After prayers, I lowered the electric coil into the bucketful of water before tucking in the toothpaste and toothbrushes in the front pocket of my luggage bag, all the while making circular motions with the tongue against the wall of my mouth to suppress the stinging. I let ten minutes pass before switching off the water heater. Pulling it carefully out of the bucket, I stared at the water and scrutinized the density of the smoke to gauge the extent of its warmth. My overused, wet napkin was crumpled within my hands, ready to spring into action whenever I sneezed.

I dragged the bucket to the tap and turned it on. Bubbles jaunted sprightly from the base of the column of running water and popped near the bucket's edge. The comfort provided by the warm water was seized by my gasping, itching, and snorting. Once I had put on my clothes and buttoned up my cardigan, I rushed to the balcony to dry my towel. There was no time to sun myself. My little daughter had to be scooped out from the depths of the blankets like a listless doll and helped through her transformation into a nicely bathed, neatly combed and impeccably dressed princess. I cupped her lolling head into position so she could sip the warm water from the glass I held to her lips. She brushed her teeth with her eyes tightly shut, standing atop a stool, facing the sink, braced against my body. It was only when I asked which of her dolls and crayon boxes I should put in the luggage bag did she part her eyelids. As I picked up her teddy from the toy rack, my hands brushed against a large, gaudily dressed doll she hadn't played with for days, and my torment multiplied manifold, riding upon a new spurt of sneezes. The itching spread across the flesh of my mouth like a destructive creeper digging into the roof of a dilapidated building.

The bell rang. I unlatched the door and let in Bina. "You will never be able to imagine how sick I was yesterday," said the maid. Her tone was not theatrical, just matter of fact. I glanced at her and nodded.

"How are you, today?" I asked a while later, sprinkling salt and pepper on the mashed potato.

"Better," she said, chopping an onion. "Don't mind *Didi*, but I really envy the health of women like you."

Women like me?

253

My daughter's bath water was ready in no time. Shelled off her woollens and then her nightclothes, she jiggled for a few seconds to beat the cold. Curtained by the descending water that I poured down from the mug, she sang at the top of her voice. Sprays of water wet my feet, triggering a new bout of itching in my throat. In order to quell this extreme discomfort, a sound involuntarily emanated from my mouth sounding suspiciously like a frog's croak. My little girl imitated me in glee, vaguely aware of the bricks blocking my nostril and the fire gutting the interiors of my mouth and ears. I promptly mopped her with a small pink towel, carefully tending to the strands of her recently trimmed hair, and swathed her in a fresh set of woollens.

My husband was awake by now and was rushing through his ablutions.

"You look fine today," he said, inspecting my face. I didn't tell him the truth as I didn't want him to worry about my health.

I checked all the items again. The fruits rolled in one carry bag. I stacked another with packets of chocolate chips, crispy biscuits and spicy, puffed rice. I also placed the Tupperware box with the potato sandwiches. Finally, the towels were brought back from the balcony. I stretched them across the contents of the luggage, padding the clothes underneath. Then I zipped up my daughter's jacket and knotted my scarf. The stairs resounded with our footsteps as we trudged down with our bags and baggage. We slammed the doors of the car, rolled down the windows and leaned back in our seats. My husband was at the wheel, taking us to the sea-side for a three days holiday. I drew my daughter close, and in my mind, I felt the itching areas lapped up lovingly by the froth, the stinging scraped aside by the sand and my nose freeing up to smell the salt like a shaken conch shell releasing the jammed up mud within to welcome the growing whisper of waves.

"There are days when I struggle to breathe; my mouth itches and throat continuously gets filled with mucus. I had visited doctors, taken vaccines and tried both allopathic and homeopathic courses of treatment, but none had led to a permanent cure. My perils get pronounced in Winter and monsoon season."

—Lahari Mahalanabish

Jaime Speed

Hypochondriac – an asthmatic poem

1.
artificial my lungs   fidget for air
heaving metal armour sticking in my chest
the hinges need greasing, aesthetics maybe
but what a very tarnished thing
            all the hullaballoo is the ruckus my sighing
this coughing makes   when I laugh
I huck my chest into someone else's   able hands
when clearing my throat feels like an admission of sick
no no coughing, I'm so so careful
now just this train's engine chugging along along

2.
I'm a loser try-hard   I'm gonna need you to like me
keening, careening   the cat I swallowed
purring in my chest again
this rattling of armour gets louder at night, shuddering
fear connected to the L bone   where I can't walk
cobwebs filling up   my throat again
tasting metal I still feel   the engine revving

3.
the net in my throat—catching
hummingbirds again, intricate as house flies struggling
against a thousand spiderwebs

this flitting of wings is an engine stalling, stuttering
staccato breaths of a hand me down relic
my medicated lungs gone metallic in the sour of blood
corroded armour plates, the way I jangle   like a charm
bracelet   pulse pounding
after shocks shuddering for days
            relying on crutches, a hobbling
organ to propel this campaign for breath
this heavy armchair arrests my chest

a chuffed anxiety, arms flapping, all-consuming
catching—as fire

4.
Before I was a hypochondriac I was heavy vapour
        dense smoke over forests of bones
like a milky dream stretching out of reach

before I was a hypochondriac I thought this purring in my chest
was just another cat, another allergy
        another engine   failing to turn   inside me
where the pistons stopped stuck, the springs—- the falls
        the whisper tickling at my spine is dendritic
with its cloaked limbs, trying to undress each one
will only make them strangle
at me faster   I've learned
to slow and control my breathing
        even when breath is too heavy to catch
to fidget and distract, counting windows, exit signs
to never admit   and when it gets so loud
everyone can hear my misfiring   to grab my shit
        and bolt

I had to learn to breathe
        before everywhere was a no   cough zone

my lungs, a nod   to vagabond delirium
before the rabble rousing of rumpus rooms
the enamoured encyclopedic flippings of childhood
        licked finger hyper, full gasoline book to book
        pull cord   my own wretched guts
loose ends loose wires on the carpet   oceans of books
        messy and blue, spreading   like a family tree

it's catching it's catching   like family tradition
a sea of apologies drowning grandpa's chest
choking my daughter's blue face, the startle
of learning to breathe again   is coming back around
the taste of metal   this knocking at my back

the kick-start the body fail
my breath   catching   onto nothing
nothing like the rabble rousing of chest pounding
anxiety in my hands, closed over a trembling bird
arms tucked into my own tree trunk
holding it in—the embrace   the smile of collar bones
cradling cages—inheriting   years of sleeplessness
the hospital walls the colour of bone shell —
        and it's nothing like being locked
in the trunk of a car   the dread of which will bolt
a flipping heart to the floor mat
held still by the black wings of sleep   there's no thrill in that
        no one's even looking   for a cure

I used to pass out, go faint, twirling—in mud rooms, entry ways
legs kicked—out from under me like an accident
of absurd angles   the lingering sickly sweet scent
of a dream dancing away   when I come to   it's like being
somewhere I've been before and finding nothing familiar
in the pattern of ceramic tiles that halo my body like chalk lines
the attack   nothing   but a feint against my will
the head rush, legs still
        kicking - I always fight back

when my breath shakes out of me in sharp staccato pulses
echoes - exacerbated - I beg you oh so sweetly
to please keep me   chugging along
but the acrid voice of the sickroom
nurse harps *it's only asthma, dear*   and so it is

The bone records (2): it doesn't work

The surgeon determines he'll operate
      an easy case
once he locates the source

He washes his hands
covers his smile with a mask
a tray of instruments
like an elegant buffet of hors d'oeuvres he sets
to rearranging me
scalpels
sutures
for finishing off the fine thread work
forceps
scissors
brushes
up on my symptoms:
says he'll have to take
a thorough look, maps
me in quarters, permanent
marker

With pointing trowel, the surgeon excavates
the archeological dig
of my body's ruins
wheel barrels of spoil removed
he thrusts deeper
tearing ulcers into layers
of soft tissue
gloved hand riding my polluted flesh
hunting for the screw, a hint,
some atrophied organ
like a wrinkled fig, a tumour, my spleen

sprouting with verdigris, he doesn't know
any better than me
what to look for
when he poises the bone
chisel at odds with my pelvis

I stay awake, muscles snapping
like hair elastics
the knife trick
my blue skin in the retractors
like a deer's fresh meat gumming up the hunter's trap
my body takes part
in this healing, he never takes
the long way around
cold-trailing recovery, he discovers
under the microscope, all tissue
is only cells, hits a nerve
that sets my body off, legs thrashing
in the rollicking allegro
of the symphony's final movement

He praises himself on the invisible
stitching he's mended
into my new seams
as he claims me whole
and sends me out to pay the bill

"Living with an invisible illness is embedded in my identity; it's always been a part of me. Along with that, there are medications, routines, triggers to avoid, self-monitoring, and an awful lot of anxiety at times. But also, there is an inherent fighter in me, who always emerges stronger, and I'm so grateful to have found her."

—Jaime Speed

METABOLIC

Nayona Agrawal

Insta ready! What she's hiding behind that smile

I'm not the shell I live in

Chronic-les. You can't keep her down

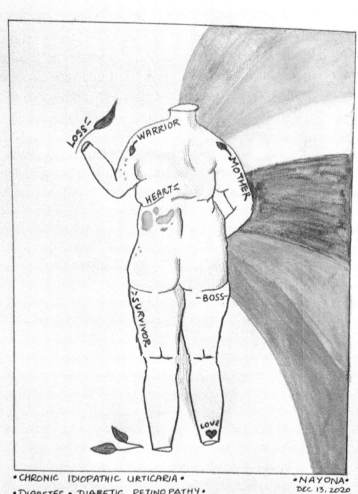

"Diabetes and diabetic retinopathy - A metabolic disease that causes increased sugar in the bloodstream. Excess sugar for prolonged periods impacts other organs, sometimes causing a deterioration in vision. In women below 40, it is a rare occurrence, and in some cases requires painful monthly injectables into the eye in an operating theatre.

Associated with this is Chronic Idiopathic Urticaria. Hives that appear all over the body without reason. It can feel like a million fire ants marching all over your body."

— Nayona Agrawal

Kasey Hill

Jail Time

"I have a myriad of health issues but, one of the ones that scares me most is my diabetes since my mother-in-law died from hers being out of control for too long. It's a fear that a young mother that I wouldn't wish on anyone."

—Kasey Hill

Satishchandran Matamp

Remember, Sweet Kills!

Sugar I loved,
For that anything sweet,
But they said stop eating
Because you're a diabetic.

Remember you're a poet
But don't write love poems
Without a bitter end, because
If only sweet, it'll kill you soon!

Kaikasi V S

A 'Sweet Disease'

Three droplets of blood, pierced and drawn out
Reshaped the contours of my disordered interiors
You are in the league of millions hounded by a 'sweet disease'
Forbids the intake of further sweetness
Reminds us of a system's untimely satiety
They said this is something that strikes people who are---
By birth
Prone to nurture a romance, the ones who—
Get excited with ideas
Wild passions
Has a penchant for lucid dreaming
And a bed of crimson thoughts
Yearning to fly high
This occurs when your passion exceeds the number of red and
white warriors within—
Multiplying everything that are supposed to remain dormant
Perching above a doldrum of hidden tastebuds
It was a quack who suggested your role in this disease inducing
game
He blamed it on me falling hopelessly in love with you
A sorcerer told me the spell you had cast alongside the river
The snake charmer even suggested the percolating power of your
eyes did the trick
Many a crystal balls have shaken, but nothing like the magic of that
icy kiss
All these and much more must have triggered a bout of this
disorder
Disheveling my dreams and altering my cartographies of desires
Pushing up the boundaries of all my organs with undue sweetness
and light
No wonder my pancreas got spared, in a bid to conquer my heart

Enslaving and forcing me to slow down
Pining for you wherever my blood greets the cells
And whenever my reason deserts for an unwilling suspension of beliefs
Strike my veins with thy coldness and ignite the rush of streams
Unlock the chambers of longing where lies the secrets to my recovery
Break in and save me, or else leave me to the mercy of imminent death

NERVE

Kindra M. Austin

My Fibromyalgia Checklist: Legit Reasons Why I'm a Surly Bitch

- Fatigue, worsened by physical exertion or stress (CHECK) ✓
- Activity level decreased to less than 50% of pre-illness ✓ activity level (CHECK)
- Recurrent flu-like illness (CHECK) ✓
- Sore throat (CHECK) ✓
- Hoarseness (CHECK) ✓
- Tender or swollen lymph nodes (glands), especially in neck & underarms (CHECK)
- Shortness of breath with little or no exertion (CHECK) ✓
- Frequent sighing (CHECK) ✓
- Tremor or trembling (CHECK)
- Severe nasal allergies (new or worsened) (CHECK) ✓
- Cough (CHECK) ✓
- Night sweats (CHECK)
- Low-grade fevers (CHECK)
- Feeling cold often (CHECK) ✓
- Feeling hot often (CHECK) ✓
- Cold extremities (hands and feet) (CHECK) ✓
- Low body temperature (below 97.6) ✓
- Low blood pressure (below 110/70) ✓
- Heart palpitations ✓
- Dryness of eyes and/or mouth (CHECK) ✓
- Increased thirst (CHECK) ✓
- Symptoms worsened by temperature changes (CHECK) ✓
- Symptoms worsened by air travel ✓
- Symptoms worsened by stress (THAT'S A BIG 10-4) ✓
- Headache (CHECK–MIGRAINE) ✓

- Tender points or trigger points (DON'T FUCKING TOUCH ME)
- Muscle pain (CHECK)
- Muscle twitching (CHECK)
- Muscle weakness (CHECK)
- Severe weakness of an arm or leg (CHECK)
- Full or partial paralysis of an arm or leg
- Joint pain (CHECK)
- TMJ syndrome (MAYBE)
- Chest pain (CHECK)
- Eye pain (CHECK)
- Changes in visual acuity (frequent changes in ability to see well) (CHECK)
- Difficulty with accommodation (switching focus from one thing to another)
- Blind spots in vision
- Sensitivities to medications (unable to tolerate a "normal" dosage) (UMM, DUH)
- Sensitivities to odors (e.g., cleaning products, exhaust fumes, colognes, hair sprays) (YES, YOU FUCKING STINK)
- Sensitivities to foods (CHECK)
- Alcohol intolerance (THANK FUCK, NO)
- Alteration of taste, smell, and/or hearing
- Frequent urination (CHECK)
- Painful urination or bladder pain (CHECK)
- Prostate pain
- Impotence
- Endometriosis
- Worsening of premenstrual syndrome (PMS)
- Decreased libido (sex drive) (UNFORTUNATELY)
- Stomach ache; abdominal cramps (CHECK)
- Nausea (CHECK)

- Vomiting (YEP)
- Esophageal reflux (heartburn) (CHECK) ⌣
- Frequent diarrhea (THANKS, IBS)
- Frequent constipation (AGAIN, THANKS, IBS)
- Bloating and intestinal gas (BEANO DOESN'T HELP)
- Decreased appetite (I WISH)
- Increased appetite (LE SIGH…)
- Food cravings (THAT'S FUCKING NORMAL, DUDE) ⌣
- Weight gain (UGH) ⌣
- Weight loss
- Lightheadedness; feeling "spaced out" (CHECK) ⌣
- Inability to think clearly ("brain fog") (THAT'S CALLED COGNITIVE IMPAIRMENT. CHECK) ⌣
- Seizures
- Seizure-like episodes
- Syncope (fainting) or blackouts ⌣
- Sensation that you might faint (CHECK) ⌣
- Vertigo or dizziness (CHECK) ⌣
- Numbness or tingling sensations (CHECK) ⌣
- Tinnitus (ringing in one or both ears) (CHECK) ⌣
- Photophobia (sensitivity to light) (DARKNESS IS MY FRIEND) ⌣
- Noise intolerance (SHUT THE FUCK UP) ⌣
- Feeling spatially disoriented (CHECK) ⌣
- Disequilibrium (balance difficulty) (CHECK) ⌣
- Staggering gait (clumsy walking; bumping into things) (CHECK) ⌣
- Dropping things frequently (CHECK)
- Difficulty judging distances (e.g. when driving; placing objects on surfaces) (CHECK) ⌣
- "Not quite seeing" what you are looking at ⌣
- Hypersomnia (excessive sleeping) (CHECK)

- Sleep disturbance: unrefreshing or non-restorative sleep (CHECK)
- Sleep disturbance: difficulty falling asleep (CHECK)
- Sleep disturbance: difficulty staying asleep (frequent awakenings) (CHECK)
- Sleep disturbance: vivid or disturbing dreams or nightmares (CHECK)
- Altered sleep/wake schedule (alertness/energy best late at night) (CHECK)
- Difficulty with simple calculations (e.g., balancing checkbook) (I CAN'T MATH)
- Word-finding difficulty
- Saying the wrong word (CHECK)
- Difficulty expressing ideas in words (CHECK)
- Difficulty moving your mouth to speak
- Slowed speech
- Stuttering; stammering
- Impaired ability to concentrate (CHECK)
- Easily distracted during a task (WHAT AM DOING RIGHT NOW?)
- Difficulty paying attention
- Difficulty following a conversation when background noise is present (CHECK)
- Losing your train of thought in the middle of a sentence (WHAT?)
- Difficulty putting tasks or things in proper sequence
- Losing track in the middle of a task (remembering what to do next) (DAMN IT!)
- Difficulty with short-term memory (DID I EAT BREAKFAST?)
- Difficulty with long-term memory
- Forgetting how to do routine things
- Difficulty understanding what you read

- Switching left and right
- Transposition (reversal) of numbers, words and/or letters when you speak
- Transposition (reversal) of numbers, words and/or letters when you write
- Difficulty remembering names of objects (CHECK)
- Difficulty remembering names of people (CHECK)
- Difficulty recognizing faces
- Poor judgment
- Difficulty making decision (CHECK)
- Difficulty following simple written instructions
- Difficulty following complicated written instructions (CHECK)
- Difficulty following simple oral (spoken) instructions
- Difficulty following complicated oral (spoken) instructions (CHECK)
- Difficulty integrating information (putting ideas together to form a complete picture or concept)
- Difficulty following directions while driving
- Becoming lost in familiar locations when driving
- Feeling too disoriented to drive (CHECK)
- Depressed mood (CHECK)
- Suicidal thoughts (CHECK)
- Suicide attempt(s)
- Feeling worthless (CHECK)
- Frequent crying (CHECK)
- Feeling helpless and/or hopeless (CHECK)
- Inability to enjoy previously enjoyed activities (CHECK)
- Increased appetite (CHECK)
- Decreased appetite
- Anxiety or fear with no obvious cause (CHECK)
- Panic attacks (CHECK)
- Irritability; overreaction (FUUUUCK!)

- Rage attacks: anger outbursts with little or no cause (LOOK THE FUCK OUT) ✓
- Abrupt, unpredictable mood swings (CHECK) ✓
- Phobias (irrational fears) (CHECK) ✓
- Personality changes (CHECK) ✓
- Rashes or sores (CHECK)
- Eczema or psoriasis
- Aphthous ulcers (canker sores)
- Hair loss (I'LL BE SHOPPING FOR WIGS SOON)
- Dental problems (CHECK)
- Periodontal (gum) disease

Catch a Chronic Illness

If you don't have a chronic illness, I suggest you find one, grab hold of it, and hand over control. Life is much simpler when you have something legitimate to blame.

If you feel like cutting out of work early, your illness is the best excuse to walk out in the middle of your shift, head held low in shame.

If you wake up in the morning in so much pain that you cannot move, you can have your spouse call in for you; then you'll have the whole day free to hurt in peace.

When you decide your place of employment expects too much of you, you can apply for intermittent leave; if you're approved, you'll have as many days off a week as you want to cry in private, and question your value as a productive member of society.

When you realize a life of leisure is better than punching a time clock, quit your job; questioning your value as a member of your family is only a small side-effect of giving up your job/career/income. Money...who needs it? Fulfillment...that's what Netflix is for.

Did you make plans with your friends, then decide you aren't well enough to even shower and dress in grown up clothes? Chronic Illness will get you out of that dinner you've been looking forward to. Your daughter is playing her last band concert as a senior in high school? The chronic pain will excuse you from attending. You were never proud of her, anyway.

Don't feel like fucking your husband? Chronic pain.

Don't feel like grocery shopping? Or cooking a meal for your family? Chronic pain.

Travelling to Grandma's for Christmas is going to be a drag? Chronic pain.

Too lazy to tie your own fucking shoes???

The benefits are limitless. Yes, you'll have to explain yourself to your friends and family who are too goddamned ignorant or uncaring to understand. But fuck them. This is about you. Everything is about you, as it should be. Because you're special.

This is your life, after all.

Fibromyalgia, You Don't Own Me

Despite the pain I live with every day, I often do forget that I'm not twenty anymore–until I hand down to my girl some vintage band tees too small for me now. Goodbye Fleetwood Mac tank top, and Rolling Stones long sleeved t-shirt. See you around, Abbey Road with the small hole in the armpit. Rick Springfield, you're next, dude. And poor Peter Frampton, my beloved...I promise you'll live on in the hands of Nicole. She'll treat you right. I just can't stretch you across my boobs anymore. Okay, so my boobs aren't the real problem. I'll be forty-three in December, and I'm a good deal heavier everywhere than I was twenty years ago.

Thank you, Fibromyalgia—you really do cramp my style, and by that, I mean, you've made me fat. My bell bottom jeans just don't fit right anymore, and I wonder who I am when I go out in yoga pants and sweatshirts. You've taken my identity and my will to give a fuck. I throw my hair up in Pebbles buns now, and wear my glasses every day. I wear slip on shoes, for fuck's sake. Granted, my shoes are colorful and cute as fuck, and I rock a messy bun, *especially* when I'm wearing glasses. I refuse to allow you to take away my good humor. You take away my concentration; sleep; self-esteem; sanity; appetite; motivation; and MY T-SHIRTS, among loads of other things...you can't have my goddamned humor, too.

I thank the Universe for Nicole. My girl reminds me who I am better than anyone. I had a lovely day with her yesterday, full of laughs and stimulating conversation. So there's another thing Fibromyalgia and my other health issues cannot take away from me—my daughter, and our beautiful relationship.

Entropy
Collaboration with Christine E. Ray

Kindra:

Every morning, I wake up. I keep
waking
up.
And
sometimes I'm angry at my opened eyes, cos sometimes
brittle fingernails
scratching inside of my skull, they split and rip and bleed and blood
leaks and shorts my circuits.
Not enough to kill me
dead,
just enough to kill my will. And so I stare up at the ceiling,
counting back the years, the weeks, the goddamned days I've
given in and left myself to
dreadful
entertainments. Circus tents of made up horrors
dressed in homemade gore—red corn syrup and hot dogs and
mushy elbow macaroni.
What am I? Incubator for the fly.
bzzzzzz
I am infestation,
lying.
Nighttime calls, and so I answer,
cos that's where I
fuckin belong.
Inside
black ink
sky—where nerve endings scream in silence of
outer space.

Christine:

Every morning, I wake up. I keep
waking
up,
fighting cobwebs of nightmares that cling to my brain
like black taffy.
My bedcovers a cotton shroud, moldering around heavy limbs.
The smell of decay and musty lavender fill my nose, make me
retch,
remind me that I'm rotting from the inside in this weak vessel of
flesh.
The sunlight creeping under the blinds is acid that burns my eyes.
I close my lids tightly, seeking escape from the awaiting nothing,
but even my ghosts have retreated for the day;
and I'm left with nothing but long hours I no longer
have the energy to fill.
What am I? An empty husk of a woman.
A corpse with a pulse,
who forgot to fall.
Nighttime calls, and so I answer
sleep's promise of oblivion.
The electric sheep I try to count
sting me like jellyfish,
leave weeping blisters on my soul
before melting into the obsidian.

Mini Babu

They Allege I Am Sick

They allege I am sick
and come peeping
just about, while
I stand, talk, and act.

And I, seeing you
smile away,
while I fall and fall
on the air
over the many layers
and bounce up and down
and you, onlookers. . .
unable to comprehend
the hurt that air
could do. . .

and my exceptionally
brilliant daughter dusts
water in the air
may be to moisten
my rise and fall
and showcase
a glimpse of earth.

Marilyn Rea Beyer

Starburst
for Cindy

On the days when the headaches come,
an entire galaxy is in flames
behind her eyes, between her temples.

Not one ounce more will fit into
the cosmos of pain, throbbing, ringing.
No thought, no comfort can penetrate.

The universe, sore inside her mind,
bangs, buckles, desiccates, and hardens
'til the sour black coal burns itself cool.

It gives a lovely light

"This both ends candle burning has got to stop," she said,
"It's all my words messing up."

He reassured her, "We're in the prime of our lives."

"If this is my life prime," said she, "shudder I to think years of gold."

Her head sagging, she sighed hard. "Keep my clothes on putting inside
out."

"You look lovely to me," he said, "Come to bed."

So she lay down next to him,

swimming in her nightgown,
thinking in buckets,
anxieties pouring down like cats and dogs.

To heal

Must I really go on living,
doing and doing and doing
in the dark of the dark?

Hanging in the bone closet,
my skeleton is frayed, corroded,
and full of holes.

It needs some work.

Perhaps with a coat of your paint,
my ravaged, ephemeral metal
will hold together a little while longer.

"You will never know. My mission is to set you at ease, to make you feel secure, to help you get where you need to be. Whatever is inside my own body must be ignored, denied, hidden, or overcome by sheer will. Seldom acknowledged, rarely admitted. It took me decades to realize three things: First, I am not the only one. Second, hurting is not shameful. Third, sharing can be healing."

—Marilyn Rea Beyer

Kayla Sue Bruyn

She

She wipes the tears away before others can see
She tucks the pain away, so she can relearn how to breathe
She straightens her spine
Utters *"it's ok I'm fine"*
When others catch a glimpse of the mess she is
She just bites her lip and lines her tongue in shiny white lies
"It's ok. I'm fine"

She often feels like her body is burning
A woman on fire
She tucks the warning alarms away
She doesn't have time to go easy today
She has a list a million points long
Despite starting the day with her spoons long gone
She is utterly exhausted
Her eyes are haunted
Trapping the ghosts of sleepless nights and un-healed hurts

She wipes the tears away before others can see
That their words have enough bite to sting
Over sensitive
Overwhelmed
Always a step behind the rest
But she tries her best
Still, she falls short

She wipes the tears away before others can see
This mess of a human being
Is me

Take Away

Today I woke up cradled in the arms of Despair
She whispered bitter sweet nothings in my ear
I choked on her insincerity and dove into her brevity
She left me empty and hallowed
A husk of a person
Is it worth it?
To go on?
My body aches and is tired
My soul weeps and wanders away from me
Protecting my sanity
Yes, despair and I go way back
She will tell you that
I am not new to watching my whole world burn
I am not new to being hurt
But this pain is of a physical kind
I've done everything I can to fortify my mind
But I'm slipping away into its hidden corners
Because this physical pain makes me feel worthless
When I cannot stand up straight
Or take care of myself
Too stupid and far too stubborn to ask for help
So I hobble on
Face scrunched up with each new wave of pain
Silently dying of shame
As I realize, this may be my new normal
So, I sink into the lap of despair
Listen attentively as she strokes my hair
And tells me all the things I can no longer do

But You Don't Look Sick

Of my limits and how this chronic pain
Will drain my youth
How it will leach away all the creativity
All of my passion
Everything that makes me, well me
And in its place will remain
A broken, hurting thing
A husk of the woman I used to be
A chronic-pain-collateral-damage, husk of a human being
But then a thought fills me
Brimming with hope
I let the despair go
I get up and wash my face
And magically I can now face the day
Even if I must hobble or stay in place
Depression won't get to dictate
My take away

Susan Burch

underground bunker

underground bunker
trying to survive
this migraine

trying to go

trying to go
a day, 2 days,
without meds
the pain as constant
as my heartbeat

serial killer

serial killer –
chronic migraines murder
my daily routine…
every day, a thousand things
that never get done

another day

another day
with a bad migraine
I fade
into the background
as usual

Jharna Choudhury

I Guess It's Thought Cancer

With a pen and paper,
one sprouted face of appalling incoherence
staring out loud through midnight's terror,
I think,
of how terribly intrigued I am
of my dough body and its pantomime.

Nothing finds me the way I do, by undressing
myself, my hair, my skin, my limbs, part by part
and then what's left in me is a whimper
tied with my innards, so strongly,
that it suffocates me.

When I lean on the headrest
my words run loose like quick animals
with camouflage;
forever turns into fever, kitten turns into eaten,
and other nonsensical slips
telling me, you are not right!

In my sleep, if I sleep,
my mind spits out people, constantly,
eyes, liver, fluids running down
and I slouch in gigantic hunger
tossing on my bed like stripped meat on a skillet,
when he asks, "are you alright?";
"just a headache", I feign,

thinking for the rest of the night,
can a torso speak,
and who has forgotten one next to me?

Portrait of My Mind

Undressing My Body

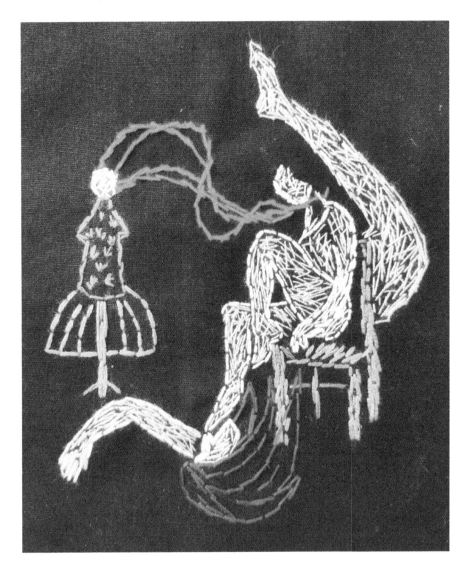

Emily Rose Cole

Ars Poetica with MS Injection

Through the syringe, light fractures—
golder now, more sinister. No sleight

of hand allowed, no tricks. You must
disjoin your shoulder's skin, inflict

a small, subcutaneous harm. Patient,
here's the lesson: Like sickness, bravery's

just a matter of mutation. The remedy's
in the wince, your thumb on the plunger.

Previously published in Harpur Palate, Summer and Fall 2019, Vol. 18, No. 1.

Pain Spell

It's as if I'm at once Odysseus lashed
to the mast, & also the sirens' shattering
counterpoint. Think rope-burn & crush
syndrome. Think Zippo, brushwood,
six months of drought. Think of pain as
the peregrine's notched beak, the bandsaw
incarnate, its suffering whine, its greedy
teeth. The fact is, no metaphor satisfies.

My best attempt so far is how our hero
didn't know whether their song was a jinx
or a blessing until he'd thrashed under
its power long enough to learn that "or"
is circumstantial at best. How he wanted it
not to be a premonition of where all loved
& unloved bodies go.

How there was nothing
he could do but listen.

Previously published in Killjoy Magazine's Access Issue, Spring 2019.

On Being My Own Wife

I take her mostly *for poorer*, but remind her how rich
we are in friends. We are forever *in sickness*. We're chronic.
But doesn't that mean, I soothe her as we scour our only
soup pot, that we're also, from a more enlightened
perspective, *in health*, too? Besides, *health* is a highly
subjective metric anyway, and don't all bodies require regular
maintenance? When she cries after the MRI, after
the visual field test, after the yearly checkup's unsilver news,
after the medical bills mob our mailbox and her breath staggers
like a twice-shot deer, I take the special-occasion tea leaves
down from the cabinet she can't reach without a place
to step. I'm careful in my preparation. I know how strong
she likes it, and that the bluebird mug is her secret favorite.

We curl on the couch. Steam touches our face like the crook
of a finger. And when she asks, like she always does, in her

spooked-antelope voice, *shouldn't I have someone?*, I hold her
mug, our hands joining over the bird's spread wings, and say,
with more certainty each passing year, *honey girl, you have me.*

Previously published in Grist issue 13.

Spell for the End of the MS Flare

Always the same, return & return, like riptide,
like nightmare. No—like the witch's warning:
what you cast will return to you three times three,
a reminder that magic begets magic begets
consequences—breakfast's black mug of coffee
reincarnates itself as a bladder spasm, an afternoon
of self-selected house arrest. Last night's extra hour
awake resurfaces as the glimmer of molasses in the brain's
gas tank. Dead engine. Each relapse makes of me an object

at rest. It's so easy to imagine this as punishment—cause
& effect. Present action equals future damage. Little wonder
that the adjective & verb forms of *degenerate* are spelled
the same way: I am *degenerate*, so I *degenerate*. Goddess,

in place of such unuseful language, grant me a new word
for disrepair. Bar from my lips all apologies. Blessed be.

Previously published in Rogue Agent, Issue 55, September 2019.
Rights are mine.

Love Poem to Injection-Site Reactions

I would say *mottled* but that's not quite true.
Mottled is stormcloud, is sculpin, is pig iron.
You're more like *curdled*, if skin were capable

of spoiling—ridged and risen and birthday-balloon
red, never the same two days in a row.

My MS specialist says driving the needle
deeper will lessen the rippling sting of you,
(unless I hit muscle; then you'll knell

through my arm for a week). She assures me
you'll vanish one day. A phase, like the spangly

cowgirl boots I outgrew when I was nine. For now,
we're stuck a few more years in this uneasy
marriage, but the truth is, I've grown to love you

a little. Every time I press the plunger down, you throb
brave, brave, brave, & I believe you. You're the proof.

Previously published in The Atticus Review, Spring 2018.

Body Horror

To keep them trapped, the doomed office
workers' heads are rigged to explode.
It makes sense in that movie-logic way—

bombs masquerading as trackers, some vague lie
about *company policy & for your own safety.*
The point is, they fall for it. The first one detonates

in a shower of bone shear, camera glamorizing
the damage, skull popped like one of those champagne
bottle explosives, a slurry of gray matter confetti

a cubicle's off-white walls. I close my eyes after that.
Give me crossbows bolted by a one-armed woman to fend
off the killer in her house, or ghosts moaning retribution

through their gummy lagoon, a rabbit hag-ridden by a witch.
But this stuff—rupturing brain, sudden loss—that's too close
to home. What's body horror but reassurance that no matter what

destruction splatters across the screen, no real people,
butter-fingered voyeurs that we are, will come to any harm?
But harm has come, instead, to me. So, retribution: I diagnose

the spunky secretary with MS, gift her my sleeplessness
& neurogenic bladder, the moth-holes in my memory.
When she scales an elevator shaft, I imagine her hands

numbing like mine do, the briar patch scratching
between her radius & ulna. She persists,
because she's in a horror movie, & she has to.

302

Her illness is never a plot point: she has chosen
not to disclose. She dies a throwaway death—
one brief bullet to the temple—the ex-Navy

antagonist's last casualty before the final
battle. Maybe that's close enough to justice
for someone as sick as me: to die

without metaphor, no cameras sweeping up her burst
brainpan. The house lights stir. I don't watch
for her name in the credits.

First published in Salamander, issue 25.1.

"In her groundbreaking book *The Body in Pain*, Elaine Scarry writes
that "To have pain is to have certainty, to hear about pain is to have
doubt." I know those words because I was diagnosed with Multiple
Sclerosis only months before entering a PhD program, where my
new disability chose my specialty for me. Disability studies helped
me navigate that tension between certainty and doubt, the tension
in the lives of everyone with an invisible illness."

—Emily Rose Cole

Amanda.x.Coleman

Buzzing in My Bones

My entire body
Is on vibrate
The length of my spine
And everything
That stems from it
Is buzzing
At a low, steady hum
Like bees
Building hives
In my bones
This body
Is stiff
And it aches
It's too young
To feel this ragged
But here it is
Swollen joints
Weak muscles
And someone I
Used to be
Begging this reality
To be a dream

Body Says:

Body says -
   "Be patient with me"
Brain says -

"I'm late again"
Body says -
  "Let me rest"
Brain says -
  "Do you do anything else?"
Body says -
  "I can't eat that"
Brain says -
  "Shut up or I'll let you starve"
Body says -
  "It hurts. Everything hurts."
Brain says -
  "Keep moving"
Body says -
  "Please. I can't."
Brain says -
  "Why are you like this?"
Body says -
  "You'll learn
  One way, or another.
  You'll learn."

"As an artist living with chronic illness, I hope sharing our experiences will help others that might be searching for answers or inspiration. There is strength in knowing that you are not alone."

—Amanda.x.Coleman

Kimberly Cunningham

Tilted Visions

Time becomes a truth keeper when one is dis-balanced. The littlest things become monumental struggles set before a person to overcome... in silence.

Do you see?

Gone are the days of standing patiently and perfectly in line. Talking to a friend while firmly planted on both feet is just another massive dreaded task. Sitting in a chair is dependent on defined conditions. Daily routines are dictated and defined by situational standards. I cannot see myself doing normal nowadays.

This is what it looks like when one has vestibular balance disorders. Or rather, what it doesn't look like to you. You probably don't see me struggle and subtly squirm just to stand up so I can complete a task completely. I don't show it. My game face stays on. You don't watch me pause momentarily against a counter or put my hand firmly on a wall while navigating my way down a hall. You don't know to look because I didn't tell you to.

My vision is as tilted as my gait appears to me. I see the wall slowly slide by occasionally. I literally feel my Earth shift crookedly under my feet. I see sideways or out of slightly opened eyes for my own safety. My sight has become blurred, but I can still see clearly in my own twisted world.

You see, I don't want anyone seeing me. I mean really seeing me. I don't want gawking glances, or sympathetic blinks or direct stares. Others can be blind to me. I can see for myself. My obscured view is all I need to gaze at the reality in front of me.

Look at my eyes.
You cannot see it, can you?

You don't see me quietly begging the universe, my universe to
have a balanced day. It does not occur to you to watch for signs.
You don't see my head slip and realign itself all in one swift motion.
You missed my muted down pleas.

Looking ahead and beyond, I see questions and doubts laid out in
front of me on a winding never ending road. I have to focus on only
what is in front of me in this moment though. Ya, I see you there,
but your view is different than mine.

If
  I
    tilt
       my
          head
             just
                right,

I can see what you see.

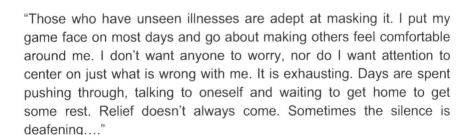

"Those who have unseen illnesses are adept at masking it. I put my
game face on most days and go about making others feel comfortable
around me. I don't want anyone to worry, nor do I want attention to
center on just what is wrong with me. It is exhausting. Days are spent
pushing through, talking to oneself and waiting to get home to get
some rest. Relief doesn't always come. Sometimes the silence is
deafening…."

—Kimberly Cunningham

Sarah Doughty

Underneath It All

*"This is what it means to be me.
And it barely scratches the surface."*

This pain I feel. It's a tangible, searing pain ripping through my body. It spreads out through my nerves like a wildfire, and I cannot help but gasp out from the intensity. The ache it leaves behind is almost worse. Because the initial pain is fleeting, and I know that it will come to an end.

It's the aftermath that haunts me. When my body locks up and my muscles contract, leaving me feeling like I've been stretched out far too much and my muscles are screaming at me to let them shrink back to their normal size. But I know they won't. They remain like that for days, sometimes weeks or months at a time.

This is what it means to live with fibromyalgia. And it barely scratches the surface.

"Spoons. Pain. These are the two biggest considerations when I wake up every morning. Can I bear standing up to begin my day? If so, how much can I do? Or is the fibromyalgia and migraine pain so severe that I can neither move to a comfortable position nor withstand any light?"

—Sarah Doughty

308

Rhian Elizabeth

special

i was practical about things at first
in fact i took a morbid interest
i stopped going out with my friends
made a new pal in google
and got excited about letters
inviting me on dates with neurologists
i marked them out on the calendar
impatiently waiting for the next chance
to piss into a cardboard pot
to get chemical dye injected into my veins
for the magnetic resonance scans
keener still to see the photographs
of my brain that they took
as if they were images
of especially arousing porn
i never cried over my brain inflaming
wasn't afraid of my spinal cord eroding
whoever got their heart broken
by damaged sheaths of myelin?
not me, i never lost any sleep
over my nerve endings being torched
like letters from old lovers
and i easily forgave my immune system
for attacking the good stuff in my body
like a violent
and abusive
mother
my own cried when i told her the news
her baby was sick, but she needn't have bothered
her baby just felt kind of
special.

all these things i think about in the mri machine

this machine is like a prop
from a hollywood movie set in space
a ship sent out into the stars
i could be an astronaut
swap this paper-thin gown
for a spacesuit
i'd love to be blast up into the stratosphere
instead they just leave me in here
flat on my back while they photograph my brain
like this is its first day at school
will they see this on the computer?
how
on those black and white images
my brain has turned into a planet
and all those lesions
have become craters
lying in this narrow white tube
that could be a coffin
i now know that i want to be cremated
it's weird
how your own body can turn on you
like a dog
who was once your loyal friend
who went mad
and ripped off your face
the radiologist is laughing behind the glass
someone must've said something funny
or maybe it was me

can she see them on the computer?
all these things i think about
in the mri machine
i can see her in the tiny mirror
they put in here
to let you know you aren't alone.

the girl who cried wolf

when i was a weird kid
i always wanted to be ill
i was jealous of the boys with plastered arms
that the girls signed their names on
in different coloured felts
i was jealous of the kid in class
with a hearing aid
and the one in the wheelchair
who was allowed straight to the front
of the dinner queue
i thought that girl with the brain tumour
was so lucky
zooming up and down
on my grandfather's stairlift
pretending i was crippled
by a disease i made up
was my favourite game to play
and once i stole his crutches while he slept
convinced my teacher that beneath my tights
the bandage i'd stuck on with sellotape
hid

a mangled leg
now i am sitting in reception
at the neurology clinic
twenty-eight years old
and i really am ill, i swear
so i think it's true
that thing they say
if you want something bad enough
you'll get it.

montauk beach

a man stopped me in the street
he was one of those god-squad folk, flapping leaflets
the folk you swerve as if they have the plague
and i have an autoimmune disease so
you know
i need to be extra careful
i think he thought i was on smack
because i was only half awake
fatigue
and drugs that make me as sleepy
as a new born baby after a feed
he told me god was here for me
here
and then i thought of all the other places
god could be if he wanted
like yosemite national park
the grand canyon
or sitting on top of the lighthouse on montauk beach

why would he be here
on this boarded and broken street?
and if god God really was that stupid
i'd ask the bastard
why did you do this to me?

afternoon tea with a unicorn

my daughter dresses up like a unicorn
baby blue with a yellow horn
and i take her out for afternoon tea
she is not impressed with the cakes
or the sandwiches
why are they so small?
she asks
and frowns
devouring each and every one
whoever knew unicorns
were so hard to please?
i put an adult nappy on
before we left this morning
and asked her if she could see it
underneath my jeans
she got annoyed
no one will notice
it's fine
whatever mum
i suppose it is a strange sight to see
your mother wearing something that
as a baby

she would put on you
i think i embarrass her
then again
she's the one dressed up
like a fucking unicorn.

"Multiple Sclerosis is a knobhead but whatever. I'm over it."

—Rhian Elizabeth

Sita Gaia

Turning on The Flashlight in The Grey Hallway

Alone on my path of sickness,
friends, over cups of coffee, were *so sorry*,
—but did they know what it was like to hallucinate
Ashton Kutcher in the shower?
Did they know the rainbow of illness
the colours cast on their floor, dim and grey?

Grief is an endless crumbled hallway.
Laughter, an echo in my stomach.
My friends don't hold their breath

when they pour a cup of tea.
Once, I forgot to hold mine,
and the kitchen floor was the coldest place

to soothe my burnt body.
Five months of bandages, the truth
under my robe as everyone said *Congratulations!*
and not, *How are you feeling?*

But one day I found a bridge
that fit into my back pocket, a community
who turned on the light in my hallway.
Strange names
with Polaroid photos
I could not
place.

Who also knew Topamax, the fork
topped high with food,

But You Don't Look Sick

which tasted like nothing
going down.

They knew
what it's like to not know
your own name
after an episode. How the body shrinks into less

of a person. My university professor saying, *Oh
you look so good!* The invalidation of sickness—
Was my body even bad before?
They knew that being too thin was also a sign of sickness.

Their stories on display, like an art gallery,
in tiny medicine cups, something
I could finally recognize.
They understood the confusion

of a sudden slumber at work, a fatigue
that hides behind your eyelids, & calls it home.
They knew the embarrassment of an unexpected
crash at the party of Zumba class, breaking

a lamp in the studio, because your brain
had a different agenda than your feet.
My friend in London struggles to make enough
money. I understand. Without my wife, I swim

below the poverty level. I tell my friend
across the pond about the polite emails
which proclaim my fingers didn't spin
fast enough to work at the coffee shop.

But You Don't Look Sick

My avatar texts two purple hearts, the colour of epilepsy,
to say *Together, we are strong like Bulls.*
Drool drips on to my chin while looking
at the recipes my pal with Crohn's posted.

Their phone dings with two growls
from my hungry stomach.
Two orange hearts to those with Multiple Sclerosis.
One friend stuck in bed for 11 weeks.

Sometimes that's all you can do.

You don't know the struggle, don't know
what to say. But know the heart said it all.

Previously published by Harness Magazine at
www.harnessmagazine.com.

Shannon Elizabeth Gardner

Crutches

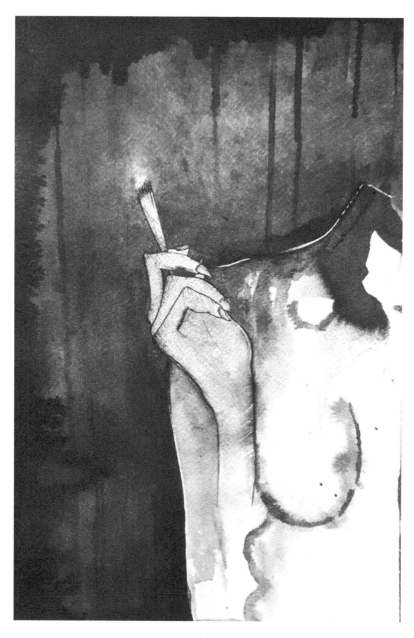

What They Don't See

Deepa Gopal

Half-baked Figurine

I am like a half-driven car
The mechanics stuck somewhere
In-between a long journey
In the middle of nowhere—
Now I am out on the lonely road
Waiting for a lift
With my thumbs ready;
As soon as I see one coming—
I am waiting…
Waiting is all I can.
Often, they look and see nothing
I look at the mirror and see nothing
What is wrong with you?
Nothing!
They claim— and yet here I am—
My bones breaking, nights shifting
Breathless and panting
Sweating and confused
What is wrong with me?!
Nothing, they say!
Nothing, I repeat!
I guess, am just a half-baked figurine—
Maybe even quarter-baked—
Probably the kiln went cold baking me.

Nowhere near 'sick'

As I hear the *azaan** through the din of children
Playing in the muddy parking lot
Behind the *Happiness Customer Service Center*
I 'move mountains' to sleep on my side
Holding my breath, clamming my hands stiff
Onto the edges of my dress, dragging myself slowly
Steadily, pausing with each inch, gasping for breath
Repeating the steps until I am on my side
Perspiring, I heave and sigh
Tears running on countless nights
Imagining a life when where I can just turn and shift
The way I want without paining a muscle
Not feeling like it's some *Herculean* task
Thinking of all those to whom this wouldn't make sense—
Of what it takes to live in constant pain
While I don't look nowhere near 'sick'
Some even judging that it's all in my head!

azaan – prayer call

We're Islands Series – Insomnia

We're Islands Series – The Pain – 2

Georgianna Grentzenberg

Fellow Traveler

Bones of Pain

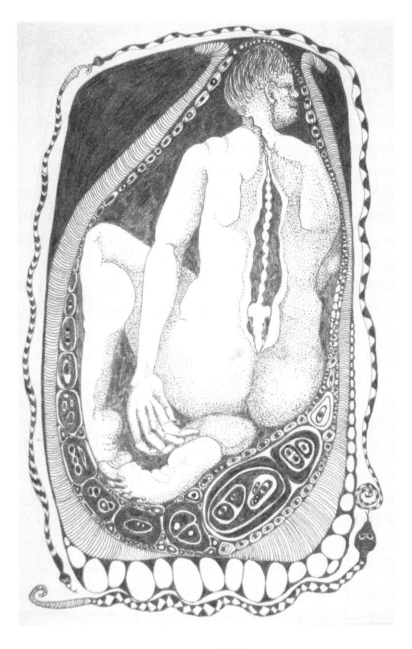

Confusions

"I grew up as an Army Brat, moving every few years. I found that not only did I not fit in, but that I had missed making connections with people, friends, and family. I spent many years in therapy trying to understand my loneliness and emptiness. Modern anti-depressants helped more, but I am still haunted by losses: people, places I haven't seen in decades, homes I can't live in any more, and weaknesses that make normal challenges at times, overwhelming."

—Georgianna Grentzenberg

Laura Hagemann

I'm Still Invisible

The realization hit me as I was laying in my hospital bed recovering from a 3-week coma, severe Traumatic Brain Injury (TBI), fractured femur, shattered pelvis, and injured neck: "At least I look sick NOW!" A strange thought for the average person to have, after surviving a near-fatal accident, that left them clinging to life. The difference between me and the average person, is that before my TBI, I was a chronic daily migraine and Fibromyalgia sufferer. I was a member of the group of people that suffer from constant pain, that doesn't present physically (noticeably), so that those who suffer from it don't look sick on the outside, but on the inside, they feel very sick.

After I experienced a coma and severe TBI I was relieved because my outside appearance finally reflected the pain and suffering I felt (and had felt to a degree) on the inside, for nearly two decades. After a near-fatal car accident, I was cut out of the car I was driving, using the jaws of life and transported by air flight to a university hospital. Once I arrived at the university hospital, my hair was partially shaved to allow doctors to drill into my head, to relieve pressure on my brain caused by the Traumatic Brain Injury. The result was a hairdo that I eventually lovingly referred to as my "TBI mullet." My hair, at the time of the accident, had been shoulder-length and bleach blonde. Post-injury, when my hair was shaved to relieve pressure on my brain, my bangs and a section of the top of my hair were shaved. When hair started to grow back in the shaved area, it was decidedly darker than the bleached blonde locks still partially there. In addition to my TBI mullet revealing the fresh trauma that had occurred to my head, I also wore a neck brace for three months following the accident, since my neck was also injured. Apparently, I was very lucky the injury happened where it did on my neck, otherwise, paralysis could've been possible.

327

In the first several months following the traumatic accident, I was primarily confined to a wheelchair. When I was first injured, my pelvis was shattered (meaning several fractures) and a titanium rod had to be attached to my fractured femur (bone in the thigh), to hold it in place. The months following the near-fatal accident required grueling physical therapy. Yet eventually, I learned to walk and graduated from a wheelchair to a walker, to a quad cane (four-footed), to the cane I now occasionally use.

Immediately following the coma, I was completely non-hearing (deaf) and instinctively read lips to communicate (I had been hearing before the accident). I had difficulty talking as well, but through meticulous work in speech therapy over months (and years), I was eventually able to speak without obviously displaying the slowness and halted speech of my brain injury. In addition to speech issues, the severe TBI has had a lasting effect on my hearing, even after I regained some ability to hear after the three months of deafness following the accident. Currently (and perhaps permanently) sound is heavily distorted, my brain can't process or understand music, and I rely on lip-reading and closed captions at all times. I have now realized that hearing loss (even though severe) is also a relatively invisible condition that I now suffer from.

It was only after months of hard work, in physical, occupational, and speech therapy, that I realized all my work and determination to survive and thrive had actually turned my visible injuries, after the accident, to invisible. So, after being relieved that my injuries and ailments were initially visible, I had inadvertently worked my way back into having a couple of invisible conditions (TBI and hearing loss) much like I did when I suffered from chronic daily migraines and Fibromyalgia before the accident. I had this realization after attending a brain injury support group where I was the de facto expert on "The Spoon Theory." It's a theory developed by Christine

Miserandino, who suffers from a chronic condition and used the example of doling out only a certain number of spoons (which represented energy in this example) throughout the day, to illustrate how she manages energy and pain daily, with her chronic condition. "The Spoon Theory" is something that is used by chronic pain and condition sufferers, to convey how they manage their conditions. As the only one in my brain injury support group with a condition like Fibromyalgia before my TBI, I was the only one who had heard of "The Spoon Theory", which made me uniquely suited to explain it. As I explained "The Spoon Theory" to fellow brain injury survivors, I realized that having a brain injury is another invisible condition (as well as the severe hearing loss I experience from my TBI) and I was in the unique situation of having gone from invisible with migraines and Fibromyalgia, to visible immediately following injuries received in a near-fatal accident, back to invisible again!

"Moving from having Fibromyalgia and migraines to a severe Traumatic Brain Injury (TBI) with symptoms that present as severe hearing loss, has been a huge learning experience for me. I enjoy sharing what I learn navigating through this new world of disability. Because if I have learned anything from my time living with invisible conditions, it's that even though your condition is invisible, doesn't mean you have to be invisible too!"

—Laura Hagemann

Patricia Harris

A Body New

Can I get a body, new?
This one is overused.
Moving aches,
Nothing but eternal pain.

It is missing pieces,
Just nuts and bolts,
That hold it together
Don't you know?

I don't want very much,
Just a body that doesn't hurt
When anything I touch.

The ability to move normally,
Like everyone else does,
Instead of screaming pain
For every step taken.

Hiding

Turning into a gremlin,
Hiding from the light,
Afraid to be seen.

Today is high pain,
And no one cares it seems.
My patience runs thin.
The couch is as far
As I could go,
Still the rest of the world
Doesn't know,
Why outside I rarely go.

Missing the sunshine,
The bird song,
Watching the flowers grow.
Stuck here wishing
For whole body replacement
To be a real thing.

Isolation

When makeup can't hide
The awful you feel inside,
And pills don't touch the pain,
It feels like you do nothing but complain.

It is so lonely and isolated,
To be alone in your pain.
The doctors don't know why
Your body doesn't comply,
For this is something all new.

You stare into the mirror
And wonder if you can ever heal.
In a huge world, surely someone else
Understands how you feel

Spoon Deficiency

The day starts with wondering
Where the pain will be,
Arm, leg, back, head, or knee.

Too hungry to ignore,
Too queasy to eat.
Stomach rebels as if
I could fix it somehow.

My energy an illusion,
Pain ran in to steal the spoon.
Broken connections as the couch
Claims me for its own,
Things sitting, needing done…
With me sitting here, alone.

"I never know how my ability to move will be. I have to take so many pills and deal with so much pain that I often forget what a pain free day can be"

—Patricia Harris

332

HLR

-algia

I can't remember
        or even imagine
what it feels
        like to not be
in pain

                                The thing about my pain is: I worry

nor can I remember
        what it's like
to not have
        a headache: I have
        had the same head
        ache for over a decade

                                that the relentless pain I feel in this
                                mess of atoms & bones & flesh

some days, the pain
        is quieter
                (dull thuds along
                historic skull
                fractures)
some days, the pain
        is deafening
                (crushing neuralgia
                that laughs in the face
                of analgesics)

                                is actually the norm for everybody

333

the pain does not live
        exclusively inside my head
no, it has spread and stretched and settled
        like a heavy dust across the entirety of my body
            (my skin, touching me, hurts me,
            my blood burns, my hair aches,
            blinking pains my eyes)

        that the entire human race exists in this same dire state
            of persistent corporeal & psychological agony

and this pain, regardless
        of its volume / strength / audacity
is always
        there / here / inside of me

        that everyone experiences the same excruciating injuries,
            at the same level of intensity as me, daily

and this pain, regardless
        of my fighting / begging / yielding
will never
        leave / sleep / cease

        that every living creature endures this
            suffering quietly, bravely & nobly

nor remind me
        of moments lived with ease
nor provide me
        with evidence of my body's capacity for healing
nor enlighten me
        as to exactly what it means to be healthy

and that only I
can't handle it

nor surprise me
          with a sudden full recovery
nor teach me
          to function properly
nor allow me
          to know peace

and only I
complain.

Emily James

Swallowed

The world I live in is a little different
Things aren't always what they seem
My body is stuck in this nightmare
While my mind still dares to dream

Everyone says I look so normal
To me normal is just a word
People say that they're trying to understand
But I can tell the lines between us are blurred

I try to hide my pain behind a smile
I don't recognize who I have become
My body is slowly failing me
My soul is becoming numb

They throw around the word lazy
Just because their eyes can't see my pain
But what they fail to understand is that it doesn't really matter
I'm already swallowed up by shame

Guinevere Lindley Janes

Morning Rituals

I lay huddled on the bed. I clutch my favorite dragon quilt in both hands, ensuring it covers me from head to toe. However, I can still sense a sliver of sunlight creeping through the tightly pulled bedroom curtains. On the bedside table next to me are the bottles of pain medication I have taken in the last 24 hours. Lined up like defeated soldiers, each of them a valiant fighter in my ongoing war with migraine pain.

My phone alarm startles me out of my pain medication haze. Without touching my migraine facemask, I blindly fumble around the bed attempting to find my phone, desperate to turn off the offensive noise. The sound of the alarm, although not particularly loud, pierces my brain. Frustrated, I pull my face mask off and throw it against the wall. I regret my decision immediately. I cover my eyes for a few minutes allowing them to adjust to the brightening morning light.

When I can see, and therefore think, I find my phone under my pillows, putting an end to the alarm. I breathe in the blessed silence.

After several failed attempts, I manage to get out of bed and stumble down the short, carpeted, hallway to my bathroom. Feeling unsteady, I keep one hand on the narrow walls to guide me.

In the bathroom, I rifle around under the sink for a while looking for my red Sharps box, alcohol wipes, syringes, and vials of medication. It takes a while to find everything I need. I keep these items tucked out of sight, out of mind.

Staring at my assembled pile on my bathmat, I am overcome by exhaustion and the effects of the last 24 hours. I curl up next to my medical supplies on my bathroom floor and sob.

"Shit. Fuck," I sob, staring up at the bathroom ceiling.

Crying only makes the pounding pain in my forehead worse. My eyes feel dry, dirty. Forcing myself to stop, I lay on the floor, wiping my nose and eyes.

I make myself get up. Looking at myself in the mirror, my lifeless eyes gaze back at me. I shudder. Friends and family tell me that my eyes betray how much pain I am in. If you did not know me, you would have no visual cues that would indicate I am ill.

Taking my finger, I trace the streaks on the glass. For a minute, my mind wanders, obsessing about housework, my low energy levels… the pounding pain in my head snaps me back into focus.

"Right then," I say, taking a deep breath, "If it were done when 'tis done, then something, something quickly." I manage a brief smile. My older sister loves Shakespeare. In times of high stress, badly misquoting lines from Shakespeare and picturing the annoyed look on her face is one of my go-to calming strategies. The standing reading lamp next to my favorite chair in the living room gives off the best light in the apartment. Ferrying the medical supplies to the living room requires two trips.

Laying a towel across my chair's ottoman, I begin. As a barber lays out the tools of their craft, I gather two alcohol wipes, a syringe, a vial of DHE migraine medication, and my Sharps box. I lay each item next to the other on the towel in neat, evenly spaced rows. The Thomas Jefferson Headache Center taught me well.

After three fumbling attempts, I finally get the safety cap off the DHE vial. Tremors from migraine pain makes precision hand-work difficult. Several times, I consider giving up and going back to bed. Instead, I wipe the tears from my eyes and forge ahead. After I have prepared the DHE vial with one of the alcohol wipes, I pick up the syringe and the vial and hold them in the light of the reading lamp. Even with direct light, my double vision makes puncturing the vial's seal with a syringe a difficult task. Between my throbbing forehead and the ordeal of getting the safety cap off the DHE vial, my patience is wearing thin.

It only takes five failed attempts at puncturing the seal, and one aborted temper tantrum, before I am finally able to get the needle into vial of DHE. Tilting the barrel towards the light to see the volume markings, I painstakingly draw up 5ml of medication.

Holding the needle towards the direct light pierces my eyes and makes my forehead pound harder. After putting the safety cap over the now long overdue injection, I hold my prize protectively over my head. Sighing, I lean back in the chair, closing my eyes. I breathe deeply in and out, timing my inhales and exhales to one another. I take a moment to gather myself

Sitting up, I turn the syringe over and over in my hands, looking at it in the light. This is my least favorite part. My doctors explained that even the tiniest of air bubbles injected into my vein can travel to my heart, killing me within seconds.

"Do I care anymore?" I ask myself out loud, "Am I happy living like this?"

Before going any further down this rabbit hole, I gently tap the barrel against the reading lamp while whispering, "Once more for luck."

Taking a deep breath, I unwrap the remaining alcohol wipe, and search for a roll of fat on my thigh that is not already purple and bruised. Swabbing it with the alcohol wipe, I jab myself with the syringe and depress the plunger until the medication disappears. Pulling the syringe out and putting it safely into my Sharps box, my hands shake. I have finished just in time, I am hyperventilating.

Realizing that tears are streaming down my face, I look at the watch on my wrist, I gasp.

"Crap," I say, shaking my head, "I'm going to be late for work again!"

"My 24/7 migraine pain changed my entire life. I dropped out of grad school. All my energies went into getting to and from work every day, talking to my medical team during my check-ups at the Jefferson Headache Center, and keeping up with my regimen of migraine medications. There was nothing left to advocate with my employer for better working accommodations or help my family understand my migraine disease. Overwhelmed and terrified, I froze."

—Guinevere Lindley Janes

Sun Hesper Jansen

Chicago to Lamy, One Way

tracknumber19tracknumbertrack
20tracknumber20numbertrack
number18tracknumbertrack

Don't let me miss this train again,
swimming through brain fog and the
quantum come-hither of tracknumber9
tracknumber8track— there is Track 8
and I break into a three-legged lope
as the red cap flies past, bearing all
those passengers unafraid to ask,
to admit they can use help.

No matter, I've won the dare again
and the first jolt of movement is
like the touch of a god, thrusting
me into another body, as graceful
as anyone here — no, I am more,
a sailor at home on the Railsea,
striding car to car with no cane,
while the able pitch around me.

I will regret lying to the solicitous
attendant about my stick, as soon
as we reach Lamy and my limbs
question my every command,
and so, this time, I tell the truth:
I am fine, but I might not be
tomorrow, and have you heard
of a little thing called MS?

But it never takes long, a day,
to heal from it all, for everything
to reset in the red rock and the
dry heat until the stick feels almost
unnecessary, its only purpose
the same as everyone else's,
to navigate inclines and resist
the fatal pull of canyons.

Returning, there's a single track.
No confusion, no noise, just wind.
Wind and the hum of regret.

What mistake am I making, again,
going back the other way when
home is wherever I'm healthy.

A coyote trots along the rails.
Pauses in the shade, facing me.
As if watching what I will do.

Wayward Bees

Reaching for *that word*
through a din of synonyms,
I suddenly think of bees
in collapse, flying blind,
their minds addled in
chemical cacophony.

At what point do bees
say 'aberrant'? When
do they realize the loss
of context and direction
and what does the hive
have to say about it?

At what juncture do I
decide I'm too sick
to be of use? Fly into
my demyelination,
pollen heavy as gold
on my failing limbs?

And in what world
can I just start building,
not a house of wax to
wall me up but a place
of honeyed welcome
for the wayward?

Maggie Messer

I will make excuses for them:
It's a walking stick, not a cane,
so it looks like an affectation
and I walk too fast for anyone
to know why I rely upon it

But You Don't Look Sick

To keep moving I have to fly,
to keep the cement from stiffening
into sculpture, to compensate for
the tilt and spin of my own world
and gods I hate a crosswalk.

I'll make excuses but not now
when I want a second chance,
to be a superhero of the darkest
kind, a Messer with a message
of educational vengeance.

I couldn't tell you the color or
make of the car, and the features
of the driver and his girlfriends
are a blur of blondness, but this
is enough for my purposes.

Next time, in an alternate world,
when I lock eyes with the driver
and point at the crosswalk, he will
stop out of shock, the screech of tires
as loud as the blood in my ears.

The knob of my stick is solid, heavy,
and when it meets the car's windshield,
glass will spider under the glorious smash.
Mild-mannered MSer become Messer,
a knife to your able-bodied heart.

He will get out of the car with a *What the
fuck* but this, I'm afraid, is not a dialogue.
Do you want to know what it's like, I'll ask,
magnificently unhinged, *to be disabled?*

Would you like to know right now?

Before he can speak, the side of his head
will meet my stick with a sickening thud.
As he crumples to the tarmac, I'll tell him
how the first time I fell in the middle of
the street, people *walked over me.*

The stick reduced the falls, but it hasn't
reduced the assholes, I will inform him
as he tries to rise and can't. I've made a
mess of his inner ear. *Feel dizzy?* I'll ask.
Buck up, honey; you'll get used to it.

You'll mark the days that you're not dizzy,
I'll say as the bleeding fool gets to one knee.
When I whack his leg out from under him,
I suppose his girlfriends will be shrieking,
mosquitos of conscience in my ear.

Oh sorry, is it hard to move those legs?
I'll ask when he tries to stand up again.
*There now, that's one more thing we have
in common, especially in the summer heat.
That's all, kids; I'm late for work.*

It is, of course, an absolutely wrong use
of superpowers and regained time. I stare
at the place my stick would be blood-stained
and wonder where all that immunity went
that I used to get from meditation.

What then, Maggie Messer? Would you
call the non-emergency police number and

wade through the automated menu and the
chain of people who will fail to understand
exactly what crime just occurred?

Another timeline, at the crosswalk's edge.
I watch the traffic for as long as it takes
to feel the sun strong on my back, and heavy;
to grasp how little rest and peace I've had.
Then I turn, and call in sick.

"I've had Relapsing-Remitting Multiple Sclerosis since 2008. I've
been in remission for the last ten years, but I rarely get a break in
symptoms, especially in the summer. Dizziness and spasticity in my
legs impair my mobility, though I can get around without a walking
stick for short distances. Fatigue, depression, and cognitive
dysfunction are the worst, limiting how much I can work. It limits my
writing, too, but it's a life-saving therapy."

—Sun Hesper Jansen

Mandy Kocsis

Deadly

She walks in darkened beauty
She walks with silent flair
Strength in every step she takes
As though she owned the air
Like a belladonna garden
With wolfsbane in the mix
As deadly as the sharpest blade
As sure as true love's kiss
You'd never guess by looking
There's no way you could know
She's so deadly that she's dying
Her body's weaker than her soul.

Scars

Don't pretend to know me
Because you've seen some of my scars
When you don't know how I got them
Or how they've gotten me this far
Don't think to understand me
You haven't seen how much has died
Or understand the fatal scars
Can't be seen from the outside.

Julia Kvist

The Spoon Theory

Count yourself truly lucky
You have a never-ending supply
Of hard-wearing spoons
In all shapes and sizes
At your disposal
Teaspoons
Soup Spoons
Dessert Spoons
Tablespoons
Serving Spoons
Even a copious amount of Ladles
That you probably never use
Strong, robust spoons
Made of stainless steel
As for me?
Sure, I have spoons too
But I am only allocated six a day
Maximum
And they are tiny teaspoons
Made of cheap plastic
So they break easily
Because they are brittle and weak
I can use up two teaspoons
Just having a bath or washing the dishes
Three spoons if I walk my dogs
If I need to go shopping
That's four spoons gone in an instant
Every day is a negotiation
An internal dialogue within myself
Of what I can and cannot
Realistically achieve in that day

How many spoons do I need for this task?
How many spoons are now left?
How many spoons have been
Snapped in the process?
Shit - I'm all out
I need more fucking spoons!
Let me ask you something
Would you like to exchange
Your infinite number of gleaming spoons
For my shoddy, inferior cutlery?
No?
That's a shame
I guessed as much
Didn't think you would
But I'm not worried
Because one day
In the not so distant future
I shall open up my cutlery drawer
And there will be no more
Cheap, plastic teaspoons for me
But glorious, unusual spoons
Fashioned from solid gold
Their handles studded with
Emeralds, rubies and moonstones
Engraved
With dragons breathing fire
Treasure chests spilling out their secrets
Sphinxes guarding ancient ruins
Peacocks with feathers ablaze
Ancient words of power
Purity and resonance
Inscribed on their handles
Hundreds of them
Thousands even

And with these
Beautiful
Intricate
Brand new spoons
Created only for me
I shall feast with abandon
On the delicious sweetness
Of all that life has to offer

Julie A. Malsbury

Memory Sclerosis

Eyes peek through the fountain of hair
cascading down her head lowered
into the cup of her raised palm. She sits,
and sighs. Weary. Sore. Photosensitive.

Patience, thinner than myelin sheath,
withers from bedtime procrastination,
each just-one-more kiss goodnight
weighs heavier than the one before.

Lights dim as little ones drift off
to dream land, but eyelids ache.
Swollen. Optic neuritis or just a migraine.
Her brain is melting.

Once firmly wrapped around neural tails,
oligodendrocytes lose their grasp.
Glia charge along the battle field of mind and body,
her nervous system forges against friendly fire.

But the oligarchy of the central nervous system
will one day fall. Unprotected axons
left behind, consumed by lymphatic combat,
to award plaque to hardened survivors.

Legions of antinuclear antibodies
consume astrocytes, slicing though
constellations of nerves and allow
lesions to eat away her memories.

Messages danced along glial cells,
synapses singing from terminal to dendrite,
will one day dangle, damaged and confused,
from a mind that can no longer fight.

"Memory Sclerosis was written for my sister. Diagnosed early, she continues work as a surgeon in Kenner, LA, wife of one, mother of two, and rescuer of dogs. When her body wages its final battle, she will retire to the beach and surf her life away."

—Julie A. Malsbury

Nikki Marrone

Hope

I still search for you
  in dark spaces,
  and quiet rooms.
  In the gaps found,
  between the words and the silences.
In city lights
  and sunlight,
  in the water.
  Warm breezes,
  and every star I ever wished upon.
I wonder where
  you could be now,
  your absence noted.
  It has been,
  years since I spoke your name aloud.
And longer since
  I spoke your name,
  through cracked lips.
  I know you well,
  we have a long history, you and I.
But I have learnt
  to live without.
  Yet in my darkest days,
  your light still shines.
  I know there will always be.

Marionette

To give yourself over to another body.
You'd give all you've got,
To be out of your own and consumed by another.
Not have to burn,
Not have to writhe,
Not have to think.
But you can't live on want
And this body's all you've got.
Touch is tainted and painted red.
A pained white grin.
Convulsive spasms in every inch.
Hands curled crone.
A climatic pirouette -
As you're snapped into stargaze.
Strings wound tight.
Blinded by the body's last drift -
Before the drop.
You're a ghost in your own skin.
Not dead -
But possessed by pain.
Bones broken but whole,
Not a crack but shattered.
The hand you hold so dear -
Turns you to ashes.
The key in the lock -
Impossible.
Sweet master of pain -
Cut your ties to me.
But before you go -
Remember to leave me,
Crippled in a tangle of limbs.
Light and free.

Road to Recovery

When survival is no longer expected,
But a war fought daily.
Think not of battlefields,
But of rain-swept country fields.

When the temple of your body,
Turns to rot and rust.
Desecrates like time caught in glass cages.
Think of maple trees and sweet scented wildflowers under foot.

When the skeletons break free of bonded chains,
Furrow deep into the breath of you,
Let them be the wind in your sails.
Clean the dust from long forgotten places.

When life and death settle down,
Build roots upon resilience.
A devastated house still shelters on,
Remember a home is a home nonetheless.

Divorce makes broken homes,
Life and death make separate claims.
Not always sure which way to go
The road is long and the burden heavy.

The choice is yours to make,
In times like these,
Think not of survival and long drawn out wars.
Think of recovery.

"I live with Bipolar Disorder as well as Complex Regional Pain Syndrome & Centralized Pain Disorder. These conditions can make life quite hard, and every day is unpredictable. I am always in pain especially in my wrists, back and legs. All three conditions are managed by a combination of physio, psychotherapies, and daily management. It is important to keep the mind, body, and emotions in balance to reduce the fluctuations in mood and pain. It's a challenging holistic process."

—Nikki Marrone

Laura Eleanor Patricia Maze

Fibromight…falling

When you look at me, I hope you see someone you like.
I hope you think I'm bubbly, that you don't see what I try so hard to hide.
When did I lose hope?
When did it change?
When did I give in, no choice but to break?

I go soul searching, for the woman I wish I could be.
Instead of the scared young girl, who is struggling to stand.
I see a girl, carrying the weight of the world,
She doesn't know what she needs, or even what she wants,
No wonder she feels so overwhelmed.
A ceaselessly pounding head, its drumming never-ending,
And the joint pain, bound and caged, constantly fraught with tension.
She feels a knife in her back, every step the twist deepens,
her muscles knotted like ropes on a ship,
her ankles and knees howl like a toddler,
she will lose her balance and dislocate her hip.
In her mind, the lights are on, but nobody is home.
Her brain cells took the day off, leaving one poor sod to get the job done.
I see a girl, hunched over in pain.
She's struggling with the weight of her shame.
Weight. The elephant in the room.
My nickname for myself when I'm feeling a bit cruel.
"You'd be so pretty, if you lost some weight."
You'd be so much nicer, if you stopped talking, mate.

ALLO-DYNIA!
What could be a cockney greeting from the east end of London,

is actually her brain, sounding the alarm,
an elaborate attempt to protect her from harm.
Imagine a feather, and tickle your hand,
It's soft and it's gentle, but her poor old brain, doesn't understand.
The feather is a threat, and so the brain must warn her,
heart rate soaring, adrenaline coursing, the anxiety swarms her,
and the feather, burns like a fire.
Her brain has ignited, to defend and attack.
She stumbles into the wall, but her brain responds as if she's been stabbed.
The caress of a cosy bed digs in, concrete.
This is all a cruel lie as a way for my brain to protect me.

Brain Fog – where should I start?
Concentration eludes me, mockingly so.
This cage I'm in is a breathless hug, I'm bowled over, it never lets go.
My mind racing ahead, through a storm of broken connections,
I can see what's before me, but nothing makes sense.
Conversation is fruitless, the confusion is too much.
 Every moment of sound and light refraction and the merest touch
Are yet more distractions that bruise my tired mind.
Faces swim before me, but I don't remember your name.
Sometimes it feels like…oh, what was I saying?

Insomnia, who joins me in bed each night.
The thoughts race as I remember
each and every single thing I've ever done wrong in this life.
Alone with the voice that tells me I'm worthless, unlovable too.
I try and laugh in response, for I am a warrior goddess,
fighting these cruel thoughts, which frankly, can get screwed.
I am a warrior goddess!
My mind's eye watches on, bemused.

The lack of sleep transforms me into a panicked hamster running endlessly,
round and round on a wheel I go.
When I close my eyes there's just a humming like a computer trying to update,
but with documents open and pictures loading and music playing,
and you can't work out where the music is coming from you just wish it would STOP!
….okay, we'll stop. Fatigue has come to say hello.
Don't think of going anywhere, or trying to achieve.
Ha. This serves you right, at least that's what I believe.

Flare ups…I'd rather give them a miss, overloading as my limbs are ripping, my brain is wire-tripping, energy levels are dipping, I'm burning and aching and chilling.
All I can do is try and scream louder than this torment is screaming at me.

And there you have it.
I'm ill, with a small 'i' for incurable.
They're wrong when they say this disease is "non-fatal,"
For every bad day I almost lose the battle.
Why should I endure this existence?
And why must I force myself to survive?
Every day the same frustrations,
All the complications and aggravations and exasperations.
In this, a life sentence for a crime I **didn't** commit.

Fuck, your self-sacrificing pity is nauseatingly mundane.
There are people literally dying out there, who are YOU to complain?

Because I spend my life in pain, wearing chains made of flames,
the aching, the suffocating, the hyperventilating, the isolating. My
pain is valid, right?
So says my therapist, and the physio, the pain specialist too.
But how can I believe their reassurance?
When this torture has no reprieve and every day I fight my body
and my mind clinging to the merest scrap of strength I can find.
I can't express this agony, *believe* me,
I've *tried*: the pen is always out of ink, and the paints are already
dry.
And…Wellness.
It feels denied,
just out of reach it pretends to hide, but winks and laughs,
I'm on the brink of despair.
Empowering myself with just a little self-care.
I just have to believe that this storm will run out of rain,
That this body will one day feel more than pain.
But you should know, the pain is not the worst of it.
Not even the flare ups, the brain fog,
or the destructive thoughts that occur more than I like to admit.

What's worse is the hope.
It's bitter, hot, freeing and burning, a sting primed in its tail.
"Maybe this is it."
"Maybe this is the moment I get better!"
"Maybe this is my cure!"

But no.
It doesn't go away. A moment of respite, perhaps.
The hope splinters.
Piece by piece, it crumbles.
Oh wait…no.
That's me.

Release

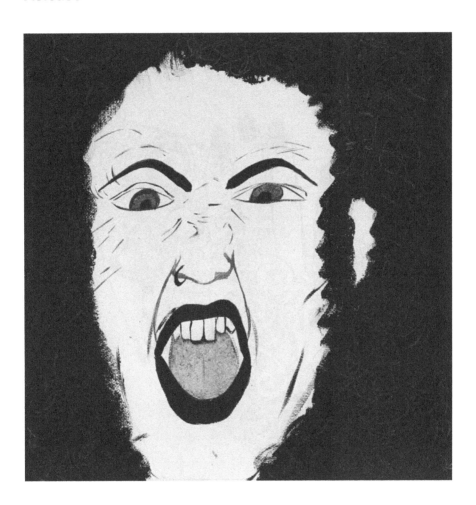

Understanding

Fibromight Warrior

A Life Sentence for a Crime I Didn't Commit

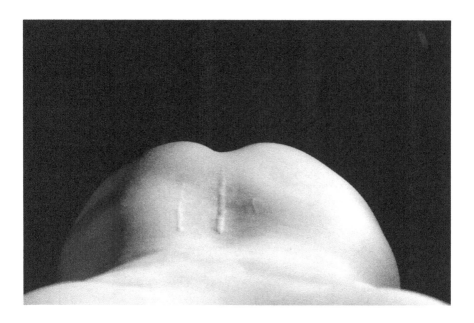

"I am a chronic complex pain warrior – perpetually frustrated and discombobulated by fibromyalgia, JMH and OCD. Every surface is a bed of thorns piercing me, but fatigue tethers me to the spot. Relief comes through screaming louder than the pain burns me. I feel drowned by these overwhelming, suffocating conditions, but my art and my family and friends bring me up for air. Without them, I would have given up."

—Laura Eleanor Patricia Maze

Laura McGinnis

Things I Have Lost - Power Heels

That sound your heels make walking down an uncarpeted hall
Click click, click click.
I feel powerful, competent, capable.
But I stumbled. I fell. I twisted my ankle,
Scraped my knee, my elbow, my hand.
Betrayed by my body; vertigo, nausea, pain.
I sit on the ground for a few minutes unable to get up.
Where are my glasses, where is my purse,
My briefcase, my other shoe?
Are you alright? You hit your head. Be careful standing up.
Slowly I finally stand, leaning on my colleague's arm,
Ashamed, embarrassed that I made such a scene.
Betrayed by my body, the days get worse.
Dark days of pain, weakness, sadness.
Where did my power heels go?
Gathering dust in the closet with my briefcase.
Bedroom slippers, flannel pants, oversized tshirts.
My throne is the couch, my scepter, the remote.
My kingdom this small, messy house.
Frustration that I can't…can't clean, can't cook, can't do
Anything.
Just sit on the couch,
Waiting to heal,
Waiting for power heels to fit again.

"Like alcoholism, my invisible illnesses will never go away. My daily regimen of pills - necessary adjustments and support for my imperfect body - remind me that I will never go skydiving or run marathons. But I have learned that I'm doing the best that I can, and my life is full of things I can still do. I have limitations, but I am a person beyond them and I will persist."

—Laura McGinnis

Dawn D. McKenzie

Fibromyalgia

Fatigue crippling your days
Intense pain, your joints don't have their way
Bowels deciding to work as they choose
Raw emotions always on the loose
Obscurity clenching you, keeping you in prison
Muscles that spasm for no reason
Yearning for relief daily
Ambling like a little old lady
Looking normal on the outside
Getting locked up on the inside
Intense Pain, respite is brief
Aches everywhere, in sight no relief.

"My Mother has been depressed. She would be so happy to see my children and me. But can my body stand the 3 hour drive, one way, over a 2-day weekend? How many days will it take me to recover from the vibrations and exertion, even if I'm not at the wheel, with pains everywhere, constant fatigue? That's a small sample of what living with fibromyalgia has meant for me in the past couple of years."

—Dawn D. McKenzie

Finn Aidan McRath

Little Blur

You danced and
Shot arrows at age
Eight! -- no way!

Then you're not
Disabled whatever feet and hands
You did use.

She said and
He said again too
Doctors! You!

Wow! I'm so
Proud of you, little "blur"
It hurts right?

I said yes,
Daddy, but I'm good.
They're mine still.

Braces, therapies, limitations
Why, I'd never noticed them
So small, cute.

The Loom

The Greeks, they say, knew three goddesses ruled your fate
Clotho, Κλωθώ, to spin the thread, the material of life in golden or
silver threads.
When and where and to whom you would be born.
Lachesis, Λάχεσις, the weaver, the shapes and colors, sorrows and
happiness,
Atropos, Ατροπος, the cutter, who seals your doom, inflexible,
incorruptible.

Strange tale to tell this body I was born to
Three weeks late and twisted in the womb
Feet folded inwards, nights laying in special shoes
I've often wondered why Clotho spun this particular doom.

Three weeks late, my poor mother and a different RH factor, lay her
baby in the womb.
Not only feet twisted but short, damaged fingers and toes.
Clotho, Goddess Fate, who spins, laughed as she spun my doom.
Too short, bent, damaged middle joint, arthritic fingers and toes.

Doctors and family and strangers laughed at my little "worms."
It's hard to fit gloves properly on such fingers.
Strange tale for goddesses Clotho and Lachesis to weave my body
into.
Everyone laughs at my cute, little, but damaged "worms."

Lachesis meant for me to sorrow and fear and anger and pain
It's hard to fit fingers into gloves and socks into toes.
Yet happiness is there too, sometimes in the tiny figures woven
around the borders.
The child who delightedly said, "your fingers are just like mine!"

But You Don't Look Sick

Everyone laughs at my pained, cute "worms"
But they play the harp well by supporting the next finger.
Lachesis sings as she weaves and Clotho sings as she spins.
Even Atropos laughs, the dark mother, as she lays her scissors in
her lap.

Strange body, cracks as I move them, strange tale they wove my
body into.
Did they not have enough thread to make normal feet, fingers,
toes?
When they wove my body on the loom of life.
Still, my soul's known no other body-home.

I wore metal braces on my feet at night and a different one in the
day.
For many years, I learned to walk and my first dance steps were in
braces.
My mother was so amused as I waddled as fast as I could, I was
called "the blur."
When the Fates wove my tapestry, they had to have some way to
hold onto my soul.

When they wove my body on the loom of life
Lachesis sings as she weaves and Clotho sings as she spins.
Dark Atropos plays the harp as she waits to use her scissors.
My soul might have blurred too fast through life without ways to
hold me down.

Clearly Clotho has lessons for me to learn.
When they wove my body on the loom of life.
Everyone laughs at my pained, cute "worms."
Clearly Lachesis has lessons for me to learn.

Dark Atropos plays the harp as she waits to use her scissors.

My small fingers, with damaged middle joint, strengthen the next fingers.
Clearly Atropos has lessons for me to learn.
When they wove my body on the loom of life.

The Tale of Gunnhild and the Fates

One day, long, long ago, when Gunnhild was very young, her mother said to her that she should take this spear and go out and meet the Norns, those old immortal witches who grant one their destiny. Gunnhild's mother said that she hoped the Norns would grant her marriage to a great king or adventurous sailor, or even a wealthy farmer. So out Gunnhild trudged along the road, carrying her father's spear with her, singing loudly to herself whenever she would pass a darkened hollow of trees along the wood. You never know what dark elf or dwarf lives in there and she wanted to be safe. But to her surprise, an arrow came flying from out of the dark woods towards her, some dark elf had let this arrow fly. It struck her, right in the back, between the shoulder blades, and she laid down injured, blood pouring. She laid there for a long time, wishing she was back at home in her warm bed, about to wake up to eat her mother's pancakes. Finally when she was sure the dark elf wasn't around anymore, she got up, with great difficulty, to see how injured she was. Well, she was in pain, no doubt about that, but the great battle mailcoat of her father's which her mother had seen that she wore protected her from the worst of the malicious arrow and despite the injury she felt she could walk along towards the Norns. After several miles of walking alongside the forest, the ground changed and became open field where many cows were grazing. She laughed to see them, chewing their cud. A bull heard her and snorted, moist breathe hot from his nostrils and he prepared to run up against her and bore her with his head-horns. Gunnhild thought to be scared a moment and then realized, what luck, she had in her pocket a large pancake, leftover from breakfast, which her dear mother had given her before she left. She quickly took it out, waved it high and spoke to the bull, saying that she had a good pancake and not to waste her mother's precious cooking. She threw the pancake in the field and the bull, a tad hungry ran towards it and snatched it up in his mouth, feeling full in his four stomachs and not at all angry anymore. Gunnhild was pleased with herself and kept on walking. She walked on and on all the day and into the night, and finally reached a large rocky crag which she knew she had to climb. She started up, despite the darkness and the lack of a light. She knew the Norns lived at the top of the crag which was next to the door to the underworld, the realm of Hel, the goddess of the dead. So she climbed, her feet sometimes tripping a bit, pebbles falling down from a great height. She was a bit afraid, but knew she needed to keep going. Now, Gunnhild, had never climbed a rocky crag before in her life, her father always said she need not, but she should stay weaving and cooking. Sure enough, her father had disappeared over the sea somewhere and her brothers a few years later, likewise, leaving only her and her dear mother. She grasped what she thought was a secure hold in the rock but then to her horror she slipped and started falling, falling, falling. Well, she was a bit afraid, and in pain from her earlier injury, but she knew she would make it, for she had her father's spear and she jammed it, as she flew past the rocks into a deep crevice and hung on tightly to the spear. With it in the rock she could get back up securely and continue using it as a help for her on the rocky journey up. Finally, she got to the top of the rocky crag and looked around her through the very misty darkness for signs of the Norns, the Wyrd Sisters, the Fates. Suddenly she heard loud cackling, laughter that thrilled her very soul and made the hairs on her neck stand up. She turned to face the three old witches, next to their cauldron, bubbling with the rot of the dead. Gunnhild thought to be scared for a moment but then knew she was come at this moment to meet the Norns and ask about her future. So, despite the Norns looking very hungrily and greedily at her, she walked up to them and asked them humbly, "Wisest Mothers, my mother sent me to you to see what you would answer as to what my fortune and future would be. My father and dear brothers are gone and my mother and I are alone in the world in our tiny farm." The Norns whispered to each other, strange, mutterings, and began to slowly walk closer and closer to her. One Norn licked her lips at the sight of the blood on the back of her mailcoat. One Norn whispered, shhh shhhh shhhh. Finally the other Norn, the wisest and oldest of them, said, "Gunnhild, you are very brave and have combatted many obstacles and fears and injuries which a lesser man or woman would break from. You will have that injury all your life, but it will not break you and you will teach others how to bend also. You will be a healer, despite your own pain. And any partner you wish to have, will delight in pride at your abilities. And you will heal kings and do honor to your family. But I ask you this, if I could heal you, would you take the healing?" Gunnhild smiled, pleased at that. She shook her head, "No, Mother, for it is the pain that will make others heal." The Norns were satisfied at this and Gunnhild returned back to her farm, and all the Norns words became true.

"I suffer from Post-Traumatic Stress Disorder (brought on by several physical and sexual assaults), Depression, and Diabetes. One of the assaults gave me a brain disorder, Pseudo-Tumor Cerebrii (which is controlled now) and difficulties with movement because of a dislocated shoulder. I suppose everything is intertwined. Stress influences depression and in turn influences stress; flashbacks and triggers happen all the time despite therapeutic techniques. People have a really hard time understanding you; even other PTSD sufferers sometimes."

—Finn Aidan McRath

Myrna Migala

Idiopathic Peripheral Neuropathy

Neuropathy
Wobbly plus dizzy
Don't appear to be sickly
You may think of me as tipsy.
Unsteady me? I stumble and sway
You might even see me laughing some days
Catch me teeter-totter — spinning dancing away!
Where are my feet?
Walking down the street
Just a little bit offbeat!
But please, I can't walk a straight line
Notice again how I look just fine
And No, I did not take that glass of wine.

"My personal statement is not to complain, but to laugh instead; laughing helps, believe me! I look at others younger than I, knowing they suffer from their crosses that are heavier than mine."

—Myrna Migala

Amy Nicole

Chronic Pain

I think of pain as a darkened room
we all have to visit now and then.
Perhaps you avoid it, or won't enter at all,
or maybe you go there, again and again.

Whatever the case, the difference between us
is that you can reach the exit, or won't.
I wish I had that choice, but my pain is chronic,
so you get to walk out, and I don't.

Previously published in Shadow Lines, 2020.

Invisible

It's up to us to share with the world
what "disability" really means,
because decades and decades of preconceived notions
are flowing through our genes.

We have to speak up and it has to be now
in a world that's no longer sensible,
because this is the time when the chronic and disabled
should no longer be invisible.

Previously published in Shadow Lines, 2020.

"My pain fluctuates, so some days I wake up feeling well and some days I wake up unable to walk. It's hard to know what to expect and harder still to explain to people why sometimes I'm 'fine' and other days I'm immobile."

— Amy Nicole

Pallavi

The Invisible Fight

some call it baby blues,
some postpartum depression,
for me, it was losing myself to a different someone
someone who was invisible
immeasurable
insolent
unreproved
someone who had taken over
my emotions, feelings, rendering me abused
there were days I felt exactly like I was "supposed" to
joyful, thankful and loved
but very often also paid a visit
were feelings of hollowness
numbness and being gloved
then there were days of
sheer doubt, pain and tears
when I would cry and yell
succumbing to indeterminate fears
I had lost myself
my smile
the love and passion for life
it was scary being someone I didn't fathom, comprehend or relied
upon
~
so I hid
behind the walls of disguise
behind the sprawl of "I am fine"
lie that all's well
I said repeatedly to others and self
lies that I was too busy
only to be sitting anchorless, wanting to set free

lies that all will be OK
only not knowing what was wrong
who to ask and where to start
lies that I was blessed
holding my bundle of joy
but deep down regretting the new me
seeing only plethora of flaws

~

I don't know when I broke free
or if at all I did
I don't know if I recovered, healed
or grew to accept
but I do remember acknowledging this invisible illness,
I do remember stopping to disguise my own weakness
I do remember this pivot in the right direction
I do remember breaking mirrors of perfection
for that, I am a hero, superwoman in my own right
for that, I am a warrior, sometimes, even now, fighting battles and
wars, out of plain sight.

"Life as a new mother is perfect or so you are made to believe. Untrue for many. About 50 to 75% of new mothers experience "baby blues" and about 15-20% develop a long lasting condition called postpartum depression. An illness which progressively gets worse or difficult to manage because rather than offering help, society makes it intolerable for mothers to even acknowledge it. Let's remove that stigma. Let's talk candidly."

—Pallavi

Suchita Parikh-Mundul

Crescendo

pain bursts with a solar energy,
like a flower in springtime,
its petals unfurling and attacking
honeybees and butterflies
with such ferocity that
the balance of nature is lost,
and all teeters on the pernicious
hold of aged fingertips and worn thread.
with each wave, I begin to prepare for loss,
and an unnamed grief begins to rise
like the dawning globe
that glitters a knowledgeable white,
as if the universe foretells it,
and is waiting for destiny to unfold.
the kernels of serenity I'd gathered
have long shrivelled, and all I feel
is a river of blindness,
a pulse that reverberates
like drum beats at a veteran's march.
the cadence elongates into
a shrieking darkness, blinding me.
I grasp the edge of civilization
with knuckles as pure as the sweet note
of an ebbing song. I can taste it on my tongue,
hold it in my fist, watch it trickle down
as another wave rushes forward,
and the orchestra begins afresh.

380

don't

don't speak to me of resilience
when my cranium burns
like the fury of a volcanic eruption,
flames and lava corroding my pupils,
so heated and bright that I can see
the past and the future with eyes shut.
don't speak to me of intelligence
when ripples from the epicentre
obliterate everything like an earthquake,
paving a path of destruction
that careens down to the base of my neck,
and into all convolutions and cells
of the headquarters.
don't speak to me of compassion
when my heart, my poor heart
allows me to live,
my betrayer, my sustenance,
marking the days and nights
I wage the war of cohesion,
of visions, dreams and decapitations.
don't speak to me of life
when I lie captive
to the deafening pain that
blinds and marauds unforgivingly,
as I give up my parts,
my hope, my mobility.
don't.

"The migraine attacks with ferocity, and has circumscribed my writing life to the extent that it now dictates my work schedule. At its very peak, the pain grows so monstrous that it debilitates me, shutting down all voluntary function, pushing me almost to the edge of existence. These migraines have grown into chronic beasts that I dream of one day mastering."

—Suchita Parikh-Mundul

Pooja Priyamvada

Yes, I don't look Sick!

Yes, I don't "look" sick
Depression is a ticking bomb
maybe in my mind
or my chest
that never rests
the deep dark well
the "black dog"
The brain fog cruel

Yes, I don't "look" sick
Fibromyalgia?
No, not fibroids
No, not fibrosis
Go, google
You see a moving robot
Do you see the muscle in a knot?
Can you imagine a flare?
"invisible" pain, do you dare?

Yes, I don't look sick
But your positivity is toxic
There is a world beyond visible disability
Fibromyalgia, Lupus and maybe some
unnamed, undiagnosed quantity

Yes, I don't look sick
because my sickness is beyond skin deep
because there are miles and piles of meds
and treatments before I sleep

Yes, I don't look sick
because this "spoonie" life
is what you don't get
it is my secret "magic!"

"Fibromyalgia, the word, the label, the condition, the something that
is a now almost a synonym to me. It changed my mind and my
body forever. It now lives like a surly oligarch in me who dictates
terms of how I live and what I can do or can't. There is no escape,
only bearing with it with all my "spoons" each day. The spoonie life
is my new lens to see the world."

—Pooja Priyamvada

S. A. Quinox

Choking On Air

Today, the air
tastes bitter.
My face
turns blue
from the oxygen
that is choking
my bones,
ties life
to my veins,
and drowns
my grasp
for the night.
The moon is
sleeping
with the sun
again, and I
am left with
her tides
still playing
with my blood
as it chains
my vessel
onto the
barren ground.
I am still walking,
I am still breathing,
and today
it just aches.

Despite It All

It stings, it burns,
it's excruciatingly
sickening,
how this pain throbs
from scalp to toe
and all the nerves
of my lips still wish
to respond with a smile
despite it all.

Immune Disease

I never really need
the weather forecast
to tell me it's
going to rain.
I can tell by the way
my joints hug each other
too tight for comfort
to keep each other
from getting wet.
Time is not linear
when you are aching.
Agony speaks

through the tiles
when more than my feet
hit the ground.
I feel like a
sack of potatoes,
expired before my age,
when I weigh down in my bed,
among the ghosts of those
who have lived before me.
They carry their
own experiences
with physical limitations.
And when the sandman
finally reaches my doorstep
and rocks me to sleep,
my soul is set free
from its physical chains.

Scorched

I walk this earth
with scorched wings.

And no, the pain is not over.
In fact, the scorching seems to
have taken quite a liking to me.
She made home of tired flesh
and nestled herself deep
within these bruised bones.

A true savage she is,
dragging my immobile feet
onto the battlefield
with no permission asked.

Now here I rest,
paralyzed within the heat
of a battle I cannot win.

"Chronic illness is like swimming with anchors attached to your legs
and spending each second fighting to remain above the surface.
Sometimes it is winning and retreating in exhaustion. Sometimes it
is drowning and being questioned by the world. You see, these
anchors are invisible, but very much present at all times."

— S. A. Quinox

Christine E. Ray

Accordion Folds

there is a point
where the pain starts
radiates out
in a geometric
arc
compresses
folds
reconfigures me
like the open fan
of a courtesan
I am
a dense network
of twisted muscle
screaming nerves
aching numbness
at pain's core
while my edges
are left thin
fragile
transparent

*Originally published in Composition of a Woman, Indie Blu(e)
Publishing, 2019*

EMG

The overhead light has a gridded metal cover
that reminds me of the old-fashioned ice cube trays
my grandmother had
with levers that released the frozen squares
with a satisfying crack.
I feel oddly vulnerable waiting alone
wearing nothing but my panties and bra
under today's utilitarian hospital gown
with its overly complicated ties
that took me too long to decode.
Vulnerable, in a way that I didn't earlier this week
when my breasts were compressed
between inflexible plastic plates
while the fancy 3D camera rotated
in a state-of-the-art 180 degree arc around my body.
There is a natural comradery
between women of a certain age
dutifully reporting for their yearly mammogram
that I miss while I wait for my neurologist
and her technician to take turns
shooting electricity through my misbehaving limbs,
the word *electromyography*
rolling on my tongue.
I stare at the ceiling as the minutes tick by,
ruminate about the other patients
who held introspected vigil in the waiting room
while I waited for my name to be discreetly called
in accordance with HIPPA,
wondering if not so long ago,
before their canes

their walkers
their motorized wheelchairs

they were like me. . .

Originally published in Composition of a Woman, Indie Blu(e)
Publishing, 2019

F Words

fatigue hangs on me
like heavy ornaments
on a late February
Christmas tree
branches brittle and bare
needles dropping to floor
carpeted
in half-finished projects
incomplete thoughts
good— but soon forgotten— intentions
so much aromatic debris
carelessly spilling
around my feet

Originally published in Composition of a Woman, Indie Blu(e)
Publishing, 2019

My Right Foot

On Wednesday night
my right foot went on strike,
declaring that unsafe working conditions,
too much unpaid overtime,
and general lack of appreciation
from the management
made continuing unacceptable.
Impossible, even.
As we were walking up a steep hill
at the time
after a very long day,
I was not amused.
I tried flattery,
cajoling,
threats,
and finally resorted to just dragging
my uncooperative extremity along,
muttering under my breath
the whole time,
accusing it of being churlish,
acting like a petulant child,
refusing to be a team player.
Reminding it that my left foot was tired too,
but it certainly wasn't complaining.
My right foot
finally started to cooperate again,
but sulked the rest of the way home.
Damn ungrateful foot.

Originally published in Composition of a Woman, Indie Blu(e)
Publishing, 2019

Glass and Thorns

betrayal is an inside job
wrecked by muscle and
joints
neurons and
neurotransmitters
mitochondrial mutiny
lays waste
to formerly silver tongue,
now struggling to find words
that used to flow like
ink through fountain pen
fatigue hangs round neck
chain woven of boulders, glass shards &
thorns
muscle spasms contort me
into balloon animal shapes
so alien, so grotesque
that they frighten the village children
like the pick axe
I plant above right eye
in hopes of blessed relief
don't mind the blood
it's barely an inconvenience
during insomniac ruminations
about long dormant-mutations
coded in DNA turned
time bombs
that ripped through my life,
casualty count still being assessed

by medics in white coats
who write cryptic words
on shiny clipboards
while I bleed

Originally published in Composition of a Woman, Indie Blu(e)
Publishing, 2019

"Those of us who live with invisible disability are often told that we
need to 'let go' of our anger and 'embrace acceptance'. At no point
in my life has someone telling me I 'shouldn't' be angry, made me
less angry. It is incredibly invalidating and infuriating to be told what
you 'should' feel. After four years, I neither deny nor accept
fibromyalgia and chronic migraine. I stand in defiance, at times with
my cane in hand."

—Christine E. Ray

Grace R. Reynolds

Spoons

My life is measured in tablespoons
Of palpitations and monotonous fatigue
Greased in scrupulous assumptions about me and my capabilities
Because no one sees how I am truly feeling

I wish they knew of the arrhythmia that is constantly pulsating
Or my fever sweats and insomnia, never quite abating
And my mind, a hazy fog, leaves me confused and breathless
But like the walking dead, I drudge on restless

Fourteen years diagnosed and twelve medication free
Committed to the belief that symptom management is the key
For my Postural Orthostatic Tachycardia Syndrome, and still
I struggle with things, like the way heat deregulates me
Like how my feet swell and pool with blood, that could leave me in
bed for days
But all I want is to run with my daughter in bluebonnet fields
Out in those loving warm sun rays

As I grow older most of my prodromes have subsided;
But the love between me and my POTS is still unrequited
This endless state of lethargy and unreliable circulation
Has finally pushed me towards the doctors for another reevaluation
So I have decided that even though they might tell me
I look normal, I'm fine
I'll keep nudging forward
For those baby blue eyes

"I was diagnosed with Postural Orthostatic Tachycardia Syndrome in 2009 after three years of searching for an answer to a multitude of symptoms that emerged out of nowhere. After many years, and a cardiac ablation to treat another coinciding heart condition, I manage each day as best as I can with symptom management. If you are newly diagnosed with POTS, I encourage you to connect with Dysautonomia International for more information and online support groups."

—Grace R. Reynolds

Shruti Sareen

Travails of a Migraineuse 2

My fingers part the coal black hair
near my right temple, as I stare
at this innocuous patch of light-skinned
scalp, which looks no different from the rest.
It does not look mischievous.
It does not look malignant.
And yet, it is the culprit.
I wonder whether pain
is an inherent property of these cells,
does it adhere to them, but then why
does it shift from right to left?
Can it be a property of the right temple cells by day
and a property of the left temple cells by evening?
Is pain a tangible, independent entity?
But if pain is tactile, where is it?
Is pain like the wandering womb?
Can I catch it, touch it, smell it, see it?
My fingers rub the patch of scalp
much like a sandpaper rubs wood.
Meanwhile, Shiva dances his tandava
nritya in my temples, right to left.

Travails of a Migraineuse 3

140 Degrees Centegrade: Cross Section of a Brain in Migraine

It has burnt charcoal edges
and vast regions of grey ash deserts,
scarred and charred
A streak of green, that spreads linearly
then grows filaments is a disease called madness
The purple lights are hallucinations
delusions becoming realities
Dancing apsaras trap me
voices and faces and whispers that exist only for me
grow fire and smoke, and screams
refuse to be stifled.
Demons in the fire want to grab me
and I am afraid.
I look at my face in the mirror
to see if its shape has changed
This is a cross section of a mad, diseased brain
in the throes of migraine, 140 degrees centegrade.

Travails of a Migraineuse 5

I hear a heartbeat in my head
as I lie at night on my bed
My migraine goes pitter patter
Is the pain dead or living matter?
Is this what they call throbbing?
It's intense enough to set me sobbing.

398

One two three four beat beat beat
Postman or policeman doing rounds of the streets
Measuring time in seconds, bit by bit
Time goes so slow when a woman's been hit
all the doctors, all the meds
can't tell you why a heart beats in my head.

Travails of a Migraineuse 7

Come over to my place every time
you have a migraine, you said
I'd have to live in your house then,
I thought to myself.
You can't tell anyone when you have a migraine, you said.
Why don't you tell us, cried my
hostel friends, leaving me confused.
You don't tell anyone when you have a migraine, I asked
I can say whatever I want to my husband, you said
I considered that really, really unfair.
(especially you being so much older than me and all that)
Gouge out my eyes and
put them in the freezer, you said.
Screw off my head, and put it away for a bit, I said. Or, cut my head
off.
And gift you my hair. I wish my head could be sliced off
as easily as an apple, removing my unholy temples.
Sometimes I wish, I really wish that migraines could be fatal.

"Chronic migraines are disabling, debilitating. We brave it and learn to control it and live with it. It is extraordinarily difficult. Nobody, absolutely nobody, understands this struggle- not your friends, not your family, not even your psychiatrist. Only another chronic migraineur would. It is so difficult to live alone when you have chronic migraines. It is so difficult to live with people when you have chronic migraines. When all possible medicines fail to provide a cure, it is difficult to even 'live' at all with chronic migraines."

—Shruti Sareen

Raney Simmon-Baker

It's Only A Migraine

Somedays I wake up,
Feeling like my head is about to explode.

An ache that not only encompasses my head,
But sometimes shoots pain in my neck too.

I try to ignore the pain shooting through me,
But sometimes it's easier said than done.

Because the pain can be so overwhelming,
I can't focus on the task at hand.

Medications Ibuprofen and Acetaminophen sometimes helped
make the pain go away,
But weren't always enough.

So I'd do best to make do with dealing with this pain,
Occasionally rubbing my forehead,
And cracking my neck in hopes it would lessen the ache.

"It's only a migraine,"
I told myself as the pain shot through my head.

But that thought provided me with little comfort,
As the migraine continued ravaging my head.

It felt as if my brain had set itself on fire,
And there was nothing I could do to put out the flames.

All I could do was watch,
As my brain melted away.

And unknown to me,
I was the one who lit the match.

"Migraines affect me on a daily basis especially in instances when I'm attempting to be most productive. They affect me when I least expect it or when I have something important I want to get accomplished but can't because it's in my way. Migraines make a day that might already be stressful even more stressful which is why I believe it's an important topic to discuss even though many people see it as a very minor illness. For me, it's the complete opposite: very inconvenient."

—Raney Simmon-Baker

Megha Sood

Amnesiac

I dread the day
when you will start
fading around me
one picture at a time
one memory at a time

like that of an old album
whose pictures
all scattered,
yet to be organized and sorted

and I keep losing them slowly
every time I open it
like they are slipping through
the cracks of time

I dread the day when all will be gone
and your presence
will be irrelevant
like unwanted solace on a funeral morning

I know it will be eventually gone
bit by bit,
piece by piece
like the impression of a
wet body of a warm bench

I know I'll lose you all
one fateful day
to this merciless time
cause every time

I open the jumble of memories
I find a few pages missing in mine.

Convulsions

"I seem to myself, as in a dream,
An accidental guest in this dreadful body."
— Anna Akhmatova

The sharp explosion
the metallic taste,
in the back of her throat
the shivers and the convulsions
which shake her to the core.

Lying helplessly on the floor
foaming at the mouth
on the same spot
where she stood before
strong and proud,
this disease is ripping away
threads of sanity
from her fabric
slowly and violently
tearing her apart.

She is hanging in limbo
the pungent state
between the dreams and the reality
broken dreams are foaming

from her mouth
she is surrounded
by the people she loved
their faces distraught.

A little whimper
groan or whisper in the night
sets a trigger
an alarm,
a frenzy in the household
where everybody rushes to where she sleeps
to check her nimble state
her body so cold.

Pain and fear have taken a new meaning
she is dragging her life
feet curled,
hands clutched
left in the fetal position
weeping.

Incessant gulping
of those damned pills
have rendered
the food tasteless,
living a single day
of life with sanity
is a war
rendered useless.

Going through life in constant fear
a battle with her
own deceiving mind,
she has severed all ties

in the fear of the
violent episodes
which rattles
and tortures from inside.

Living with a monster
taking refuge in your soul
cutting and ripping it apart
and drilling holes.

Gnarls and the gashes
blood from the incessant
clutching of teeth
leaves her trembled core,
helplessly asking gods for the mercy
to spare her soul.

Trajectory of Pain

The trajectory of the undulating pain
travels on the arched back of mine
on the trail of this crooked spine

my brittle bones are cracked
seem to respond to every monsoon call
tendons frayed at the end
sinews seem to burst apart

Pain,
which has its own path

it twists and morphs me
making those
sailor knots out of me

Oh! dear
your balmy presence
and your peachy afternoons
trick me for a
fickle of a moment

the reticent mind
forgets for a fleeting moment
that pain has its own
trajectory
and it never diverts.

Amrita Valan

Bad Nerves

I was diagnosed with
Fibromyalgia in 2017.
Fibro-what? Doctor said
I have "bad nerves".
That shoot faulty signals
Magnify trivial pain.
I shot him a dirty look.
He assured me my pain
Was real. Without real cause.

All this time that I thought
My bones were dissolving
In acid, becoming jelly
My nerves were misfiring.
Because? I can control this.
Brain, Not Really Sick.
I ordered.
I meditated, mediated, negotiated
In a Pregalin haze, Tryptomer veins
I lay down terms and conditions
For my brain.

After two months I self-weaned.
Those drugs harm more than heal.
A poet of pain, I made my brain
Reread signals again.

Three years later,
I am more or less free.
The bad days I let them be
Love myself some more.

You may not see my agony
Or even know how aches, pains
Tremors come and go. I write,
Make light. Sometimes late nights, I brood
Wandering back to days when I
Ran, rode a bike, an ATV
On a mountain hike, Badass mamma
Of two adorable boys.
I can't smash down an easy badminton lob.
Wrists go broken china shards when I try to
Power through a game.
Well, table tennis then.

I hide my list of no can dos
Tell my kids to smile
Kiss the boo-boos life deals
I paint and sing and dance with them
All on my crazy neo-alien knees.
I pray I have many more beautiful days
Filled with minor achievements like these.
Bad Nerves, I own them,
We made peace.

How Does It Feel?

Getting up holding the sofa couch
Armrests. Sitting down on the floor.
To chop vegetables and forget the knife.
Screaming for someone to fetch it.

But You Don't Look Sick

Attempting to knead dough on fingers
frozen rictus brittle digits.
Another twist and curl of the dough,
You might break it.

You think I fake it?

I hold a hot and heavy gridle and holler
I don't want to drop something
I cooked for an hour
Where are the coasters for the love
Of God?

God is on sound cloud, ears plugged.

I wear bright lipstick
And pay attention to details.
I do up my hair and let a curl trail.
I team up my sweaters with
Pants that fit well.

No, I'm not well.
Would you prefer me
To dress down
And look like my hell?

I have fallen so many times
In front of my friends serving
them a dish, I fell at their feet
wobbling like fish.

Confused blushing like a beet
Menu du jour, pizza facing floor,
Cheese topping with extra dirt.

I toppled downstairs on
High heels,
Ah! Those early ignorant days
Into a manhole my right foot.
My left one made the safe.
I teeter and totter
My joints jitter and shudder
Like bugs crawl in my veins
No cause. No diagnosis.
Life in Fibro Lane.

So, Nothing's Wrong, Really.

As a bride of twenty six
Standing and washing dishes
At the kitchen sink, shocked by
Swollen ankles and bloated knees.
Doctor said mild rheumatoid arthritis,
I laughed, forgive me for being twenty six.

My grandmother had it, and a great aunt,
It's the hereditary haunt.
I mustn't sleep on floors, sit cross-legged
Use Indian toilets, the doctor said.
I wisecracked, "In other words Doc, I must
Be dead."

And I continued doing all three,
Played badminton with hubby

Jogged from home to office to meet him.
Incorrigible. Indomitable.
But at least arthritis is legit.
In the social roster of diseases.

At forty five, in a new city,
I ascribed constant shooting joint pains
"Oh that old arthritis, back again.
Friendless. In a bad patch, lonely and sad.

These pains made no sense. I didn't have them
While mopping the floor, walking outdoors.
Always when I lay down to rest, closed my eyes
Saw resilient aged parents, barely survive,
Felt like a deserter.

Slow spaced out fusillade, Acid laser phaser rays
Started flogging my body, crucifying me at nodal
Points, penetrating every joint, as involuntary shudders
Anticipated another cycle.

I was no brave heart kick ass young woman,
A week later crawled to the doctor.
No, not arthritis flaring up again,
Bad new beast in town,
Fibromyalgia by name.
Heart sickness, misguides the brain
misfires its arsenal on itself.

"So nothing's the matter with you?",
Sigh of relief, beyond belief, from
bosses, relatives, best friends.
No, I'm not cooking up a tale,
To get pity, attention, few days off work

Whatever you suspect.

I cannot give due evidence nor cause
The pain is surreal not fictional.
I can't explain what I don't
Ever want you to get.

Believe this, your ignorance,
Is not your loss.

"Everyday, I step out with a dread of falling down or otherwise embarrassing myself, exercising control through caution. What I can't control is the reactions I face, ranging from disbelief to amusement. 'What kind of a sham disease is that?!' This unvoiced thought on people's faces makes me cringe. Fibromyalgia's real heartbreak is that there are no apparent causes or solutions, except to avoid undue nervous stress or strain. Weak nerves is not weak character."

—Amrita Valan

Dr. Archana Bahadur Zutshi

Through the Looking Glass

It was a stifling call.
Suffering of absences
Traject espousal of neglect and abuse.
Seething flares, the silent monsters you feed within.
Diminishing the dynamic dimensions drastically!
The existential
Advent of mulling woes in a cryptic culmination.

Thirty two, is too young for a degeneration
To knock you out, frigid with fright
The new malady slithers in, though
Quite difficult days follow or churn
Fibromyalgia ramifies life in limitation.
Of long term engagement with malevolent ruinous turn
Looking through the glass of abnegation.

I never pulled the trigger,
Still I should walk around
Look for some ground to recover
my ground in life.
Onto the grind I must hail my confidence as it stutters.

Each year displayed its shifting zones
There were fractures in the tectonic churning,
I fell. I was within the ring of fire.
Silently the shocks rumble through me.
Fibromyalgia is a simmer zone, uneasy, smouldering
By day and night, the colossal shifts,
The fiery spurts, the painful knocks

414

All lie underneath the rocks.
Life seems cumbersome, but the will says carry on!
The stiffening takes place and you are consumed!
The vulnerable body dithers you first,
Love yourself there is nothing outside you,
You have cut yourself brutally with self-criticism
Now is the time to look no further, than your own self.

Elizabeth Wadsworth Ellis

Failure to Thrive: Falling of the Bell Curve

Failure to Thrive was a syndrome we often saw and diagnosed in the Emergency Room. An ambulance would be called when neighbors detected a strong odor from an adjoining apartment and their neighbor, an elderly man was brought to the Emergency Room. No longer employed, his spouse deceased, and his children moved away, he had given up. Any friends he had were gone or passed away. He had given up his *raison d'etre*, as the French would say, his reason to live. An aide once told me his 90-year-old charge- a man- had committed suicide.

Failure to Thrive falls at either end of the Bell Curve afflicting the very young child or the very old. Mammals (which we humans remain, despite our big brains) call out their loss when deprived or separated. Rupture of an attachment-bond results first in protest; then in despair. In despair, a coherent physiologic state, mammals like humans, slump; dejected, sad. "If they feel they have nothing to live for," veterinarian James Herriot wrote, "They will very often die." In the animal shelter where I volunteered, we saw that same effect in mammals: quiet, withdrawn. The puppy whimpers.

In the Emergency Room this syndrome of loss and despair, this injury of attachment, this inconsolable grief, is known as *Failure to thrive* from prolonged separation of affection, but on the other end of the bell curve from the geriatric man, is the child. *Failure to thrive* refers to babies and small children who whither and fail to grow and develop.

An old wives tale was that a spouse dies within 3 years of its mate. Scolding someone, "Oh, just get over it!" doesn't work. "Warm human contact [read *attachment*] generates internal opiate release, delivering the magic of forgetfulness from the twinging ache of

419

mammalian loneliness. Loneliness outweighs pain." (*A General Theory of Love*, Vintage Books, 2001 Affect, attachment, memory: contributions toward psychobiologic integration.)
—Psychologists Amini Fari, Lewis Thos., Lannon Richard.

The human mind," Peter Hessler wrote after studying Egypt, "has changed very little in thousands of years. Basic desires and instincts remain the same, with certain societal patterns repeated endlessly." Love is the safety of protection, caretaking, sacrifice, concern. Affection is love, too, as well as the "life sustaining power of attachment," Lewis, Amini and Lannon wrote, and helps blossom children's full potential. "A distraught baby reaches for his mother because an attuned parent can soothe him when he cannot soothe himself." Eventually he'll learn to 'self-quiet.' A father once told me when their baby couldn't be consoled they gave the child a t-shirt with his mother's scent to soothe swoon and swaddle. "Without emotional shelter infants die." (Lannon et al.)

In *Man: his first million years*, Ashley Montagu defines love as 'behavior which confers upon others survival benefits in such a manner that their potentialities for being human are afforded an opportunity for optimum development.' When we are not loved we are lonely, insecure, feel worthless. We detach, quietly withdraw; become weird, reclusive, antisocial; unmoored, adrift. Human behavior results from human need.

"A 21-year-old woman was arrested Tuesday evening," the St. Paul Pioneer Press reported, "after ramming the car of another woman who was allegedly seeing the same man." The threat of losing attachment exacerbates into violence. The puppy growls.

Loneliness isn't the only psychological pain that wears us down. Stress debilitates as well. A man I knew named Bill said he survived the Outward Bound Survival School, despite grave hardship. He was confined in the kind of hot box without enough room to stand up or stretch out we hear about in prisons for solitary confinement. "Then," he told me, "They threw a snake in there."

According to Lewis, Amini and Lannon, "One person we know was trapped in a dismal relationship simply because she could not get around the pain of loss...At each attempt to break w/him a taller wave of wretchedness welled up...so her inner scales regularly tipped in favor of staying. 'I'm constantly fighting w/myself over it,' she said. Therapy clarified her misery, but did not diminish it. Attachment penetrates the neural core of what it means to be human." Like this woman, we feel inner restlessness, a powerful urge to contact the beloved; looking/seeing signs; being vigilant, nursing blind hope, and a drive to reestablish contact. Even cortisol, the stress hormone, gets involved and elevates alertness.

How tough we need to be. When I swore prison inmate Michael Smith in to the proceedings in the courtroom, I made my usual routine eye contact. Thirty-five years later I can still see his eyes were cold. My amour, on the other hand, is warm as an easy-bake oven. Ernest Gaines (b. 1933, Louisiana) wrote, "Some tough people and mean people could control their women—most of them would brag about having more than one woman."

"People stumble, lie, change, move, die, and there's nothing we can do about it. This kind of pain is the price you pay for loving," Carolyn Hax wrote

When I was a little girl the mother figure in my life pushed me away. "You get too close." Humans need to be loved. Someone once sneered, "You seem so needy!'

In a 2015 newspaper article a man choked his girlfriend. "Caring makes you completely vulnerable. But that's something to get used to, not over." Carolyn Hax wrote. In another incident two dogs were killed, "because of a jealous lover." A man I know threatened suicide when divorce snapped the tightrope he balanced on. This was reminiscent of the day I tied a sheet to the sturdy closet rod.

People are like trees: whittle them away long enough pretty soon you have nothing left.

People aren't like the steering wheel.   I can't grip voluntary friendships, expecting them to go where I want.

People's feelings fishtail and veer direction; are not mine to demand.

People are valued and not dispensable like aspirin or disposable like Kleenex.

Attribnyt

Seashore

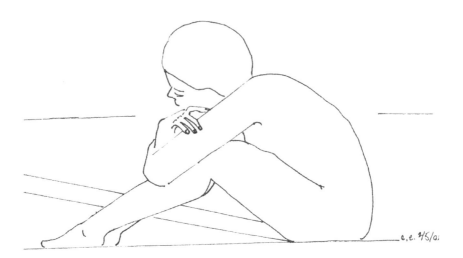

Pooja Francis

Wings

It's the unknown that scares us.
We've been in the dark for so long, we start perceiving it as our comfort zone.
It's not. It never was.
No matter how scary it may seem, you need to take a step.
Just because you don't see your wings, doesn't means, you don't have them.
They aren't always feathery moveable things attached at your back.
Your wings, they are your blood.
your heart, that's beating, no matter what the situation is.
Your soul, that's always loyal.
That whisper, yelling at you to never give up.

You.

Stop searching your wings.
Stop searching something, that's within you.
Start believing.

Steps

It's not about how many steps we take further, or how many steps we take back.
We're humans, we will fall at some point in time.
No matter how strong we get, or how brave.

We need a soul.
We crave affection.
We need a shoulder, a helping hand.
Whether we show it or not.
We always wish, having a soul, someone with pure intention,
someone who'd understand.
Maybe a friend, a partner, or family.
Just,
Someone worth fighting for.

Mark Andrew Heathcote

But there's hope tied to every mast?

Time is often—
dreamed as longer than time exists to be?
No need to smell the rank-rose to discern,
the dying abominate bee. As with each new flower,
a wellspring stem seeds the souls of men again.
But then some tortuously linger on
like hybrid tea roses, beset with rust and black spot.
That's never illness-free of some disease or disorder—
the likes of— bipolar, diabetes, lupus and such.
The likes of— multiple sclerosis, muscular dystrophy and cancer
But there's hope tied to every mast, breath that lingers
no matter the fatigue, there's a willingness to do battle
that precedes all victories and losses, one of identity.
It's a tug of war, we can't afford to ever lose.
It's a raft of overwhelming hope in the fiercest of storms
whatever the wreckage indelibly there'll be
something serenely calm and recognisable of me.

Terry House

It's Like That

She said, Remember the grass which grew
through the sidewalk's cracks?
It's like that.
She said, In the black of panic,
you find a path.
You become the blade of grass.

She said, It's true; illness changes you.
But living continues within whatever limits illness sets.
Even the feeblest breath still trills an aria of accomplishment;
even the weed sprouting through concrete still spins a pirouette.

She said, Baby, ask yourself this:
what if all you had left was a spyglass glimpse of sky or
the pinprick of a jay's reflected flash? What then?
What if there were no end to what you might contain?
What if terror did not teem within your veins?
Well, it's like that.

Originally published in the chapbook Speaking of Sculpture,
September 2019, by Old Frog Pond Farm & Studio, Harvard, MA.

Punam Chadha-Joseph

I wonder if they can see, what's really happening to me?

"Sharing made me realize I'm not alone and that gave me strength."

—Punam Chadha-Joseph

Louise Kenward

Storytelling

We are all born of storytellers. It courses through our veins and pumps through our hearts. Narratives are created for every eventuality, every set and every circumstance. Since the start of Time there has been a story.

I have begun to conjure stories of my own: of my body, of illness, of absence. I have created multiple versions of what happened and why. With every scrap of new information it twists and turns, maybe this is the right one, or this?

Once upon a time, I stopped. Everything about me stopped - as if I had died but had forgotten to finish the job, it lacked commitment. I spent weeks, then months, in bed. A half-hearted end. My early stories are lost. I either didn't have the capacity to create them or lost the ability to remember.

As time went on, other people made up stories about me. My GP thought I'd had a virus. He thought my body was taking a long time to recover from it, but he couldn't tell me why. He couldn't even be sure there was a virus, it was one that skips about, that can't always be seen, one that everyone has. My mum thought I was burnt out. Like an old car on bricks, blackened with charcoal.

Other people created stories for other people unable to get up, absented from life. I started reading them, and then I stopped.
There were stories of personality disorders, hysteria and anxiety, of illness stretching years and lifetimes, tales of no return. These were filled with fear and anger. They gave me nightmares.

Over time I got better without a story. But eventually it found me again, insisted I needed one. I got sick, again, for longer. My doctor had promised that wouldn't happen. I was angry with him. I'd written down his words. "It will never happen again as badly or for as long as it happened before. Don't ever hold back on life." But it did and I have had to.

Have you tried...?

In the absence of a story and sometimes with, there is no end to the possibilities of things that 'might help'. The potential number of stories is matched only by the number of possible cures –

From the statutory kale and yoga to more nuanced and wild possibilities.

There are the standard ones of course: drink more water, eat more greens, reduce intake of caffeine or sugar. Then there are the ones that sound plausible, hold traction, make sense: increase your protein levels, improve your gut, take magnesium supplements.

The further down the rabbit hole you go, the more wild and wonderful it gets: avoid mould, bungee jump on valium, drink cow urine.

We become so embroiled with stories and, more importantly, with happy endings, that we search and search. We do not easily give in or give up as it's helpfully phrased. There are no stories of the things we don't know. There are no stories to explain, none that help us navigate when our lives do not follow the rhythm of a narrative. There has to be a moral or a reason and an end. When this is missing it is tempting to go on looking, there will be a prince or a prize. Perhaps I just didn't try hard enough, or look in the right places. I am still lost in the woods with a witch - unless I am the witch? We never hear the witch's story. Perhaps they are right? I am neurotic, hysterical - a witch. My end is to be burned at the stake, dunked in the river to see if I drown. The wildness of stories.

So I construct my own.

I am structurally unsound

I am structurally unsound.

I have long believed this to be true.

A gorilla sits around my neck, crushing at my head and my shoulders when not sleeping in the small of my back.

I am filled with jelly and all things insubstantial, it's not quite set.

Bits of me move around a bit more than they should.

I'm stretchier than is entirely necessary.

Perhaps an exoskeleton will help? I am a crab without its shell.

Part amoeba, part xylophone, my body has not properly evolved to deal with gravity.

Or maybe I should just never leave water?

Paige Kezima

Ditching the Party
Real Reasons why People with Chronic Illnesses have Shitty Social Etiquette

Last Friday I went to my friend Miles' surprise birthday party. The execution was classic. Folks arrived early, and eagerly plotted how we would craft the moment of shock. One person gave live updates of Miles' whereabouts, another decorated the cake, someone else found the perfect party song to play after the surprise wore off.

Finally, we got the warning. Miles was two minutes away.
Lights off. Crowd hidden.

The door creaked open as Miles and our accomplice Stephanie walked in.
"SURPRISE!" we screamed.
The execution was classic.

I was ecstatic and determined to have a good time at the party. Not because I love parties (which I do), but because I had been experiencing a chronic illness flare-up all week. This included sick days from work, canceled plans, and an overall feeling of helplessness and despair.

So badly did I want to celebrate. So badly did I want to forget what was going on in my personal life. So, so badly. About an hour in, I noticed the pain start creeping up, resulting in me having another drink. This was an unsuccessful method of treatment.

2 hours in and I was plotting my escape. As my pain increased, my mood fell. The noise was too loud. The vodka hadn't made me drunk. The cake was gross. I was pissed.

As I slipped into a quiet room of the house, the overwhelming nature of my condition captured me: "Gotcha"! As the crowd roared mere rooms away, I started to weep.

Thoughts of both pity and hatred alternated in my head: "this isn't fair" and "you're so weak".

The pity goes something like this: "What did I do to deserve this? Surely, I must be a bad person if this is my life. It's not fair."

And anger? "What a loser," I thought. "You've been resting for days and can't manage to straighten up for a few hours for someone's birthday. You're pathetic".

As soon as the tears dried up, I fled. Mumbling goodbyes to a few folks, I basically sprinted to the door. When I closed the Uber car's door, I swear I was so angry I could have bashed my head into it. I arrived home and swiftly went straight to bed, as to avoid processing what had just happened.

To an onlooker, I just ghosted the party. The bitch who ditched, I'm sure they would call me. Except inside, there was a painful battle to get me to that point.

When someone abruptly cancels plans, or even ghosts, it's easy to get angry at them. The thing is, you're not getting the whole picture. That bullshit line of "everybody has a story", well, it becomes true. Last Friday it was my physical pain that got in the way. Next Friday it could be my mental illness. There are a plethora of reasons that can interfere with social plans.

While my coping mechanisms aren't great either, as they mostly consist of anger rather than self-soothing, I take responsibility for them. I am actively engaging in ways to be less self-destructive.

Your responses, on the other hand, I can't really control. That's up to you.

So, check in your flaky friends. Keep inviting them to things, even though half the time they won't show. If you really care, you'll take time to learn what's really going on behind the ghost.

Aishwariya Laxmi
Side Effects

Pills. Pills. Pills
White ones, big ones, small ones, broken ones.
Eighteen of them in a day
You choke back vomit
As you swallow them
That's all you've known for the last two decades.
Your-once slim frame bloats to twice its size
And there's not much you can do
You give up and resign to life as a new person
You wonder what was wrong with the old one
That this had to happen.
You walk, exercise and eat less to lose weight
Until a new disease strikes
And you repeat the process all over again
You wonder how much more your body can take
Whether any day of your life
Was worth this pain
And then you remind yourself to be grateful
You enter the good things in your life
Into your app
And read them again
When your mood plummets
You stay positive
Coz if everyone says life is a gift
It must be
You don't want to give up
Before you reach its end naturally.
You exhale

But You Don't Look Sick

The next time someone makes a thoughtless remark
Like "you don't look sick"
It glides off you
Like water off a duck's back
And you face a new day.

Rihan Mustapha

Strong

I'll stay strong – won't be
a withered rose dying from
inner thorns of pain.

Anita Nahal

I did not say, *I love you*, to my mama

It had drizzled that morning and the soil was still damp as my son and I took the Uber to the hospital. New Delhi is very earthy when it rains. Unpretentious, it strolls into one's heart and settles in a hug next to your soul. Its fragrances blossom and its smells, its traffic nuisances, its busy body-ness, its capital city pretentiousness, recedes. The vibes change from testiness to serene. This time the tranquility metamorphosed into unnerving. I had this feeling this would be the last time I would see my mother alive. She lay on the hospital bed, no movement. Complaining was not her habit in any case. Cancer had spread rapidly in a matter of two months. She opened her eyes on hearing our footsteps. "*Can you take me to the bathroom?*" The care worker got up in reflex. "*No, not you, my daughter will take me.*" She looked at the unruly hair strands falling from her bun in the mirror after washing. "*You are so beautiful, mummy.*" I muttered. She smiled and we both sat on the windowsill for a while. I, just holding her. Later, I held on to her real close that evening before rushing to the airport to catch our flight back. She looked directly into my eyes right through to my inner being. This is it. This is goodbye my darling she seemed to express. Laying on the bed, other relatives watching, she couldn't say anything more. "*We will return very soon, mama.*" I whispered as I kissed her on her forehead. At the elevator door, I said, "*I think I did not say, I love you to her.*" You did, you did, others consoled. In the lobby downstairs, I ran into some relatives, "*I think I did not say, I love you to her.*" My son comforted me, "*You did, you did.*" Before entering the Uber, I turned and looked my mother's way, "*I think I did not say, I love you to her.*" "*You did, mama, you did.*" As the plane left the tarmac with a distraught drizzle still engulfing New Delhi, my uncontrollable tear drops felt an incomprehensible barrenness. I think I did not say, *I love you*, to my mama.

"I left my birth country with my 14-year-old son, resigned from a tenured professorship, and started afresh in the US so we could have a safe and peaceful life. Although I am a very strong women, deep invisible scars have left their mark. I sometimes stand on a tightrope between the new life and the one left behind. Our closest relatives passed away without us having touched or spoken to them. I don't realize our trauma until something triggers it. Folks call us emotional refugees."

—Anita Nahal

Akhila Rajesh

Pain and me

If pain could grow wings
It would still fly around in circles in my veins
How do I free it?
And would I ever want to part with it?

It gives a sound to my voice as never before
My stentorian voice, gone unheard for years
Is now heard even in whimpers

Funny, how the badge of pain marks my wins
I wasn't a hero for the marathons I gallantly finished
But I became one for the last mile that I limped

We strayed into and then stayed in each other's cages
Two hollows filled with each other's sympathies
I wonder if it has made me or I have made it my muse-
Painting the other with each other's blues

Pain is a pathetic painter, but no love lost
My painting has found its long due spot
In the myopic eyes that people possess; after all
Caricatures do get more recognition than stoic portraits...

Tina Sequeira

Behind the Sangfroid Silence of the Cursed Frogs

As much as I hate fairy tales and gag at their sickeningly sweet happily ever after endings, I dare to hope for a better world.

Where the silent frogs would be free to croak as loud as their hearts' desire—

Where the cursed frogs would not have to live in the bone-chilling fear of grating the listeners' senses—

And where they don't perform as an involuntary joker in a debauched world.

An unspeakable conspiracy pits the world against frogs with an ugly, choked voice. So ugly that it casts a frosty spell and hardens the hearts of people. Left with little choice but to burn the voices of the nasty, cursed frogs with matches of pealing laughter, stripping mockery, feigned apologies, and condescending tributes.

They roll the red carpet out in honor and set the stage for those with a golden voice. All this while they force the cursed frogs to retreat into visible invisible existence.

How does it feel to be a cursed frog with an ugly voice?

Ask me.

I came out of my mother's womb with two dangling swords. One on my tongue. One on my chest. I'm born with a stutter and asthma.

As a child, I went up on the podium, spoke in front of hundreds of students in the school assembly, and won the elocution competitions. But I got tongue-tied off the stage without the rehearsed speeches. I harbored the fear of being ridiculed if I spoke spontaneously. I feared rejection for being me. And so, I wore the cloak of silence as my armor.

Despite my nil social skills, my classmates would regularly vote for me as their class leader. Since I performed well on both the academic and extra-curricular front, I became one of the school captains with the unanimous votes by the students, teachers, and discretion of the school principal. Maybe my silence worked in my favor. I wasn't sure. But now, I carried three swords. I suffered from Imposter's Syndrome as well.

All seemed well until I stepped into college to pursue science, a discipline that I had no interest in. I wanted to pursue journalism or English literature. But like most middle-class Indians, my parents reasoned that these weren't high-paying jobs, and I should stick to the conventional choices of a doctor or an engineer. I chose the former option. It was a perplexing phase, and for the first time, I detested learning. The guilt of not cracking into the highly competitive MBBS entrance exams and appeasing my parents manifested into depression and, in my speech, with an exacerbated stutter.

It took me years to heal and feel good. I went up to people on my own, introduced myself, and made new friends. A luxury that I'd denied myself in my growing years owing to my stuttering condition. I've always loved people, and this newfound confidence and joy of making small talk and graduating to more meaningful relationships gave me the impetus to feel less like an imposter.

However, the lack of opportunities for reading out loud, as in the classroom, and taking part in competitions threw me out of gear where public speaking was concerned. Those were rare occasions, but the mean jokes and scornful glares were enough to haunt and give me nightmares for long.

But it's not the mockery of the speech disorder that sends shivers down my spine as much as the myths that surround people who stutter. We perceive people with flawless speech as more intelligent, confident, and successful. We label those who stutter as unintelligent, unconfident, unsuccessful, untrustworthy liars, and incapable people. These flawed perceptions all boil down to one thing alone -

A mere stutter in speech. Much like a scar on the skin.

Those with scars have makeup to the rescue. But stutterers live in an unnatural state of miserable, shamed silence. Little wonder that apart from a few within the family and celebrities who came out with their stammering condition, I'd encountered no one else with it.

An educated older adult attributed my stuttering to bad karma. This flawed mindset justifies the insensitivity, bullying, and rejection that stutterers undergo because somehow they deserve it. Telling you're cursed lifts the entire blame from society and rests it entirely upon your head.

Throw in asthma, which flares up during every seasonal change, and it's a wild roller coaster ride in my dark inner cores. Unlike stuttering, asthma is an invisible disability. I look perfectly fine to the world, which cannot understand why it's hard to take a few steps, climb stairs, lie down in bed, or carry basic tasks.

Sometimes it's a mountain of an effort to breathe and get a single word out. But it's the darkest days that strengthen my resolve to come out of hiding and take center stage. Even in those quiet moments of resignation, with warm fat tears rolling down my cheeks, Hope kissed me on the lips and embraced me in her ample bosom.

"I'm glad you've made a start somewhere."

"I was raw at first, too. Practice, and you will get there like me."

"Wow, I am so impressed by your courage today."

These were some comments that I'd received when I'd put aside my fears and disabilities to host an event after a very long time. When I narrated the incident to my husband, he said that stuttering is a part of me, and it's not something I should be ashamed of or hide from public view.

It's why I dare to dream of a better world. It will not be a smooth, straight road to the light. And it's going to take time for the world to accept our glitched voices as the norm.

I'm no longer apologetic but grateful for my disabilities because it has made me — empathetic, resilient, and human.

To all my fellow ugly cursed frogs, we croak, and let's keep croaking till the Sun goes down!

"I share my lived experiences of being an asthmatic with a stutter and how misrepresented our conditions are in the mainstream world. People with a stutter face undue mockery and rejection. Stuttering has nothing to do with cognitive abilities, anxiety issues, or nervous disposition. Asthma is an invisible condition that plays havoc in our daily life, and we still face a lot of stigma and stereotypes such as 'weak,' 'lazy,' and 'nerdy' in our society."

—Tina Sequeira

Chandra Sundeep

My Anosmic Life – An Unseen Reality

For some, life is a bed of roses, while for a few it's a garland of thorns. I belong to the latter category. My sufferings remain unseen to the world, deemed not a 'real disability' by most. It's a crown of invisible thorns which pierces my soul and makes my life a horrendous journey. Only my closest ones are privy to this part of my life. For the world, there's forever, a smile plastered on my face. A mask to hide the real me.

My illness, though unseen, is certainly not imaginary. I suffer from Anosmia, or in simple words, I lack the sense of smell. Humans are born with five senses; and I am one of the chosen few born with just four of them.

Loss of limbs, eyesight, hearing or mental abilities is considered as disability. But the world hardly sees my condition as a loss of faculties. What people fail to realize is just because it is unnoticeable, it doesn't make my sufferings lesser and meaningless. Sight and hearing are perceived as 'necessary senses,' whereas touch and smell are taken for granted, and remain undervalued, and least appreciated.

The smell of fresh baked bread, or the aroma of steaming coffee; the briny smell of ocean, or the crisp mountainous air – you have experienced them all. You can distinguish between the scents of rose or gardenia. A walk in the wilderness or passing a landfill; exquisite perfume or disgusting poop; to me it's all the same, no difference at all. I have read all about them, but found no words which could describe the smells the way they really are. I know what I'm missing in life, but still would never really know; and that's the greatest irony of my existence.

Mimicking the behaviors of people around me is my defense mechanism. A trick I learned early on in life, thanks to my class-mates who bullied me in school. Scrunching my nose when others do, or inhaling and smiling as if having attained nirvana. The web of lies around me is so strong, sometimes I forget it's a farce, and confuse it to be my reality.

The smell of your mother's embrace kindles forgotten childhood memories. The whiff of tobacco, metallic smell of blood, or even the stench of rotten wastes; every smell forms an association, becomes a part of your life. My life remains an incomplete canvas. None of my memories are associated with smell, or rather they are all associated with a lack of smell.

Imagine you are in a restaurant. What's the first thing you notice even before you dig into your food? The presentation, and the aroma, right? The aroma tingles your taste buds, generates saliva signaling the brain and tempts you to enjoy your food. For someone like me, who cannot smell the food, most of the time I cannot enjoy the flavor too. Frankly speaking, I eat for the sake of living and pretend to enjoy the food in front of others.

Mental and physical disabilities are noticed, and acknowledged. People suffering from any of the 'seen' disabilities have governmental support, empathy of friends and family; but what about the rest of 'us'? The world leaders talk about inclusion, diversity and tolerance; yet conveniently choose to turn a blind eye to those battling unseen disabilities. And because I don't look 'sick,' even the society is largely ignorant of my challenges.

As per scientists, the average human being can recognize up to 10,000 separate odors. Can you imagine, I haven't smelt a single fragrance or odor all my life; and probably never will. Next time when you are dancing in the rain enjoying the petrichor, I hope you'll not take your sense of smell for granted. Remember, there are many like me, craving to enjoy the small pleasures of life.

Ranu Uniyal

You can't let me down

This will not do, he growled.
You have always been unkempt,
untidy and uncouth. Your
laughter shrill and body smug.
The sickness in you, terminal.

Change or you will miss
the bus – full of happiness
and children. Spring and cities
thrive in the company of youth.
And you are turning grey – inside out.

I heard his rant,
winked at the only cacti
with a tiny dash of pink
and thought of a tribe of women
dancing in the desert. What fun?

"I believe in protecting the rights of people with disability and for
me, inclusion is a means, not an end."

—Ranu Uniyal

Mehak Varun

Lost in our struggles of twists and turns

My whole world is shaken

WOMB

Mona Dash
Living with Endometriosis

It is hard to know where to begin, which part to pick up and display, like a jeweller, showing off rubies, sapphires. Blood hums and makes its way through generations. The complex chromosome mapping, citing the colour of eyes, the height, the shape of limbs – the way you hold your hand under your chin, the way you tilt your face, why that is exactly what grandfather did! It comes down with the hum of blood in our veins. And through that comes the mutations, the nonsense mutations in the gene encoding, the common gamma chain, protein shared by receptors, sorry can you please speak in English? The chromosomes speaking their own language, indecipherable, the story written and ordained, the conditions given to us and those that we pick up, not knowing how, not knowing why.

We could stand in a circle here and sing together, for we will die one day. We shall all die one day after all. Babies, children, adults all. Hysterically we can sing, but calmly we live on, and on.

'Come with us,' she said, 'we must visit a shrine, of the Goddess, who heals.' I followed her – dazed mother, desperate; educated I, sceptic. When Science has cast its dice, where is God, what can he do? Only Science can help my body. Only the right hospital, the right doctors, the right place. Not here, not here. Yet I followed the procession of women, maids, cleaners, cooks, all mothers, fertile women, and reclined in front of the large-eyed Goddess.

Help me God. The world is hollow.

I cannot follow, but I must escape, somewhere else.

They said, grief is like a stone in your shoe, even if you don't always step on it, you know it's there. They hadn't said, grief also rose phoenix-like, and enveloped you in her cloying feathers when you least expected it.

Months passed into a whole year, but unlike last time, the storks were refusing to visit us, while the entire world around us was producing babies.

The GP said, 'It could be nothing, but we can run a few tests.'

It had to be nothing. Why would infertility join the tropes in my motherhood struggle? I had other crosses to bear.

A scan showed the path of blood gone wrong. Globules of congealed blood, forming cysts in delicate ovaries, trapping eggs in their rigidity and never releasing them for conception.

They called it Endometriosis.

Frustration, sorrow, anger finally sequinned on that one word.

They asked me about the pain. 'How do you make love, surely you double up with pain?' I blushed and answered, 'no not really.' 'How do you have a monthly cycle, without lying useless in a ball, curled in pain?' I replied, 'there is no pain.' I sail through, I holiday, I work through my periods, not knowing. 'You are lucky, so lucky,' they say, 'to have endometriosis and not know its pain.' But this is it. I never knew, while I lived, whizzed by on effervescent wings while that something inside was bleeding, bleeding wrongly. That something inside was silently growing into my ovaries, and there was I, on the outside, knowing nothing. Endometriosis grade 3. Yet not knowing, there I was planning, diligently, charting temperatures, making a monthly routine of love, to no avail.

But there was help. The gynaecologist was stubbornly positive, the surgery to remove the cysts and adhesions. I lay on a bed in the private hospital looking out at the tranquil snow filled grounds, hoping I would conceive soon.

Months later, nothing, nothing.

Then other words came up, Clomid pills, cycle after cycle. Prayers, alternative remedies. Failure.

Pray. There are enough Gods to choose from. In India, I saw thousands of families, praying to the 'Gurundu Gopala,' the crawling baby Krishna, the symbol of cheeky childhood. Outside, I too bought a small idol, the black stone in the shape of a little boy, heavy on my palm.

'He will give you what you want,' everyone assured.

When I eventually conceive. Believe.

Two years passed. Another acronym floated in. IVF. Why not? You conceive in a test tube, and you offer your womb to the one who isn't agreeing to be born. You write your own fate. Drugs, sprays, injections now sat next to the juices and milk in my fridge.

The flow of blood was unfailingly regular, sometimes even before time. In August, a couple of days late, I felt reckless enough to try the pregnancy stick that was packaged optimistically with the ovulation predictors I had been buying regularly for months. And just like that, so simply, the lines turned double dark pink.

All the belief, all the hope, all the prayers lined up to say – Yes, you were right!

Never Give up Hope. I tell myself.

Endo-what?

The technician handed me a robe, 'Change there.' She pointed at an area in a corner of the large room.

I went to the corner and found that I could see the waiting area where the millions waited patiently – needless to say, they could see me too.

'How am I supposed to change here?' I grumbled. 'Don't they have better facilities?'

'Is there a cubicle or something?' my sister asked one of the nurses politely.

The nurse looked around blankly.

'Oh well, I will manage,' I scowled.

I lay down on the examining table and my insides came alive on the screen. I was fully convinced nothing could be wrong. Concentric circles, the probe pushing inside, some more greyish circles. The radiologist paused for a moment and asked my sister, 'Has she ever had endometriosis?'

I had never heard of this term before, which meant I couldn't have had it. I searched my brain – what on earth was endometriosis? The name didn't ring any bells, not even from the far past. I knew my sister well. I knew her every expression. The familiar face had frozen at the question.

'No, never,' she replied.

'Well, she has endometriosis now.' The nurse pointed at some blurry shapes on the screen.

'What is endometriosis?' I mouthed, when I finally caught my sister's eyes. She had been looking at the screen, the radiologist, anywhere but me.

She shrugged helplessly. 'It's a cause of infertility.' Then turning to the radiologist, she asked, 'Where is it?'

'There are chocolate cysts in both ovaries. But here, in this right ovary, it's not clear whether this is a chocolate cyst. It's massive, almost looks solid.' My sister and the technician exchanged worried glances. I didn't know what a chocolate cyst was, but if there was a solid cyst in an ovary, even I could see that could be a problem.

'You might need to have a blood test as well,' the technician said.

'We will meet the doctor now. We will ask her.'

I changed back into my clothes, this time without protests, and we walked back to the doctor.

'Why does this thing…endo whatever, happen?' I asked.

'It's one of those diseases where the cause isn't very clear. Something to do with periods, and the blood instead of flowing out, flows inwards and deposits inside the uterus. But I never knew it could happen only in the ovaries... nothing in the uterus,' she said, looking at the report. I didn't know if it was bad or good to have it in the ovaries instead of the uterus.

Dr Sundari saw us in a few minutes. Even she looked shocked. She certainly hadn't expected I would come back with something like this.

'Big chocolate cysts in both ovaries,' she said, looking at the report, 'but in the right ovary, the cyst seems more solid.'

'What are chocolate cysts?' I asked again, like a parrot.

'Chocolate cysts are a characteristic of endometrioses. They are not solid, almost like a liquid chocolate, hence the name. We are not worried about those. But the solid looking one in the right ovary here needs to be tested. We need to rule out it's not cancerous. She needs to have a blood test for CA 125. Come back in the afternoon as the blood tests are closed for the moment. CA 125 is a marker for cancer, so if the factor is high, it could indicate cancer, and we would recommend a biopsy of the cyst.'

'But what about the endometriosis? Would she need surgery?' sister asked.

'She needs to have a laparoscopy. Since she is in a hurry to conceive the sooner the better. You could admit her tomorrow and we can do the procedure.'

'I am leaving the day after. I can't get admitted tomorrow,' I said.
Dr. Sundari shrugged. If it was this important, then surely I should have it done, her expression said.

'But surely you must have had some symptoms?' she asked, looking at me for a moment, 'Painful periods, painful intercourse?'
'No, I didn't, not ever.' She didn't look convinced.

'I mean, I would know, wouldn't I?' I said.

'It is strange that she has such severe endometriosis, but no symptoms at all,' she told my sister, almost as if I was deliberately tricking everyone.

My sister was quiet, driving back, her face scrunched up with disbelief.

'Endometriosis…but how could you get it? No one in our family has something like this. It's not even very common you know, among Indian women.'

'Since when have I had it, do you think?' as if knowing the exact moment of onset would help somehow.

'It's hard to tell. But both the ovaries are affected quite badly. You need to have the surgery done soon. A laparoscopy is not a very complex operation.'

Back home, my mother was waiting anxiously. As I cried silently over the rice, dal and prawn curry I was served for lunch, my sister told my mother about the diagnosis.

'But there is a cure, isn't it? It's so good that we know now.'

'Cure?! And now they are saying I also have cancer,' I said as if it was all their fault.

'They aren't saying that you have cancer. They are just wanting to rule it out, so that you are fine. Ovarian cancer can be serious. So, we can go for the blood test in a couple of hours and I will get the results tomorrow itself.'

'There is no way I am going back for a blood test, cancer or not,' I said and stomped off to the bedroom. The computer sat in a corner. And once again, I gave search, yet another unfamiliar term.

Endometriosis – the cause unknown, the cure unknown. One theory was that working women were more prone to endometriosis.

The best way to stop the onslaught of the condition, in some catch 22 travesty, was to get pregnant, except that the endometriosis would prevent a pregnancy.

I called my husband to explain. I wasn't this normal healthy person I thought I was. I had something called endometriosis, Grade 3. E Globules of congealed blood, forming cysts in delicate ovaries, trapping eggs in their rigidity and never releasing them for conception. Endometriosis so bad that both the ovaries were covered with chocolate cysts, making them useless. Endometriosis so rampant that I had to be treated as soon as possible with a laparoscopy to clear it. Yet endometriosis with no symptoms at all, nothing to warn me before it had spread so much.

Extract from *A Roll of the Dice: a story of loss, love and genetics* by Mona Dash (Linen Press UK, 2019).

Childlessness

(I) have forged across seas
trekked in deserts
flown over mountains
fallen from the skies
lived in the arms
of strong men
watched the hunt of
helpless large kudus
felt the love of raging elephants.

(I) have done it all

When will I have you
to hold, to watch
as you sleep
to love you as no other?

But You Don't Look Sick

(I) have travelled the world
owned sapphires and diamonds
possessed and loved
when do I get lucky
like my harassed neighbour
mother of four?

"Invisible illnesses are the worst, or are they the best? It's great when a trace of the illness doesn't show on your face or body, when you look as good as the person next to you. The traces which instead appear inside, creating little things like infertility for instance, are only yours to know about. The pain of the inside, never coming up to the surface, but resolutely beating inside you, enveloping you...you can always scream in silence..."

—Mona Dash

Ingrid Wilson
Le Horla, Mental Health and PMDD

In this essay I would like to discuss PMDD, and other mental health conditions, in the light of a powerful and disturbing short story by Guy de Maupassant. My father first read *Le Horla* to me when I was a child. Presumably he wanted to terrify me. The story certainly left an impression:

The narrator, an aristocratic gentleman of Rouen, falls ill with a fever at the beginning of the tale, which is told in the form of a diary. Through successive entries, he charts the progression of his strange and most disturbing illness. As the protagonist becomes more ill, he develops a growing awareness of a being which resides within his home, feeding on his vitality and sapping him of his energy and willpower.

As the tale progresses, the narrator feels increasingly that his spirit is being dominated by this strange being, which he comes to know as *Le Horla*. Unable to leave his house or properly command his own body, in a desperate attempt to kill the demon, he burns down his house, trapping his servants inside. Realising with horror in the end that the fiend is still alive, he concludes his diary (and the story) as follows:

'No, no...without a doubt...without a doubt...he is not dead. Then...then...there is no other solution but to kill myself.'

Context of the Story

The story was published in 1887, five years before Maupassant attempted to commit suicide by slitting his throat, and six years before he died in a Paris asylum. He had been suffering from tertiary syphilis which can cause 'dementia, personality changes, delusions, seizures, psychosis and depression.' (Source: Wikipedia).

In describing *Le Horla*, Maupassant was most likely describing his own struggle with his failing mental health. The narrator of the story questions his own sanity several times during the course of the narrative, for example:

'From whence do these mysterious influences come, that through discouragement change our good humour and confidence into distress?'

The narrator wakes up happy, with a song in his heart, only to return from a short walk completely desolate 'as if some evil waited upon [him].'

The story was written at a period when the profession of psychiatry was in its infancy, when the medical profession was only beginning to probe the depths of the human psyche. Upon returning to this story, reading it in the context of my own battle with mental health issues, I can only conclude that we have not come very far in this field since 1887.

My own experience with Mental Illness

I always found it a little strange that my father chose to read this particular story to me as a child, not least because my mother had killed herself at the age of 32, when I was 8. I think for this reason it stayed with me. Perhaps it offered some kind of explanation for what she did.

To say that suicide is selfish is surely one of the most insidious and counterproductive misconceptions about mental illness. I know we

465

say 'mental health' these days, but in my opinion if someone kills themself they do so because they are very ill. Only those who have experienced the battle with failing mental health and inner demons can possibly hope to understand the desperation and mental torture which can drive people to take the most unnatural of actions.

I am now going through my own personal mental health battle, in the form of PMDD. Though apparently caused by an overreaction in the brain to a drop in oestrogen during the luteal phase of the menstrual cycle (i.e.e, a physical cause) its manifestations are mainly psychological. I fly into blind rages over the smallest of things. I feel overwhelmed, at times completely defeated and without hope, even though I know the condition is only temporary. My family tell me, and I feel myself, as if someone else has taken over my body. Very possibly just how Maupassant felt when he wrote *Le Horla*.

Hope on the Horizon

PMDD, like many other conditions which affect a person's mental health, is treatable. And I believe, it is beatable. Unfortunately, and I suspect tragically, it has only been recognised as a condition since 2013. I think of all those women throughout history who were believed to be 'possessed by demons,' some of whom were probably burned alive or drowned as witches. I think about my mother, who I remember flying into rages for now apparent reason, who I remember suffering from very heavy periods. No one had heard of PMDD back then. I will never know if this was Le Horla which led her to take her own life. I only know that it was not an act of wilful selfishness.

I only know that PMDD, like other illnesses which affect the mind, can only be cured by understanding. We have to listen to sufferers and try to understand their experiences, as herein must lie a clue to the root cause of their suffering. Every month, I worry that this thing will kill me. Every month, I worry that my family will turn against me because of the monster I become. I go through one week of hell and I get two weeks of reprieve. But I have the support of my family, and more recently, of other sufferers.

If you think you might have PMDD (telltale signs include extreme bouts of anger and depression which come on in the weeks leading up to your period and disappear with the onset of menstruation), you should of course seek medical advice. However, if your doctor has never heard of the condition, or shrugs it off (as has been my experience) do not lose hope: there is much information and support available on Twitter. Follow #PMDD, and use the resources @IAPMDGlobal, @MEvPMDD, @DPmdd and @viciouscyclepmd. Reach out to other women who are suffering and let them know they are not alone. There is no *Le Horla*, there is only ignorance, whose greatest enemy is understanding.

"PMDD is a condition in which the body has an adverse reaction to the luteal phase hormones of the menstrual cycle. This can cause extreme physical and mental discomfort in the 7-14 days prior to menstruation.

I began to experience the condition after the birth of my first son. Sometimes the symptoms can be severe and include suicidal ideation and bouts of depression and rage. I currently manage my symptoms using yoga and meditation."

—Ingrid Wilson

BIOGRAPHIES

Annessa Ann Babic is a freelance writer, artist, and professor in New York, New York. She specializes in women's studies, US social and cultural history, public health narratives, and transnational studies, emphasizing the modern Middle East and US-Turkish relations. She has a hefty academic publishing background (with a handful of books and a gaggle of articles), is a long-standing community activist, and publishes outside academia. Currently, she is looking to publish her first novel. She lives in Manhattan with her rescue-pup, Bourbon.

Mini Babu is working as Assistant Professor of English with the Department of Collegiate Education, Government of Kerala and is now working at BJM Government College, Chavara, Kollam. Her poems have featured in journals and magazines. Her debut collection of poems is *Kaleidoscope* (2020)

Lorelei Bacht is a European poet currently living in Southeast Asia with her family, which includes two young children and a lot of chaos. Her current work focuses on gender, aging, parenthood and other complicated things. Her recent work can be found and/or is forthcoming in *OpenDoor Poetry*, *Litehouse*, *Visitant*, *Quail Bell*, and *The Wondrous Real*.
She is also on Instagram: @lorelei.bacht.writer

Christina Baltais is an artist from Toronto, Canada who has lived with Myalgic Encephalomyelitis (ME) for over fifteen years. She uses art, photography, and writing to raise awareness for ME, and to help process the experiences of living with a highly contested illness. 'Anthology of ME' was inspired by the works of artist Johan Deckmann, who uses books and their titles, to convey universally relatable truths about life.

Prof. Dr. Laksmisree Banerjee is a senior poet, writer, literary critic, educationist, scholar, rotarian (a multiple Paul Harris Fellow) and practicing vocalist. She is a Senior Fulbright Scholar, Commonwealth Scholar, and National Scholar in English from the Calcutta University, India. A University Professor of English, Poetry & Culture Studies, and Ex-Vice Chancellor, she has lectured and recited in universities and literary festivals across the globe. Dr. Banerjee has eight books of poetry (two forthcoming) and 120 academic and creative publications.

Doctor by profession, **Supriya Bansal** longs to live in a world with a constant supply of extra dark chocolate and filter coffee. She and her husband share their home with two extraordinary kids and a lifetime supply of books. Writing is her me-time, her happy place.

Shannon Barnsley is a writer, poet, and chronic illness bard from New Hampshire, currently living in Brooklyn. She holds a degree in Creative Writing/Mythology & Religion from Hampshire College. Since graduating, she has given tours at an 18th century Shaker village; translated English-English into American-English for an independent publishing company; and tackled the epic, unrelenting journey that comes with having multiple chronic illnesses. Her first book, *Beneath Blair Mountain*, was published by 1888.

Susan Bellfield is a cancer survivor, a dog momma, and a lover of interior design who holds a Master's degree in English/Creative Writing. Her poetry placed first and second in Lindenwood University's 2018 Annual Poetry Contest, and has appeared in *The Loch Raven Review*, *Tuck Magazine*, *Sorrows Words*, and on her website susanbellfield.wordpress.com.

Marilyn Rea Beyer's writing springs from her everyday Midwestern upbringing, seeking the dark or the fanciful in it. Her poems have appeared in the Indie Blu(e) anthologies *We Will Not Be Silenced*

(2018) and *Through the Looking Glass* (2021), plus *Whisper and the Roar*, and *Oddball Magazine*. She holds a Master's in Oral Interpretation of Literature from Northwestern University. Marilyn and her husband, author/filmmaker Rick Beyer, raised their family near Boston. She proudly hosts WFMT's The Midnight Special, Chicago's longest-running music radio show.

Suzette Bishop teaches at Texas A&M International University. Her books include *Horse-Minded*, *She Took Off Her* Wings and Shoes, *Hive-Mind*, *Cold Knife Surgery*, and most recently, a chapbook, *Jaguar's Book of the Dead*. Her poems have appeared in many literary magazines and anthologies and received an Honorable Mention in the Pen 2 Paper Contest and first place in the Spoon River Poetry Review Contest. She is a contributor for *The Mighty*. Her website: https://suzettemariebishop.com/

Nashville, TN native, **Kayla Sue Bruyn**, is a breakout poetess. As a pansexual, bipolar and perpetually depressed and anxious, plus sized woman who deals with chronic pain, Kayla Sue has an entire wheelhouse to pull from to connect with others through her art. She likes to think of herself as an advocate for mental health, body positivity, disabilities, and ethical non monogamy. She can be found on Instagram @kayla.sue.writes.too and @kaylabcreates

Susan Burch is a good egg.

Amie Campbell is an emerging poet based in Austin, TX. She enjoys spending her time with her children and rescue dog, and trying to keep her succulents alive. She has been published in Indie Blu(e)'s anthology, *SMITTEN This Is What Love Looks Like*, antilang's *Pithy Politics,* and the online literary review *Evocations*.

Formerly a Counselor, Systems Analyst, and Small Business Owner, **Deborah Hetrick Catanese** spent four years of semi-retirement helping a friend create *Project Motherhood* blog, for which Deborah wrote over 85 Editor's Posts. Other publications of her poetry and nonfiction include *Voices in the Attic*, Carlow University; the *Pittsburgh Post-Gazette*; *The Microcomputer Facility*, ALA; *Dreamers Anthology*, and *Is It Hot in Here?*, *Beautiful Cadaver Project*; *Ekphrastic Review*; 6 awards for poetry, *Konect E-Zine*, and daily participant and contributor to Online Mindful Writers Group.

Jharna Choudhury, 27, from Assam, India, is an embroidery artist, poet and PhD student working on grotesque bodies and illness narratives. Her creative writings have been published in *The Assam Tribune*, *The Sentinel*, *Muse India*, and forthcoming in *The Little Journal of Northeast India*. Previously covered by Shawatales, Ladakh, in a talk series 'Hand-Embroidery & Storytelling', she insists on making poetry via threads and paints. Reach her in Instagram: @_embroidery_stories_.

Wanda Morrow Clevenger lives in Hettick, IL - population 200, give or take. Over 700 pieces of her work appear in 193 print and electronic journals and anthologies. Her debut book *This Same Small Town in Each of Us* was published in 2011 through Edgar & Lenore's Publishing and four of a five-volume chapbook set (*where the hogs ate the cabbage*) has been published through Writing Knights Press. Clevenger is currently serving as a contributing editor for *U-Rights Magazine*.

Emily Rose Cole is the author of *Thunderhead*, a collection forthcoming from University of Wisconsin Press, and *Love & a Loaded Gun*, a chapbook of persona poems in women's voices from Minerva Rising Press. Her poetry has appeared in *American Life in Poetry*, *Best New Poets 2018*, *Poet Lore*, and the *Los*

Angeles Review, among others. She holds an MFA from Southern Illinois University Carbondale and is a PhD candidate at the University of Cincinnati.

Amanda.x.Coleman grew up and lives on Cape Cod. She began sharing her work on social media in 2015. She also has a passion for music and graphic design. She was diagnosed with Lyme Disease as a teenager, and has lived with fibromyalgia since. She was also recently diagnosed with occipital neuralgia and gastroparesis. Find Amanda online: www.amandaxcoleman.com

In late summer 2020, **Natalie Cummings** (42) faced a breast cancer diagnosis. Through her personal fight with anxiety, she's supported a daughter with similar battles beginning at a young age. This Maryland wife and mother of three watches her brother's struggles with, and has lost close family to, autoimmune disease. The soft hues of her beloved sea glass revealed deeper meaning and a desire to shed light on the overlooked and unseen. Natalie believes, like her treasured glass, there is beauty to be gained after being broken by the sea.

Kimberly Cunningham has written three published books, *Undefined*, *Sprinkles on Top*, and *Smooth Rough Edges*. In addition, she has written over 35 pieces of published works. She has work included in *We Will Not Be Silenced*, *As The World Burns*, *Into the Rabbit Hole*, and *The Brave*. Kimberly is a special education preschool teacher residing in central New York with her husband, daughter, and two curious cats. Find her on Amazon-Kimberly Cunningham.

Mona Dash is the author of *A Roll of the Dice: a story of loss, love and genetics* (Eyelands Book Award), *A Certain Way*, *Untamed Heart*, and *Dawn-drops*. Her work has been listed in leading competitions such as Novel London 20, SI Leeds Literary award,

Fish, Bath, Bristol, Leicester Writes and Asian Writer. Her most recent work is a short story collection, *Let Us Look Elsewhere*, published by Dahlia Books UK. She works in a global tech company and lives in London. www.monadash.net

Jane Dougherty lives and works in southwest France. Her poems and stories have been published in magazines and journals including *Ogham Stone*, the *Ekphrastic Review*, *Ink Sweat and Tears*, *Nightingale & Sparrow*, and *Brilliant Flash Fiction*. Her poetry chapbooks, *thicker than water* and *birds and other feathers* were published in October and November 2020.

Sarah Doughty is a Smashwords Most Downloaded Author with one poetry and multiple fiction books available, with more in the works. In addition, she has contributed to multiple current and upcoming books with standalone pieces or collaborations, such as *Wild Is She*, *Poetica*, *Yellow*, *Crown Anthologies*, and more. She lives in Indiana with her husband, young son, and a pack of misfit, therapeutic pets.

Dorinda Duclos is a poetess, one who thrives in the darkness, and seeks out the shadows in the light. She is also the author of the blog, *Night Owl Poetry* (www.dorindaduclos.com). She writes, because it is her escape from reality, a chance to release the passion she holds in her being.

Rhian Elizabeth's novel, *Six Pounds Eight Ounces*, was shortlisted for The International Rubery Book Award and her poetry collection, *the last polar bear on earth*, was recently published by Parthian Books. She is a Hay Festival Writer at Work and International Literary Resident in the town of Tranas, Sweden.

Tiffany Elliott is a mental health professional who received her Master of Fine Arts in Creative Writing from New Mexico State

University in 2020, where she was awarded the Mercedes DeLos Jacobs Poetry Thesis Prize. Her poetry explores the ways we mythologize our lives, the lasting impacts of disability and trauma, and how recovery and resiliency allow us to remake ourselves. Her work has appeared in *Spectrum, Riggwelter, isacoustic, Inlandia, MUSE, Pacific Review*, and others.

Elizabeth Wadsworth Ellis was an outside child, conceived outside marriage, wed outside her culture, served outside her country in Serbia, Sofia and St. Petersburg, Russia, holds beliefs outside her upbringing, and jumped outside airplanes.

Following a successful 30+ years career in IT, **Trevor Flanagan** is currently studying for a BA in Creative Writing at the University of Bolton, UK. Further details on Trevor's writing and creativity can be found at: https://trevorflanagan.com/creative-writing/

Pooja Francis lives in Lucknow, India and is pursuing a Masters in Clinical Psychology. She believes that if people listen and provide unconditional acceptance, then healing and growing is always possible and that love for oneself should always be deeply rooted. Her poetry is filled with motivating words that are relatable, and understood. She desires not to fix or give advice to others but simply to be there, to listen, because sometimes, that's all we need.

Molly Fuller is the author of *For Girls Forged by Lightning: Prose & Other Poems* (All Nations Press) and two chapbooks *Tender the Body* (Spare Change Press) and *The Neighborhood Psycho Dreams of Love* (Cutty Wren Press). Her work has appeared in *The Hopper, The Fourth River*, and *Bellingham Review*. Fuller was the winner of Gris Gris's 2020 summer poetry contest. You can find her on Instagram and Twitter @mollyfulleryeah.

Sita Gaia is a TEDxAlumnae, and has previously been published in *Harness Magazine* and *PoetrySoup*. She has been writing since grade three, loves owls, and drinks way too much coffee. She resides in Vancouver with her wife and their plants. She has a chapbook coming out early this summer through Prolific Rise Press.

Jordan Garcia earned her Bachelor of Arts degree in Political Science from Barrett, The Honors College at Arizona State University in 2019. Jordan is currently a law student at Arizona State University Sandra Day O'Connor College of Law working towards her dream of becoming an attorney. Jordan's passions include politics, law, social justice, and disability advocacy as well as fashion and poetry. Follow Jordan on Instagram @jubielance.

Shannon Elizabeth Gardner incorporates elements of occult symbolism and iconography in her work. She explores Earth's forgotten beauty while imitating natural imperfections. The use of watercolor and India ink create beauty within flaws. Allowing ink to flow unconfined produces an ominous burnt feeling attributing to a worn allure seen throughout her work.

Roopali Sircar Gaur, Ph.D. is a columnist and writer. She is the Founder-President of YUVATI, working for girls and boys across India. Roopali was a professor of English at Delhi University, and taught Creative Writing at the Indira Gandhi National Open University. Her book *The Twice Colonised: Women in African Literature* is a seminal text on women's issues. She is also the co-editor of two international poetry anthologies, published in 2020 and 2021.

Kelly Glover is a Crohn's Disease warrior and single mother of three living in Greensboro, NC. With an honest and in your face approach, her poetry and prose touch upon the darker aspects of life. Her work can be found in various online journals and international anthologies and Kelly currently has three collections of poetry available on Amazon. She would be tickled if you followed her writing journey @Serenitysavagewrites on Instagram.

Mary Rogers Glowczwskie has been published in several online publications and appears in the anthology, *We Will Not Be Silenced: The Lived Experience of Sexual Harassment and Sexual Assault Told Powerfully Through Poetry, Prose, Essay, and Art*. Her writings have been featured on *Elephant Journal*, *Gathering Stories*, *House of Citrine*, *Huffington Post*, *The OC87 Recovery Diaries*, *Redflag.org*, *The Tattooed Buddha*, and *The Urban Howl*. Passionate in all that she does, her favorite pastime is getting naked on paper.
Facebook: https://www.facebook.com/woodsandwander/
Instagram: @woodsandwanderer

Deepa Gopal is a visual artist and a creative writer based in Dubai. Author of the blog, *Hues n Shades*, she has a Masters in English Language and Literature. Her works are often "mindscapes"– introspections into the emotional and psychological. She likes to play with dreams, myths and visions. Her poems have been published in four anthologies – *Whispering Poiesis* (2018) *Beyond Words* (2020), *The Kali Project*, and *Through the Looking Glass: Reflecting on Madness and Chaos Within* (2021) respectively.
Instagram: @dee.huesnshades
Blog: https://deepazworld.blogspot.com/

Georgianna Grentzenberg has been active in the arts in the Philadelphia area for over 40 years. She attended the Pennsylvania Academy of the Fine Arts from 1978-1982. She has shown in many juried, and one person exhibitions. Her primary work takes the form of fantastical visions and gardens done in ink and colored pencil.

She also works in ceramics, mosaics and mixed media. She is grateful for her many loyal friends, supporters and patrons. Her work can be viewed online at www.artbygeorgi.com.

Deborah Dubas Groom is a West Coast multimedia writer. Her work has appeared in *Canadian Stories* magazine, and seventeen anthologies in the U.S., the U.K. and Australia. She is a member of the Langley Writers' Guild. She has been living with lupus, migraines and depression for most of her adult life. She is the proud mother of Josh, a sci-fi and fantasy geek and a secret superhero fighting the tyranny of everyday cooking.

With advanced degrees in English and Library Science **Laura Hagemann** has been writing her whole life. When Fibromyalgia and daily migraines stopped her from pursuing her dreams of being an author a coma and severe Traumatic Brain Injury (TBI) actually refocused her to write her story. She's writing her story with blogs at https://writingbylaura.com/ and has ambitions of publishing a memoir. Twitter: https://www.twitter.com/wordsbylaura
Instagram: @writingbylaura

Patricia Harris is a dreamer, crafter, gamer and artist who loves creativity in life. She is a devoted mom who can be found doing a variety of art when she isn't penning poetry and writing words. She is half of the publishing company Fae Corps Inc.
www.Facebook.com/mouseypoet pattimouse.wordpress.com Her books can be found at www.books2read.com/rl/PatriciaHarris

Mark Andrew Heathcote is an adult learning difficulties support worker. His poetry has been published in many journals, magazines and anthologies. He resides in the UK, from Manchester, he is the author of *In Perpetuity* and *Back on Earth*, books of poems

published by CTU publishing group ~ Creative Talents Unleashed.
mrkheathcote@yahoo.co.uk
https://www.facebook.com/mark.heathcote.18

Monica Marie Hernandez is a writer from Texas who has 3 rare diseases. She writes to help her deal with her illnesses and the challenges that she faces.

Sister Lou Ella Hickman's poems and articles have appeared in numerous magazines and journals as well as four anthologies. She was nominated for the Pushcart Prize in 2017 and in 2020. Her first book of poetry entitled *she: robed and wordless* was published in 2015. (Press 53)

Kasey Hill has lived in Franklin County, VA for most of her adult life. Spending two years in journalism in high school, and a few articles published in the Franklin News Post, she built much of her young adult life around reading and writing. She has several novels published and many more stories circulating for anthologies as she pushes her passions forth into the writing community.

HLR (she/her) writes poetry and short prose about her real-life experiences of mental illness, trauma and grief. Her debut prosetry chapbook *History of Present Complaint* is published by Close To The Bone (2021). HLR lives in north London, where she was born and raised.
Find her on Twitter @HLRwriter / www.treacleheart.com

Terry House is a two-time guest contributor in poetry at the Bread Loaf Writers' Conference. Her work has appeared in numerous journals and anthologies including *The Berkshire Review*, *Arkana*, *Birdsong: Poems in Celebration of Birds*, *Lines in Landscape: Plein Air Poetry at Fruitlands*, and *The Anthology of New England*

Writers. She is a past president of The Robert Creeley Foundation and the current poet-in-residence at Old Frog Pond Farm & Studio. She lives in Massachusetts.

Rachael Ikins is a 2016/18 Pushcart, 2013/18 CNY Book Award, 2018 Independent Book Award winner, & 2019 Vinnie Ream & Faulkner poetry finalist. She is author/illustrator of 9 books in multiple genres from fantasy to memoir, to a nonbinary poetry collection. Born in the Fingerlakes she lives by a river with her dogs, cats, salt water fish, a garden that feeds her through winter, and riotous houseplants with a room of their own. Dragons fly by.

Emily James is the pseudonym used by Lori Weyandt. Lori's soul roams from the mountains of Pennsylvania to the mountains of North Carolina. She shares her life with her fiancé Brian, her daughter Kirsten and her littlest love, her granddaughter Miss Elliott Rose.

Ashley Jane is an indie author and book editor with a background in psychology, research and substance abuse. She has been writing off and on most of her life and currently has 3 books of poetry available. You can find her on most platforms at @breathwords. She loves music concerts, traveling and true crime dramas. She currently lives in Alabama with her husband and their one child, a rescue cat named Shadow Monkey.

Guinevere Lindley Janes grew up in New England and spent most of her 20's going to school in the Midwest. She now resides in the suburbs of Philadelphia, a train ride away from the Thomas Jefferson Headache Center. Guinevere process knits, only drinks Fair Trade Certified Coffee, loves storytelling, reads voraciously, and is a devoted APG. Guinevere writes to still the voices in her head. A lifelong Quaker, Guinevere eagerly anticipates whatever happens next.

Sun Hesper Jansen is a poet and writer working in the darker genres of fantasy, science fiction, and magical realism. Her work has appeared in the Indie Blu(e) anthology *As the World Burns: Writers and Artists Reflect on a World Gone Mad* and in *The Chamber Magazine*. She is the author of the blog *Away from the Machine* (awayfromthemachine.wordpress.com) where she writes on/as literary therapy for multiple sclerosis. And yes, she calls herself a Messer, and hopes it catches on...

Carol H. Jewell is a musician, teacher, librarian, and poet, living in Upstate New York, with her wife, and numerous cats. Her first collection of poems, *Hits and Missives*, was published in 2017, by Clare Songbirds Publishing House. Carol lives with several chronic illnesses, and has been an advocate for people with disabilities since 1985.

Eva Joan was born in 1960 in Augsburg/Germany and now lives in Glücksburg at the coast of the Baltic Sea. Eva is a pharmaceutical-commercial assistant and course instructor for autogenic training. During her free time, she writes, reads a lot, listens to music, and likes to knit. She suffers from irritable bowel syndrome/chronic fatigue syndrome and anxiety disorders.

Hotelier, advertising professional, writer, poet, artist. **Punam Joseph's** much-acclaimed book of poems- *The Soulful Seeker*, also features her sketches. Her achievements include poetry readings at various literary festivals and watercolor paintings adorning homes within India and overseas. She is the recipient of several awards, with poems and artworks featured in publications like *Portraits of Love*- a coffee table book, *She the Shakti*- an anthology of poems about women and the women-powered *The Kali Project*.

Jennifer Juniper loves to travel and has an innate curiosity that often leads to adventure and intrigue. Pulling from life experience, she chronicles connections and interactions that inspire. Her writing has been featured in *Decimos: We Say* and *The Chamber Chowder* (Key West's business publication). She is an award-winning poet living life on the road, indulging her sense of adventure and currently writing her memoir.

Louise Kenward is a UK based Writer, Artist and Psychologist. She holds an MA in Fine Art from London Metropolitan University (2011). Published by *Elsewhere*, *The Clearing*, and *Sussex University Life Writing Projects*, Louise also collaborated on an anthology of women's writing about illness in *Disturbing The Body* (Storytelling is an edited extract from Underland, Boudicca Press), and her work appears in *Women on Nature* (Unbound). She is currently working on her first full-length manuscript.

Paige Kezima is a newbie writer creeping into the field. She writes about her personal experiences with numerous conditions, including but not limited to Borderline Personality Disorder, and Endometriosis. She loves cats and desserts. Paige is a white settler and grew up on Treaty 4 Land in Saskatchewan, Canada. As a curious equity dreamer, she relishes in opportunities to learn and unlearn and is always interested in personal growth. Paige uses the pronouns she/her.

Former educator presently navigating life through the lens of chronic illness. Writing, photography and art, fill the gaps in an otherwise sedate life. Creativity also serves as a vehicle for healing and ultimately transformation. Visit **VJ Knutson** at her blog vjknutson.org, Twitter @vjknutson or Instagram @1womansquest

Born and raised in Detroit, Michigan, **Mandy Kocsis** is a legally deaf spinal meningitis survivor diagnosed with fibromyalgia almost a decade ago. She bleeds in poetry from She Hates It Here, Indiana, where she cares for her elderly mother and her teenaged son. You can find more of her work at *Mandy's Land* on fb, and her book, *Soul Survivor*, is currently available on Amazon and other online bookstores.

Tracey Koehler is a poet and writer. She suffers from a genetic connective tissue disease called Ehlers Danlos Syndrome and has lived a life of physical and mental abuse. She is a small-town Indiana girl sharing the chaotic rantings of her heart and soul, hoping to inspire others and give them the courage and strength to live their best life and fulfill their dreams.

Vandana Kumar is a middle school French teacher, translator and recruitment consultant in New Delhi. She contributes poems to online publications like *GloMag*. She has also been published in international journals like Toronto-based *Scarlet Leaf Review* and Philadelphia-based *North of Oxford*. One of her poems was recently published in the Winter 2020 paperback edition of the Houston, Texas-based *Harbinger Asylum* which is available at amazon.com. She was recently published in the heritage newspaper *Madras Courier*.

Julia Kvist is an award-winning Theatre Director, Writer and Poet based in the UK. She also has the joy of living with a spinal injury and Fybromyalgia on a daily basis.

Brandy Lane uses her experiences, metaphors and analogies to help readers relate to the topics in order to draw out emotion. She has been diagnosed with osteoarthritis at 17, PCOS at 28, Hashimoto's at 33, fibromyalgia at 34, then finally Ehler's Danlos at 40, and has suffered various allergic reactions and migraines and

depression throughout her life. This wife and mother of four hopes to inspire others through sharing her words.
https://www.instagram.com/wherebeautifullives
https://www.facebook.com/wherebeautifullives
www.wherebeautifulinks.com

Aishwariya Laxmi is a writer, editor, blogger and poet living in suburban Chennai. She has been in the field of content and communication for the last twenty years. Her flash fiction has been featured in anthologies by the Half-Baked Beans, The Macabre Ladies and in magazines such as *The Amp*. Her articles are on *womensw*eb and *WeQip*.
Her bookstagram is https://www.instagram.com/ashtalksbooks/.
She tweets at https://twitter.com/Aishwariya

Professor of English at Lock Haven University, **Marjorie Maddox** has published 13 collections of poetry, including *Transplant, Transport, Transubstantiation* (Yellowglen Prize) and the forth-coming *Begin with a Question* (Paraclete) and *Heart Speaks, Is Spoken For* (Shanti Arts)—*What She Was Saying* (prose, Fomite); 4 children's/YA books—including Inside Out: *Poems on Writing and Reading Poems with Insider Exercises* (Finalist 2020 International Book Awards), and *I'm Feeling Blue, Too!*—*Common Wealth: Contemporary Poets on Pennsylvania* (co-editor); *Presence* (assistant editor). www.marjoriemaddox.com

Lahari Mahalanabish's book of poems entitled *One Hundred Poems* had been published by Writers Workshop, India (2007). Her work was shortlisted for Erbacce Prize Poetry Competition (2009 & 2010), Eyelands Book Awards (2019 & 2020) and long-listed for the Grindstone Short Story Prize (2020). Her short stories/poems have found places in anthologies such as *Yellow Chair Review 2015 Anthology, Freedom Raga* (2020), *The Kali Project* (2021), *The*

Ocean Waves (2021), *2020 Grindstone Anthology*, *Where the Kingfisher Sings* (2021), and *Moolah* (2021).
She blogs at http://theserpentacursedrhyme.blogspot.com.

Sudipta Maity is currently pursuing her Master's Degree in English Literature. She is an artist and a writer, composing in English as well as in her mother tongue, Bengali. Her work has appeared in numerous magazines, journals, and international anthologies. She occupied third position in the State Level Essay Competition in 2016 and lives in West Bengal, India.
https://www.facebook.com/sudipta.maity.14661
https://www.instagram.com/sudiptaamaity

Daniel P. Malito has been living with Rheumatoid Arthritis for over thirty years now, and he has developed a unique way of telling his tales- with humor. Nothing is as absurd as living with invisible illness, and if you can't stop and laugh at the craziness of it all, you'll cry. Laugh along with him as you learn, feel, and smile.

Julie Malsbury received her MA in Writing Students from Saint Joseph's University and teaches writing, rhetorical, and literature at various universities in the Philadelphia area. She lives with her partner in crime and 3 strange cats. In her spare time, she hoards books to read "one day," sings with Anna Crusis, the longest running feminist choir, and occasionally updates her blog www.weebly.ConjugationalVisits.com.
Follow her @ConjugationalVisits (Facebook), @jou1es (Instagram), @JulieMalsbury (Twitter).

Nikki Marrone is a spoken word performer, poet, photographer, and coffee addict. She is motivated through feelings, of which she has plenty. Nikki has won multiple poetry slams and has featured at various spoken word nights and festivals internationally but is based in the UK. Author of *Lost & Found: A Poetry Passport*,

Psychogenic Fugue, and *Honey & Lemon*. When she's not wandering around the world or documenting her adventures, she splits her time between motherhood, performing, creating, and starving as an artist.

Satishchandran Matamp, a retired English Professor at St Gonsalo Garcia College, Vasai, University of Mumbai, is a bilingual writer of poems, stories, and journalistic articles, writing in English and his mother tongue Malayalam. His publications include *Uncanny Land of Rocks, Mockpoems, The Cloth Show, An E mail From Mars, i momed a rath mimsy*, and *The Flight & Other Stories*. Recently, his poems were included in two anthologies: *Hibiscus, and* Shimmer Spring published by Hawakal and Global Pandemic Crisis by Transcendent Zero Press.

Hey, I'm **Laura Eleanor Patricia Maze**, a chronic pain warrior living with fibromyalgia, JHS and OCD. My artwork often has a sombre edge as I try to express the challenge these conditions pose. Normally, I have a cuppa tea in one hand, paintbrush in the other, Queer Eye on in the background, and my black Labrador Jack keeping me company. Originally born in New Zealand, I was raised in England, and am currently studying in the Netherlands.

Laura McGinnis is retired from a career in project management, after being disabled with multiple physical and mental challenges. She writes to share her experiences, and empty her head of racing thoughts.

Having grown up in Europe, **Dawn D McKenzie** followed her husband to the USA. There, fibromyalgia was already recognized, and she was diagnosed, which helped her accept the illness and the limitations it placed on her life. Not all those supposed to love her did, though, and writing helped her feel heard and believed. Following a divorce, she is now ready for more daring writing projects, while tending to her children and pets.

Finn Aidan McRath is a history teacher, a writer of fiction and non-fiction, a harpist and guardian of the Parrot of Perpetual Pandemonium and the two Rabbits of Righteous Relaxation. Her hobbies include the constant recitation of Anglo-Saxon and Old Irish texts, and trying to get a song out of any musical instrument, pot, pan or string she can find.

Marion Michell is a London-based visual artist, blogger, writer. She has severe M.E. and P.O.T.S., and creates with fervour, but at a painfully slow pace, and often in the supine. In December 2016, her book *SUPINELY SUBLIMELY* (poetic prose) was published by Palewell Press.
Art: www.marionmichell.com
Blogs: https://chronicjots.wordpress.com
https://supinesublime.wordpress.com
Twitter @marjojo2004 Instagram @marjojo2017

Myrna Migala: About my humble life! Having reached the young age of 80, I recently found poetry after raising my six now-adult children. This submission is my first attempt to publish. I post on my WordPress blog titled: *myforever.blog* as well as on the poetry site *Poemhunter* (https://www.poemhunter.com/myrna-migala/poems/). I enjoy my grand/great children and am happy to have found the world of creating through writing. Yes, I live with Neuropathy.

Donna Motta (poet/author/novice play-write) who lives and breathes in the beautiful Berkshires with her family. Motta thrives, while successfully kicking the ass out of muscular dystrophy- and all the accompanying challenges. She is also a student of trees, bees, herbalism, ecology and life. Much peace.

PT Muldoon is a poet from the Irish Hills of Southern Michigan. His books are available through Amazon and can be found on Facebook (*PT Muldoon*) and on WordPress (www.ptmuldoon.com). He struggled for several years with neurological challenges before being diagnosed in 2019 with MG (Myasthenia Gravis), a rare disease that attacks the body's neurotransmitters. PT continues to ride and compete as a timed event rodeo athlete despite the limits of MG.

Rihan Mustapha: I am a teacher by day and a poetess by night. I view myself as a fighter, lover and strong believer of good karma, purity of the heart and kindness. I like reading, writing, watching movies, other languages and different cultures. Also, I've got a romantic soul and very fond of the sea. That's why I love to write under the name 'Romantic Mermaid.' For more information:
https://www.facebook.com/MyWordsinProseAndPoetry
https://www.facebook.com/MyWordsinProseAndPoetry2
https://www.facebook.com/OceansOfMyEmotions
Instagram: @rihan_h_mustapha and @rm_coffee_and_poetry

Anita Nahal is an Indian American poet, flash fictionist, children's writer, and columnist. Anita has three books of poetry, one of flash fiction, four for children, and three edited anthologies to her credit. Her third book of poetry, *What's wrong with us Kali women*, was recently released by Kelsay Books in August 2021. Anita teaches at the University of the District of Columbia, Washington DC. More on her at: https://anitanahal.wixsite.com/anitanahal

Nayona and her partner Venky, reside in Bangalore and are passionate about two things; their kids and good food. A mom of two - Sid (human) and Groot (no, he's a French bulldog), her daytime job is in consulting, while dabbling in "creation" to unwind from it. She teaches herself new forms of art and finds it to be very meditative and relaxing. She is personally on a very long journey of healing from chronic conditions and is nothing if not a fighter.

Amy Nicole has worked with *The Sacrifice Anthology, Aelurus, The Bird and* Dog, and *Wild Photon*, and is published in four *Chicken Soup for the Soul* books. Her two published books are *Invisible*, about living with an invisible disability, and *Shadow Lines*, a collection of poetry. Reach her at contactamynicole@gmail.com, follow her on Facebook @ShadowLinesWriting, or check out her blog at http://shadowlineswriting.tumblr.com/

Christine Obst is a Philadelphia writer whose poetry has appeared in anthologies and in the *Daily News*. Christine wrote articles for *The Odyssey* and she is currently working on a memoir about dating successfully (and not so successfully) in the 1980s, which will be published through Auctus Publishers. Christine works as a Mental Health Therapist and professor of Psychology in Newtown, PA. Previously, she taught English Literature and Creative Writing in the School District of Philadelphia.

Pallavi writes on a myriad of issues pertaining to motherhood and womanhood. The topics that especially tickle her fancy are the ones that are occasionally thrown under the rug or tell an engaging story. Some of her writings have been published in *Go Dog Go Cafe, Whisper and the Roar,* and *Free Verse Revolution.*

Suchita Parikh-Mundul is a freelance writer, copy editor, and poet. Her poetry has appeared in Sahitya Akademi's *Indian Literature*, online literary magazines *The Pine Cone Review*, *Hakara*, *Cerebration*, *Muse India*, and in anthologies. A collection of poems, *Liquid Apnea*, was published by Sampark, Kolkata in 2005.

Jess L Parker lives in Madison, WI where she works in Business Strategy. Her work has appeared in *Poetry Hall*, *Millwork*, *Wallop Zine*, and *OPE!– A Pop-up Anthology of Madison Writers & Artists*, and elsewhere. Jess holds an M.A. of Spanish Literature from the University of Wisconsin-Madison and an MBA.

Deepali Parmar, 48, works at Altering the Human Experience with Presence & Creativity. She is a Creatif & unschooler, an artist, poet, thespian, story-teller, and creative educationist. Her art, writing, plays & educational models have been appreciated, published, awarded and curated well enough. She lives an empowered life with her young child and tribe of Creatifs & Unschoolers in India. Presently, she curates *The Artist Within Sessions* Online. Ping her deepalistable@gmail.com or https://www.instagram.com/the.artist.within.journeys/

Lilan Patri is an American-born writer and visual artist based in Berlin. She contracted a progressive case of Myalgic Encephalomyelitis (ME/CFS) in 2003. Prior to becoming housebound and mostly bed-bound in 2010, Lilan worked as a creative writing teacher, translator, and journalist, and the editor of numerous print and online publications. She holds an MFA in fiction from the graduate writing program at Sarah Lawrence College.

Pooja Priyamvada is an author, columnist, translator, online content & Social Media consultant. An awarded bi-lingual blogger she also offers psychological/mental health first aid, and has been associated with several reputed national & global portals. She has translated *A Night in the Hills* to English and Caregiver's Handbook for Down's Syndrome to Hindi. Her ebooks *Mental Health: A Primer* and *Papa & I* are available on Amazon Kindle.
Twitter: @Soulversified

S.A. Quinox is a young, Belgian and modern poet who writes for the aching, the yearning and the mad wanderers among us. She loves to write about the dark night of the soul, the parts that we so desperately try to keep hidden. Quinox has been suffering from Fibromyalgia and Chronic Fatigue Syndrome since her early childhood, which inspires many of the pieces she writes. Quinox can be found on social media through Facebook and Instagram.

Akhila Rajesh is an IT professional with poetry at her heart. Her journey with poetry began in her school days and continues to get intriguing each passing day. Her first published book of poems is – *From Womb to World*. The second book *Enchanted Verses* was a collaboration with fellow colleagues. Her poems have also been published in multiple anthologies of Poetry Society of India, Xpress Publications, The Significant League, Poetry Corner, Asian Literary Society, etc.

Smita Ray is the mother of two lovely kids and hails from north-eastern India. Her perpetual displeasure arising from the hypocrisy in society underneath the semblance of religion, culture as well as the conditioning for compliance urged her to put down the impressions in her mind. In her spare time, she likes to have some culinary adventures along with her kids.

Grace R. Reynolds writes about the dark and obscure fantasies of life. Her writing invites readers to look at the everyday things around them to wonder what gruesome scenario they will find themselves in next. When she is not writing she is reading or attending to the daily responsibilities of a domestic engineer. Connect with Grace on Instagram @spillinggrace or visit her website www.spillinggrace.com

Shruti Sareen holds a PhD in literature from the University of Delhi on "Indian Feminisms in the 21st Century: Women's Poetry in English" which is now forthcoming as two monographs from Routledge (UK). Apart from having a plethora of publications in journals and anthologies, her debut poetry collection, *A Witch Like You*, was published by Girls on Key Poetry, Australia (2021) She is currently seeking publishers for her novel, *The Yellow Wall*.

Neelam Saxena has authored 5 novels, 1 novella, 6 short story collections, 32 poetry collections and 14 children's books. She holds a record with the *Limca Book of Records*, 2015 for being the Author having the highest publications in a year in English and Hindi. She has won several international and national awards. She was listed in Forbes (India) as one of the most popular 78 authors in 2014. Website: http://neelamsaxenachandra.com/ Facebook page: https://www.facebook.com/NeelamSaxenaPoet/

Winner of the Rashtriya Gaurav Award (2019) in association with the Government of Telangana, Orange Flower Award (2017) by *Women's Web*, Literoma Nari Samman (2020), GrandQueens Leadership Award (2020) by Lions Clubs International, and Women Lit of the Year Award (2020) by I.N.S.P.I.R.E Beyond Motherhood Awards, **Tina Sequeira** has published several short stories, poems, and essays in international journals and publications. Find her at www.thetinaedit.com and @thetinaedit.

My name is **A. Shea** (Angie Waters). I am 49 years old from Atlanta, GA. Poetry has been a part of my life since early childhood when I first started writing. In my teens, the few books I had from classic romantic poets really stole my heart. Now, the inspiration is endless from my own life struggles with chronic illness and past trauma. You can find my work on Instagram @a.shea_writer and Facebook at www.facebook.com/a.sheawriter

Raney Simmon-Baker is a 28 year-old class of 2015 graduate of Columbia College in South Carolina. She graduated with a Bachelor of Arts degree in Writing for Print and Digital Media. Her love of the written word can be seen on her blog https://rainyday.blog/ where she writes book reviews, talks about video games and occasionally shares her poetry. Her favorite genres of fiction are young adult and fantasy.

Pankhuri Sinha is a bilingual poet and story writer from India, who has lived in North America for 14 years and has two books of poems published in English, two collections of stories published in Hindi, five collections of poetries published in Hindi, with many more lined up. Has won many prestigious, national-international awards, has been translated in over twenty two languages. Her writing is dominated by themes of exile and immigration, gender equality and environmental concerns. Follow her on Facebook: https://www.facebook.com/pankhuri.sinha.56/

Sanhita Sinha, native of Tripura, is a teacher, a bilingual poet. Her poems got published in different prestigious national and international anthologies, journals & magazines. Her first book *Silent Bystander* was published in 2020. Her poems were published in *POESIA 2021* and many other works are in the pipeline. Her poems were translated in Russian also. Apart from writing, as a regular elocutionist-actor she is actively connected with stage, National television and radio too.

Megha Sood is a Pushcart-nominated Award-winning Poet, Editor, and Blogger based in New Jersey, USA. She is an Associate Editor at MookyChick (UK), Life and Legends (USA), and Literary Partner in the project *Life in Quarantine*' with Stanford University, USA. Author of Chapbook *My Body is Not an Apology*, Finishing Line Press, 2021) and Full Length (*My Body Lives Like a Threat*,

Flower Song Press, 2021). She blogs at https://meghasworldsite.wordpress.com/ and Tweets at @meghasood16

Jaime Speed lives, works, and plays in Saskatchewan, Canada. A fan of reading, gardening, throwing weights, and dancing badly, she has recently been published in *The Rat's Ass Review, Dear Loneliness Project, Hobo Camp Review, Anti-Heroin Chic,* and *OyeDrum Magazine,* with work forthcoming in *Psaltery & Lyre, Channel,* and *They Call Us* along with collections by Ship Street Poetry, Gnashing Teeth Publications, and White Stag Publishing.

Eira Stuart is a creative writer (poetry) and a guest writer for the M.E. Association. She has two poetry collections: *Sophistry, Metanioa* and *Eudaimonia* (non-fiction). Her recent publications include an M.E. care article in *More Notes for Carers* by Greg Crowhurst, a collection of poems in *Screaming from the Silence* (Vociferous Press) and featured micro poetry in Nightingale and Sparrow's "Heat" press release. Eira was nominated for Sundress Presses *Best of the Net Anthology 2020.*

Chandra Sundeep discovered the passion for writing on one of those days when everything seemed to go wrong! In the complex puzzle that life is, words came as a breath of fresh air and rescued her. Having worked as a social worker across cultures and classes, her stories reflect her understanding of society. Her thoughts have found a place in a few anthologies and various online forums. She blogs at https://wordsopedia.com/

F. Cade Swanson is a queer dad living with his three kids, his two dogs, his husband and his HIV in the Pacific Northwest. He grew up in southeast Virginia and runs a community center. His published works can be found at fcadeswanson.com

Brent Terry is the author of three collections of poetry, the latest of which is *Troubadour Logic*. His next collection will be released in January 2021 from Unsolicited Press. His first novel, *The Body Electric*, appeared in 2020, also from Unsolicited. He is currently writing more poems and a novel. He teaches at Eastern Connecticut State University, but yearns to rescue a border collie and return to his ancestral homeland of the Rocky Mountain West.

Nicole Townsend is a writer of poetry, stories and song lyrics from Jamaica. She has self-published two books on Amazon titled *Serenity* and *Thoughts of Me*. She has had multiple publications in *Harness Magazine* and *Page and Spine*. She has been awarded second-place position for the over eighteen age group in the Common Wealth Youth Council's *Unseen and Unspoken* poetry competition, as well as second place in the *Tales of Autumn* poetry competition. Facebook: @NicoleTownsend
Instagram – @Lizabethcole Twitter - @Lizcolewriter

Ullie-Kaye is a Canadian poet who began writing as a young girl, bringing her imaginations to life with her pen. As an adult, she learned of the power words could have. She writes in a vulnerable and empathetic style and seeks to build connections with readers by offering hope through her relatable and thought-provoking pieces. A word nerd and neologist, Ullie loves photography, experimenting in the kitchen and getting lost on hiking excursions.

Ranu Uniyal is Professor and Head, Department of English, University of Lucknow. She has published three poetry collections: *Across the Divide* (2006), *December Poems* (2012), and *The Day We Went Strawberry Picking in Scarborough* (2018), translated in Spanish in 2020. She is a founding member of PYSSUM, an organization for people with special needs in Lucknow. She can be reached at ranuuniyalpant@gmail.com. Website: ranuuniyal.com

Ms. Kaikasi V.S. is presently working as Asst. Professor of English, University College, Thiruvananthapuram. She is an accomplished creative writer and bi-lingual translator whose poems have appeared in several national and international anthologies including *The Poetry of Flowers*, *Mytho Madan*, Musings, Borderless Journal, The Kali Project, and in academic journals like *Gnosis* and *The Criterion*. In the year 2021 she received the first prize in the World Poetry Day Competition conducted by Christ Nagar College Maranalloor.

Amrita Valan is a writer from India, mother of two boys and a keen observer of life, who likes to write on everything under the sun. Her debut book of poems, *Arrivederci,* was published on Amazon in May 2021, and her collection of short stories, *In Between Pauses*, is awaiting publication. Her poems have appeared in anthologies, like *Poetic Swords, Divided: A Poet's Stance, Down the Rabbit Hole, Fire and Ice*, and in zines like *Cafe Dissensus, ImpSpired,* and *Spillwords.*

Antonio Vallone. Associate Professor of English at Penn State. Founder: MAMMOTH books. Editor: *Pennsylvania English*, *The Watershed Journal* Literary Group. Collections: *The Blackbird's Applause*, *Grass Saxophones*, *Golden Carp*, *Chinese Bats*. Forthcoming: *American Zen* and *Blackberry Alleys*. In progress: *The Death of Nostalgia*. He can be reached at ajv2@psu.edu.

Mehak Varun was born and brought up in Jammu and settled in Chandigarh. She has been bestowed with the 100 Inspiring Authors of India award in Kolkata. She has also been honored with the Women of Influence 2019 award presented on women's day in New Delhi. Recently she has been awarded the Gitesh-Biwa Memorial Award of excellence for her article on woman power 'I Just Need A Chance'.

Juli Watson is a disabled artist from the north east of England and was co-founder of Newcastle Literary Salon spoken word night. Her poetry chapbook, *L.O.V.E. Feelings* was published in 2014 and her collaboration with photographer Gemma Dobson, *Stagger-path*, was released in 2019. She currently makes artwork that combines found objects, collage and cut-and-paste poetry as well as exploring self-portraiture.

Julene Tripp Weaver lives in Seattle, where she writes and has a psychotherapy practice. She has studied Chinese and Western herbal medicine, is certified a green witch in the Wise Woman Tradition, and wildcrafts for personal use. Her second full size poetry book, *truth be bold—Serenading Life & Death in the Age of AIDS*, was nominated for a Lambda Literary Award and won the Bisexual Book Award.
Find more of her work at www.julenetrippweaver.com
Twitter: @trippweavepoet

Allison Whittenberg is a Philadelphia native who has a global perspective. If she wasn't an author she'd be a private detective or a jazz singer. She loves reading about history and true crime. Her novels include *Sweet Thang, Hollywood and Maine, Life is Fine, Tutored,* and *The Sane Asylum.* She has scleroderma.

Ingrid Wilson is a British poet and writer living in Slovenia. She has had poetry published by *Spillwords Press, Free Verse Revolution, Secret Attic,* and in several anthologies. Her non-fiction work has recently appeared in *Route 7 Review.* Ingrid is creator and editor of *Experiments in Fiction,* where she writes poetry, short fiction and journals, and provides a platform for other writers to share their work. You can find her on Twitter @Experimentsinfc and Instagram @experimentsinfiction.

Dr Archana Bahadur Zutshi is a poet of Indian origin, author, translator and educator. She contributed to several literary journals and blogs. Her scholastic interviews have appeared in both print and media. She has co-authored sixteen anthologies and authored three books of verse: *Poetic Candour* (2018), *The Speaking Muse* (2019), and *Careless Verse Whispers* (2021). Dr. Zutshi and *Poetic Candour* were featured by *The Culturium* (March 18, 2019). *The Speaking Muse* was featured by *The Asian Extract*. Contact her at zutshiarchana@gmail.com.

The *But You Don't Look Sick* Team

Kindra M. Austin is an author from Michigan, USA, and the co-founder of Indie Blu(e) Publishing. She is an advocate for mental health awareness, sexual trauma survivors, and for the LGBTQ+ community. Her debut novel was released in 2017; she has since written and published two other novels, as well as four poetry collections. A neo-noir novella is planned for release in Fall, 2021. Other written and editorial publications include contributions to *We Will Not Be Silenced, SMITTEN*, and *As the World Burns*. Austin has also written for *The Mansfield Pride* magazine, an annual periodical out of Ohio. You can find her books at Amazon, Barnes and Noble online, and other major online retailers.

Candice Louisa Daquin is a Senior Editor of Indie Blu(e) Publishing and a Psychotherapist specializing in adults abused as children. She freelances as Writer-in-Residence for *Borderless Journal* and Poetry Editor of *The Pine Cone Review*. Daquin is the primary editor of the 2020 National Indie Excellence Awards Finalist *SMITTEN This Is What Love Looks Like* (2020) and Co-editor (with Megha Sood) of the 2021 National Indie Excellence Awards Finalist *The Kali Project: Invoking the Goddess Within/ Indian Women's Voices*. She has written five poetry collections and her sixth poetry collection, *Tainted by the Same Counterfeit* is due 2022 from Finishing Line Press. Daquin is an advocate for raising awareness of mental health/ invisible illness and eradicating stigma.

Matthew DJ Eayre is a non-binary pansexual poet living with mental illnesses and physical conditions which cause them chronic pain. A poet and artist, a parent and spouse, Matthew is published in six poetry anthologies and has a collection of poems in the works, expected in 2021. "Hope is the only gift I can give you; it's all I have."

Victoria Manzi is the Marketing and PR Specialist for Indie Blu(e) Publishing. She received her B.A. in English: Professional Writing from Centenary University in New Jersey. Victoria has completed research on the relationship between students' writing and their university's writing center by looking at race, ethnicity, language, and (dis)ability backgrounds of undergraduates. She has presented at the National Conference on Peer Tutoring in Writing/International Writing Centers Association's (NCPTW/IWCA) joint conference on the effectiveness of the writing center and writing program development at a small, liberal arts college and at the Conference on College Composition and Communication (CCCC) on the relationship between multilingual/English as a second language (ESL) students and their writing, in spaces where standard vernacular English is dominant and oppressive to individuals with different language backgrounds. Victoria is passionate about raising awareness of the challenges sexual assault, domestic violence, and dating violence survivors (SADVS) and LGBTQIA+ members face, as well as supporting the voices of underrepresented and often silenced groups.

Christine E. Ray (She/Her) lives outside of Philadelphia, Pennsylvania. A former Managing Editor of Sudden Denouement Publications, she co-founded Indie Blu(e) Publishing with Kindra M. Austin in September 2018. Ray is author of *Composition of a Woman* and *The Myths of Girlhood*. Her writing has also been featured in *Through The Looking Glass: Reflecting on Madness and Chaos Within*, *As The World Burns: Writers and Artists Reflect on a World Gone Mad*, *SMITTEN: This Is What Love Looks Like*, *We Will Not Be Silenced: The Lived Experience of Sexual Harassment and Sexual Assault Told Powerfully Through Poetry, Prose, Essay, and Art*, *Anthology Volume I: Writings from the Sudden Denouement Literary Collective*, *Swear to Me* (Nicholas Gagnier), and *All the Lonely People* (Nicholas Gagnier).

Read more of her work at https://braveandrecklessblog.com/.

Mel Sherrer (She/Her) is a writer, editor, and educator. She received her B.F.A. from Hollins University in Roanoke, Virginia, and her M.F.A. from Converse College in Spartanburg, South Carolina. Mel teaches and conducts Creative Writing and Performance Literature workshops. Her work is featured in *SWWIM*, *Interim Poetics*, *The Racket Journal*, and others. She currently resides in Las Vegas, Nevada.

Another Indie Blu(e) Title You May Be Interested In:

As the World Burns

As the World Burns is an anthology of poetry, prose, essay, and art inspired by the unprecedented events of the year 2020. It embraces fierce and raw creative works relating to life during the Covid-19 pandemic, Black Lives Matter, Donald Trump, and the economic uncertainty and horror of the events of 2020. It is both a story of survival and an act of resistance.

https://www.amazon.com/As-World-Burns-Writers-Artists-ebook/dp/B08MYTJ5VC

Another Indie Blu(e) Title You May Be Interested In:

the kali project

The Kali Project draws in the voices of women as women, adding a sharper understanding of the inner realities that patriarchal structures seek to silence, sanctified by society, religion, community, and class. The gamut of experiences is vast and reiterates the idea that art and poetry are the essential vehicles which carry the hurt and, in the process, also healing within them.

https://www.amazon.com/Kali-Project-Invoking-Goddess-Within/dp/1951724062

Another Indie Blu(e) Title You May Be Interested In:

THROUGH THE LOOKING GLASS

THROUGH THE LOOKING GLASS
REFLECTING ON MADNESS AND CHAOS WITHIN

Join 158 writers and artists from across the globe as they journey Through the Looking Glass to unveil the truth about life with mental illness. Diverse, raw, and urgent, the poetry, prose, and art work in this anthology dig deep into the experience of living with depression, anxiety, bipolar disorder, and other neurodivergent conditions, as well as the challenges of loving someone who struggles with such an illness.

https://www.amazon.com/SMITTEN-This-What-Love-Looks/dp/1951724003

Another Indie Blu(e) Title You May Be Interested In:

WE WILL NOT BE SILENCED

We Will Not Be Silenced is a siren call to survivors everywhere. It should simply be available to everyone and anyone who has ever been violated, and to everyone and anyone who would be brave enough to speak out and speak up in an era when victims still aren't being heard.

https://www.amazon.com/Will-Not-Silenced-Experience-Harassment-ebook/dp/B07KXCTVX7

Indie Blu(e) Publishing is a progressive, feminist micro-press, committed to producing honest and thought-provoking works. Our anthologies are meant to celebrate diversity and raise awareness. The editors all passionately advocate for human rights; mental health awareness; chronic illness awareness; sexual abuse survivors; and LGBTQ+ equality. It is our mission, and a great honor, to provide platforms for those voices that are stifled and stigmatized.

Made in the USA
Monee, IL
27 August 2023

41732217R00312